FRAGILE POWER

Leadership lessons in life, business and sport

GEORGE D. NORRIS

RYAN PUBLISHING

First published 2021 by Ryan Publishing
PO Box 7680, Melbourne, 3004
Victoria, Australia
Ph: 61 3 9505 6820
Email: books@ryanpub.com
Website: www.ryanpub.com

 A catalogue record for this book is available from the National Library of Australia

Title: FRAGILE POWER: Leadership lessons in life, business and sport.

ISBN: 9781876498092 : Paperback

Copyright © 2021. George D. Norris

Apart from any fair dealing for the purposes of private study, research, criticism or review, as permitted under the Copyright Act, no part may be reproduced by any process without written permission. Inquiries should be addressed to the publisher.

Internal and cover design by Luke Harris, Working Type Studio, Victoria, Australia. www.workingtype.com.au

Front cover painting of the author by Australian Artist, Neil Wyatt, entered for the Archibald Prize in 2006.

To my children Nicole, Melinda and Campbell and my grandchildren Eve, Ewan, Declan, Kieran, William, and Caitlin who inspire me every day to continue my journey.

ACKNOWLEDGMENTS

To my clever brother John who has been an inspiration to me throughout my life and been there for me also as a friend throughout life's ups and downs.

To my loyal Executive Assistant Christine Griffiths who for the past 15 years has helped and guided my business and affairs with such insight and dedication.

To my long time golf friend Lo Magill who pushed me to write my business autobiography, believed in me and helped me with the first courageous and ruthless edit.

To my amazingly talented cartoonist friend George Haddon who picked me up once when I was down and brought companionship, humour and memorability into my life.

To my long time friend of over 40 years, Ed Davis who has encouraged me to continue my writing and continues to educate me with his intellect, knowledge and wisdom.

To my golf friend Trevor Main for being a light house of wisdom, friendship and support over the past 10 years and reinforcing my belief in myself and the human race.

To my Editor, Publisher and golfing friend Graeme Ryan for his courage, advice, knowledge, patience and passion to help me publish this my fifth book.

Author Details

George D Norris

FAICD, FAIM, FAMI, CPM

CORPORATE/EXECUTIVE COACH, SPEAKER,

MENTOR-IN-CONFIDENCE, FACILITATOR

Norris Management Pty Ltd

HIGH PERFORMANCE STRATEGISTS

Suite 1110, Yve, 576 St Kilda Road,

Melbourne Victoria 3004

T +61 3 9521 2292

M 0418 561 271

E norrismanagement@bigpond.com

www.norrismanagement.com.au

BUSINESS COACHES & SPEAKERS GROUP

LEADERSHIP • COMMUNICATION • CULTURE

FOREWORD

It is my pleasure to write the Foreword to introduce you to George Norris and his fifth book *FRAGILE POWER: Leadership lessons in life, business, and sport.*

The year 2020 was a challenge for most, and in Melbourne, Australia, it was particularly difficult as we were all in house lockdown for nearly five months. Many people became lonely, depressed, and anxious while others saw the situation as an exciting opportunity to achieve what they had not done before.

George was one such person and used the many months locked in his home to write his business autobiography covering the past 60 years of his life. To write it in his 80th year is even more incredible as it took a lot of dedication, passion and especially discipline in time management to enable him to achieve his goal.

He still enjoys working three or four days a week as a leading corporate coach, management mentor, motivational speaker and facilitator providing leadership strategies for success, high performance psychology and words of wisdom. He is remembered for his many years on Melbourne radio as 'The Life Coach'.

I first met George 37 years ago at the end of September 1983 when he called me from Vancouver, Canada, while on a business trip. My family and I were in Hawaii on our way home to Australia after celebrating the 1983 America's Cup win by Australia II. His tenacity impressed me, and we met in person later when we had both returned home to Melbourne. We then discussed my role as the

Keynote Speaker and Guest of Honour at two motivational business conferences his company was conducting in Sydney and Melbourne. They both were great successes, and I was able to share many leadership insights we had used in winning the 1983 America's Cup with the delegates.

His book *FRAGILE POWER* is aptly titled, for I know how fragile power can be when you and your crew are trying to win the America's Cup from the Americans for the first time in 132 years!

You will find George's book a captivating journey of his experiences in life, business and sport but remember you only have very Fragile Power when you're a skipper or leader of people in life, business and sport.

Good luck and good reading!

John Bertrand AO
Skipper of Australia II,
Winner 1983 America's Cup.
Chair, Sport Australia Hall of Fame.

PROLOGUE

A Look back in Time

This book sets out my journey in life, business and sport over 60 years and I hope will act as a source of encouragement, inspiration and knowledge for many people, both young and old.

When I started my corporate career in 1958 the microchip had just been invented. It was the year of the great Chinese famine. The first trans-Atlantic passenger airliner service began. The Munich air disaster happened with the resulting death of seven Manchester United players. The US military predicted that satellites would orbit the earth to make detailed maps from space and NASA was officially formed.

In Australia, the first Opera House lottery was drawn in NSW. Qantas commenced their first round the world air service. Sydney's Cahill Expressway was opened. Cyclone 'Connie' damaged or destroyed nearly every building in Bowen, Queensland. The Monash University was established by an act of parliament. Trams ceased running in Perth. Wreckage of the airliner 'Southern Cloud' lost in 1931 was found in the Snowy Mountains. Trams ceased running in Adelaide.

Australia's first nuclear reactor at Lucas Heights became operational. Bandstand, hosted by Brian Henderson began on television. Herb Elliott ran a world mile record of 3 minutes and 54.5 seconds.

The estimated population of Australia was 10 million. The Clean Air Act was passed in Victoria and was the first state to control air pollution, and I started my corporate life at Caltex Oil.

TABLE OF CONTENTS

FOREWORD 1

PROLOGUE   A Look back in Time 3

PART 1   **THE MANAGEMENT CADET** 9
    CASE HISTORY 1   Caltex Oil (Australia) Pty Ltd 11
        Chapter 1   Joining the Club 12
        Chapter 2   Coping with Adversity 15
        Chapter 3   The Challenge of Change 21
        Chapter 4   A Career in the Country 28
        Chapter 5   War in the City 37
        Chapter 6   The End of an Era 41
        Chapter 7   A Clash of Cultures 44

PART 2   **THE INTREPID ENTREPRENEUR** 47
    CASE HISTORY 1   George D Norris & Associates Pty Ltd 49
        Chapter 1   A Leap of Faith 50
    CASE HISTORY 2   Collingwood AFL Football Club 53
        Chapter 1   Mission Imperative 54
    CASE HISTORY 3   L'Oreal of Paris 61
        Chapter 1   The Golden Frog 62
    CASE HISTORY 4   Wurlitzer 69
        Chapter 1   The Musical Mouseketeer 70
    CASE HISTORY 5   Renault (Australia) Pty Ltd 74
        Chapter 1   The French Connection 75
    CASE HISTORY 6   Ansett Airlines of Australia 79
        Chapter 1   Back to the Future 80
    CASE HISTORY 7   Caltex Oil (Australia) Pty Ltd 84
        Chapter 1   A Strategy for Success 85
        Chapter 2   Bali Bound 89
        Chapter 3   First Time Flyers 93

Chapter 4	Negotiating a Nightmare	96
Chapter 5	Beauty and the Banquet	100
Chapter 6	A Birthday Surprise	104
Chapter 7	Attitude and Aptitude at Altitude	112
Chapter 8	Teamwork in Action	115
Chapter 9	Sleepless in Jakarta	120
Chapter 10	A Calming Influence	125
Chapter 11	He ain't Heavy	129
Chapter 12	Home on AutoPilot	132
CASE HISTORY 8	**Tooth Hotels Pty Ltd**	**136**
Chapter 1	The Horse's Mouth	137
CASE HISTORY 9	**Indian Tourism Board**	**146**
Chapter 1	Incredible India	147
Chapter 2	Forbidden Fruit	150
CASE HISTORY 10	**Operation 84, America's Cup Conferences**	**155**
Chapter 1	Sailing into the Future	156
Chapter 2	A Light Bulb Moment	160
Chapter 3	Needle in a Haystack	165
Chapter 4	Catching a Marlin	169
Chapter 5	Syncing with the Skipper	**174**
CASE HISTORY 11	**Australian Motor Industries Ltd: TOYOTA**	**180**
Chapter 1	Trust comes by Foot	181
Chapter 2	The Cook from Essex	188
Chapter 3	A Path to Perfection	193
Chapter 4	A Golden World	199
Chapter 5	Rabbits in the Hat	205
Chapter 6	Trust leaves by Horse Power	211
Chapter 7	Hitting the Canvas	216
CASE HISTORY 12	**Australian Vintage Travel**	**219**
Chapter 1	Bouncing back Up	220
Chapter 2	A Vintage Year	223
Chapter 3	A Vintage Betrayal	227
CASE HISTORY 13	**The Australian Bicentennial**	**232**
Chapter 1	Living a Dream	233
CASE HISTORY 14	**In Touch and In Line**	**239**
Chapter 1	Foundations for a Future	240
CASE HISTORY 15	**Calder Park Thunderdome**	**245**
Chapter 1	Learning from a Legend	246

Chapter 2	Skating on Thin Ice	252
Chapter 3	Realising Reality	260
CASE HISTORY 16	**Norris Management Pty Ltd**	265
Chapter 1	The Phoenix Rises	266
CASE HISTORY 17	**Jetset Travel**	272
Chapter 1	One Night in Bangkok	273
Chapter 2	Success Through Service	277
CASE HISTORY 18	**Anthony Tesselaar Plants**	281
Chapter 1	Smelling the Roses	282
CASE HISTORY 19	**Herb Herbert Pty Ltd**	286
Chapter 1	The Growing of Herbie	287
CASE HISTORY 20	**General Motors Holden**	292
Chapter 1	Renewing Relationships	293
CASE HISTORY 21	**Telecom Mobilenet**	299
Chapter 1	Searching for Excellence	300
CASE HISTORY 20	**The PGA of Australia**	305
Chapter 1	The Business of Golf	306

PART 3   THE CORPORATE COACH 313

CASE HISTORY 1	**Grey Advertising Pty Ltd**	315
Chapter 1	Insights in a Bubble	316
Chapter 2	Many Shades of Grey	321
CASE HISTORY 2	**BMW Australia Ltd**	325
Chapter 1	The Beauty in the Beast	326
Chapter 2	Breathless in Bavaria	332
Chapter 3	The Benefits from the Brand	337
CASE HISTORY 3	**Radio 3MP 1377**	
Chapter1	A Shot of Inspiration	346
CASE HISTORY 4	**Melbourne and Hawthorn AFL clubs**	349
Chapter 1	Coaching the Coaches	350
CASE HISTORY 5	**Radio Magic 1278**	358
Chapter 1	The Life Coach	359
CASE HISTORY 6	**National Foods Ltd**	362
Chapter 1	Food for Thought	363
CASE HISTORY 7	**Royal Sydney Golf Club**	366
Chapter 1	The Cellar Dweller	367
CASE HISTORY 8	**Kelvin Boyd Advisory Pty Ltd**	371
Chapter 1	A Watching Brief	372

CASE HISTORY 9	**Greystone Wines**	375
Chapter 1	A Strategic Solution	376
CASE HISTORY 10	**Cookers Bulk Oil System Pty Ltd**	382
Chapter 1	Cooking with Canola	383
CASE HISTORY 11	**Victoria University**	387
Chapter 1	Worshipping Wisdom	388
CASE HISTORY 12	**AFL Coaches Association**	394
Chapter 1	Meeting the Master	395
CASE HISTORY 13	**Mercedes Benz Dealers**	400
Chapter 1	The Silver Stars	401
CASE HISTORY 14	**HLB Mann Judd Pty Ltd**	406
Chapter 1	Taming the Tiger	407
CASE HISTORY 15	**Renault (Australia) Pty Ltd**	413
Chapter 1	Renewing the Connection	414
CASE HISTORY 16	**Logic Information Systems**	416
Chapter 1	Flying High on Golf	417
CASE HISTORY 17	**m3property**	421
Chapter 1	The Vision Equation	422
CASE HISTORY 18	**First National Real Estate**	427
Chapter 1	Putting Culture First	428
EPILOGUE	**The People's Pandemic**	**432**

PART 1

THE MANAGEMENT CADET

CASE HISTORY 1

Caltex Oil (Australia) Pty Ltd

CHAPTER 1

Joining the Club

I joined Caltex Oil (Australia) Pty Ltd as a 17-year-old management cadet in January 1958 after leaving as one of 'The Original' students in 1954 at the now famous Victorian Secondary School, Balwyn High School.

My first day at Caltex was one I will never forget.

I first was welcomed by the Accountant, Lloyd William Cowdell, a gentle, quiet well-mannered senior manager who made me feel at ease on my first day of work. He then ushered me into an adjoining office where I met the Assistant Accountant, a fearsome large man called Jack Cocks who would set out my role and mail room responsibilities.

Standing well over six feet in height with slicked down wavy dark hair parted in the middle and wearing his trademark brown brogue shoes, he had the ability and the reputation, I would later learn, to put fear into the heart of the most confident young person.

He welcomed me then proceeded to lay down the law, so to speak, about what I would be doing in the 'Mail Room' as my first role.

However, after leaving his office he called me back and said, "Shut the door and take a seat." He then made a comment which I now realise was most insightful, but strange and in some ways threatening at the time.

He said, "George, I just want to make the point that you don't have to like everyone you work with, you just have to get on with them and do your job." So began my corporate career with Caltex Oil.

He had perhaps realised that as a new boy the other management cadets may give me a hard time on my first day and some initiation in joining their 'Club'.

It was great advice, which I have since given to many people in management positions that I have coached and mentored, as it was of utmost assistance to me on that first day.

On 7 January 1958, the Mail Room was the nerve centre for incoming and outgoing correspondence and parcels. The cadets would, for example, open, sort and allocate the incoming mail into pigeonholes for the relevant departments and key executives and frank the outgoing mail through a franking machine. This would print the value of the stamp on the envelope depending on its size and weight or print a stamp label to be affixed to larger parcels, envelopes, or boxes for mailing.

On my first day, as you might imagine, I was trying to please 'the boss' of the management cadets, a stern but amicable, ex-military man named Leo Armitage, and was asked to frank a couple of hundred standard envelopes. They were to be franked at the rate of $3\frac{1}{2}$ pence. I was shown how to set the machine for this amount, and to feed the envelope through to be stamped.

I started and got going, I now realise too fast compared with the other cadets, so the Head Management Cadet, a tall, blond, powerful, assertive guy called Brian Patton asked me a question to make me lose concentration. I looked over to where he was pointing and took in his comments and walked over to see and learn about the other feature of the mail room.

I then went back to franking the mail and soon worked up a good turn of speed, when after about 10 minutes he came over in front of the other cadets and 'the boss' Leo and exclaimed, "Do you know what you've set the value of the franking machine at George?" I replied, "3½ pence."

"Well you haven't, you've set it to 3 shillings and 3 pence."

I was mortified as he calculated that I had franked 157 envelopes costing Caltex a lot of money and yes, on the morning of my first day!

I couldn't believe I had made the mistake and was devastated. However, when we had our tea break one of the other cadets, Wayne Tyler who I became close friends with later, told me that when Brian had got my attention earlier he had arranged for the other cadet to alter the franking value on the machine so I wouldn't know, as my initiation to the company and the 'Corporate Club' on my first day.

It was a hard lesson to learn, yet it taught me two things, one to check everything consistently and two, people can be threatened by others who are more enthusiastic than they are and as a result they will often try to bring them down to their level of mediocrity.

This lesson on day one of my working life was to be reinforced and displayed may times in my experiences in life, business and sport.

Leadership Lessons:

1. Believe in yourself.
2. Be resilient and brave.
3. Stay focused on the process.
4. Don't make assumptions, check the details.
5. Be careful not to threaten peers.

CHAPTER 2

Coping with Adversity

My first day at Caltex was therefore a day when I learnt about coping with adversity and inspired me to create the saying I have used many times since, "Out of adversity comes advantage, it's just that at the time of the adversity we don't yet see the advantage."

My career as a management cadet, who never went to university and commenced in business straight from high school flourished, and the lessons I learnt on that first day, of pride, passion, enthusiasm and focusing on a process, enabled me to rapidly progress through many roles and departments.

I must have been earmarked by management as I became the youngest management cadet in Accounts Receivable, Cashiers, Sales Reporting, and Credit Control. I was then promoted to Area Credit Manager responsible for all retail accounts in Victoria and Tasmania at the age of 24.

However, it was at this tender age and in this position that the Assistant Credit Manager told me arrogantly at lunch one day in front of my peers, that my problem was, "I had no ambition!"

By then I had given up playing cricket for Balwyn Sub-District where I had taken 6 wickets for 33 runs one Saturday only to be given two more 'overs' for the rest of the season because my captain was also a leg spin bowler.

This was another case of someone being threatened by enthusiasm, pride, process, talent and passion.

Balwyn Sub-District Cricket Team
Author in back row second from right.

Disenchanted, I left and joined Kew Sub-District Cricket Club which was a blessing as it was closer to my home in North Kew. I became an opening bat and leg spin bowler, but soon found that the same culture was embedded in cricket no matter what team you played with.

If you were a threat to a senior player or captain with similar skills and talent, you didn't prosper because they had the power of influence and they could quickly put out your flame of passion.

CHAPTER 2 Coping with Adversity

It still happens today in cricket around the world as senior players seem to hold the power and their places for too long in most teams and have the power to influence and stop opportunity for the young and talented because they are threatened by them.

Again, disenchanted, I changed my sport, and this was to be the best decision I ever made for my self-development and wellbeing.

While playing and practising at Kew Cricket Club I would often watch the athletes of the Kew Harriers Athletic Club train and compete in various athletic events. At Balwyn High School I had a keen interest in running, and became the senior champion in 100, 220 and 440 yards.

So, one momentous day I put my cricket bat away in the cupboard, bought a new pair of running spikes, joined Kew Harriers, and never looked back.

I found that in athletics you control your own destiny, as in golf, and your talent, enthusiasm, endurance, commitment, discipline, dedication, technique, passion, process, and pride enable you to perform with excellence, if you want to attain that level.

I had shown speed from an early age at school sports, and I soon started to show progress and promise as the leading club sprinter and went on to become the club champion over 100, 220, 300 and 440 yards.

After a couple of years of consistent performance, I was elected captain of the club and started to impart the coaching knowledge I had gained from being coached by one of the starters at the 1956 Melbourne Olympic Games, Stewart Embling, who was also a sprint coach.

During this period, I recruited a number of champion athletes to the club, the best being the Australian 100-yard sprint champion and record holder, Byron Williams. Byron was a shy, retiring, gentle guy who was totally dedicated to his sport and who also was quite a deep thinker, strategist, and philosopher.

Byron was a member of the powerful Box Hill Athletic Club but would train with his cousin Peter Denny at the Kew Harriers Club at the Victoria Park oval on most evenings.

I soon became close friends with Byron, who has become a loyal, lifelong friend and one day when training with him he suggested I try out for the 880 yards as he thought I had the speed and endurance to compete well over this distance.

It wasn't long before I influenced him to join the Kew Harriers Club. I then became the 440 and 880 yard champion and left the 100 and 220 yards to him.

Byron, I and two other sprinters, Ray Brunton and Bruce Falconer from Old Scotch, soon became a dedicated group of four and we trained throughout the winter with 10 to 12 mile training runs twice a week after work, training on the track two nights a week and working out at the gym on the fifth night.

It was a seriously daunting training schedule, yet we improved our times significantly for our respective events and formed a great bond of friendship and support for one another that lasted many years.

It was not unusual on our long runs to return bleeding and sore with blood on our shorts from the chafing of the skin between our legs. However, we couldn't stop as our pride, passion and dedication wouldn't let us give in to the pain.

Then, near the end of 1965 as decimal currency was about to be introduced in Australia, I was told by the Victorian Manager of Caltex, that a massive computer in Sydney was going to replace our jobs in the Melbourne office.

He then surprisingly told me that I had been selected for a new position as the Area Representative for Caltex, based in Colac in the Western District of Victoria.

The role would cover the flourishing area from Lorne to Apollo Bay on the coast of Bass Strait, to Port Campbell with the famous tourist attraction of the 12 Apostles in the west, up to Lismore above Camperdown in the dry north and east back to the little town of Cressy north of Colac.

It was a big decision for me to leave my family, home, friends, girlfriend, athletic club and life in Melbourne, yet I agreed as I had learnt in my business career at Caltex that if you ever refused a promotion, you went into the 'black drawer' and forever would experience non promotion!

The Manager immediately challenged me saying, "Tell me George, what makes you think you can do the job and be successful in a lonely, country environment after living in the city all your life?"

I thought for a moment and replied, "Well Mr Aitchison, when I'm eight miles from home on a training run and bleeding from the chafing between my legs and I haven't got any money to catch a bus, train or a taxi, I continue to run home, and guess if I can do that consistently, I believe I can do this new job!"

He was stunned into silence and simply said in reply, "Okay, George, you've got the job." So, I started an adventure that was to dramatically change my social, sporting and business life forever.

In January 1966, at the age of 25, I set off by myself in a new company car, a Valiant sedan, as part of my role to 'carve out a career in the country' that built the foundations for my future life in performance management and especially, leadership.

Leadership Lessons:

1. Out of adversity comes advantage.
2. It's okay to have ambition.
3. Try to control your own destiny.
4. Have courage in decision making.
5. Be authentic and your true self..

Chapter 3

The Challenge of Change

I arrived in Colac late January 1966. I had my time taken up settling into living in a town I had never been to before let alone lived in, meeting the diverse range of customers, forming a relationship with my Distributor, Lyn Paslow, who was also the Mayor of Colac and finding my own accommodation after living all my life to this age, at home with my parents and my brother John.

Finding suitable accommodation during that time proved difficult so after about six weeks my Distributor said to me one day, "If you can't find accommodation George, why don't you advertise for someone to share a house with you?"

Shortly after I arrived at the Caltex Depot the next day, I received a message from my Distributor that a local senior businessman, who owned the largest clothing store in Colac, had called to enquire who I was and asked me to meet him at his home.

I called him and met him that morning at his beautiful home next to Lake Colac and we struck up a friendship straight away.

His name was Ted Clayton. He was seven years older than me, had recently separated from his wife, owned a fully furnished house, a 16-foot Merlin Sabre speed boat and the latest Grundig home entertainment system which was considered then to be very 'up-market'.

He explained that I would have my own room and work desk and we would share the household chores. He had a housecleaner who came in once a week and a boxer dog called Kate who could jump as high as the fence, but thankfully not over it.

Ted also happened to be President of the Colac Chamber of Commerce and President of the Corragulac Football Club. In the course of discussion, I also discovered his birthday was 29 November, the day after mine!

Author kissing Ted Clayton at his 70th Birthday.

I had fallen on my feet by taking the advice of my Distributor which was another lesson in leadership, in that to overcome a significant problem it helps if you think creatively or laterally to get a solution.

Once I moved in and was settled, I started to plan and perform again with the pride, passion and keenness I had exhibited in the Melbourne office which had enabled me to be selected for this daunting role in the first place.

Before arriving in Colac, I had surprisingly beaten Noel Clough in the time of 1 minute 58 seconds in the 880 yards event at the Mentone track in an early season regular track meeting in October. However, the following week I unfortunately suffered a serious hamstring tear and couldn't run let alone walk properly for the next eight weeks.

The 1996 Commonwealth Games were to be held in Jamaica in August and I wondered how Noel, who coincidentally also worked for Caltex and who had finally qualified and been selected, would perform in the 880 yards. Amazingly he won the gold medal for Australia in 1 minute 46.9 seconds and all at Caltex and I were elated at his achievement. However, I have always wondered what would have happened if I hadn't torn my hamstring!

It wasn't long before my injured leg became strong enough to start running and training hard again. I found a great track close by the house, overlooking the lake through the Colac Botanic Gardens that I would use every morning for a 3-mile run.

Soon my fitness returned and late one day I asked the Mayor, "Does Colac have an athletic club?" He answered, "Yes it does, but I believe there is a meeting tonight at the Colac Chiropodist, to wind it up or close it down." I said, "Why, what's the problem?" He replied, "I'm not sure, but I think it's because of a lack of parent support."

I thanked him and left for the day, not really knowing what I'd uncovered.

That night at 7pm I arrived for the meeting. No-one challenged me, spoke to me, welcomed me, or asked who I was, and it appeared that everyone was anxious and stressed. The meeting eventually commenced, and I listened to the discussion for about an hour. The discussion seemed to focus on how it was all too hard, too difficult, and too onerous to help the children and young adults of the City of Colac and surrounding towns to enjoy their athletics and achieve their potential.

Finally, they took a vote of those present on whether or not to disband and close down the Colac Athletic Club. I voted 'NO' and as I was the only person to do so, the Chairman in some form of shock, looked at me for the first time since the meeting started with a startled look of disbelief on his face.

"Hello," he said, "I noticed you didn't vote 'YES'. I am sorry we haven't met so can I ask you who you are, why you are here and why are you of that opinion?"

I filled him and the others in on my name, job, and the fact that I had only recently arrived in Colac and that I had recently been the Captain and Coach of the Kew Harriers Athletic Club in Melbourne.

I also said it was amazing and disappointing that the adults and parents of Colac would abdicate their responsibility to support the health, well-being, and sporting interest of their children, and in fact that they should be ashamed of themselves.

They then asked if I would be prepared to act as Captain and Coach of the Club if it continued to operate, to which I replied, "I would if the parents helped with transport to support me in assisting their children."

They agreed and that night the Colac Athletic Club was given a new lease of life. So was I, because the role enabled me to meet and mix with the business people and prominent residents in the Colac area.

In fact, it enabled me to quickly establish myself in my new role and grow the business for my Distributor, the Mayor, who I was indebted to for helping me gain accommodation and unexpected involvement in the Athletics Club.

We competed every Saturday at the John Landy Athletic Field near the Barwon River in South Geelong, so it was important that up to six parents volunteered every week to transport the athletes, their children, to and from Geelong. They did and the club flourished!

A consistent training venue was arranged at the Colac Oval where I conducted training and coaching on Tuesday and Thursday evenings from 5pm and the Club grew to over 25 athletes.

The well-known 3CS sports announcer Doug Jennings asked me to present a Friday night athletics program which gave me a great opportunity to promote the Colac Athletics Club, the Colac athletes, and my own Caltex profile too.

Little did I know that this would be the foundation for a later career on Melbourne radio that would last for nearly 10 years.

We won the premiership two years later and the businesses of Colac donated all the trophies for the best performers of the season. The Mayor and the Mayoress presented the trophies and spoke of how the club had gone from oblivion and closure to being premiers in just two years. The Mayor thanked me for my efforts in helping the youth of Colac.

I was happy, yet humbled by his comments, which together with a photograph appeared in The Colac Herald the next day.

Colac Mayor and Mayoress with sprint champion, Terry Doak. Author at rear.

It was an amazing couple of years in my young adult life. It proved yet again that with courage, good communication skills, a community caring culture and some positive resilience we are all able to move mountains and harness the efforts and talents of a team of people who have the same common goal.

It also proved to me again that out of adversity comes advantage. It's just at the time of the adversity, you don't yet see the advantage!

Leadership Lessons:

1. Setbacks are just emotional hurdles.
2. Think laterally to overcome problems.
3. Be humble yet happy in success.
4. Have the courage of your convictions.
5. Good communication skills are critical.

CHAPTER 4

A Career in the Country

My life in Colac blossomed and I settled in well, still keeping in touch with my longtime friends in Melbourne John Robarts, who I had known since the age of three and John Harrington who John and I had met at the weekly Saturday dance at the Heidelberg Town Hall.

John Robarts and I decided to have an adventure together over the Christmas holidays and on 17 December 1967 we set off in my new Valiant to drive to Perth and back. I had the front bench seat made to fold down so we could sleep in the car and we took a lot of food that our mothers cooked for us together with John's air rifle, just in case of an 'incident'!

We departed Melbourne and started out for Ballarat about 10am. No sooner had we left Melbourne than it was reported on the radio that the Australian Prime Minister, Harold Holt, was missing at Cheviot Beach, Portsea. By the time we arrived at Ballarat he was considered drowned, and by the time we stopped for our first night at Clare near Adelaide he was presumed dead!

What an historic day to start our adventure.

We continued the next day in some sort of shock and reached Ceduna at the start of the Nullarbor Plain and the Eyre Highway. In 1967, the highway was unmade and looked like the bottom of a river

CHAPTER 4   A Career in the Country

*The Age Business Basketball Team.
Author at right and long time friend John Robarts third from left.*

bed. In fact, it was necessary to drive down into the road it was so low and dangerous. The 'bull dust' holes, as they were named, were often so large and deep that they had tree roots in them to warn drivers to avoid them. We were also given a reality check as we started to descend to the 'highway' by a large sign that read, 'This is your last reliable water supply for 770 miles'!

We took it in turns to drive in two hour shifts for safety reasons and that night stopped off the road behind some bushes, locked the car doors, put the windows down about half an inch and slept peacefully. Early the next morning we were woken by a guy tapping on the window. We had been warned that there may be nomad people wandering about, hence John had bought his air rifle which was under the front seat. John reached for it while I asked the guy what he wanted. It turned out to be a false alarm as he was a road worker and his grader's battery had gone flat and he wanted us to alert the Road Team at the next town to bring him a new one. We did and continued on our way.

Our journey took us through many interesting towns like Penong, Yalata, Eucla, Mundrabilla, Madura, Cocklebiddy until we finally reached Balladonia.

As we hadn't had a shower since Melbourne and we had finally found water, we both decided a shower was in order. However, we discovered another significant fact when after I had washed my hair and John wanted the 'Seagull' Soap I couldn't find it, only to be told by John that it was still tangled in my hair. The water was so hard that it got caught up and stuck in my hair, and I hadn't noticed!

We continued through Norseman and Coolgardie to Kalgoorlie and then proceeded on to Kambalda where we were made members of the Western Mining Social Club and given some nickel as a memento of our visit. The next day we continued to Perth where we spent Christmas Day eating Kentucky Fried Chicken on the banks of the Swan River.

The next day we flew to Rottnest island on a MacRobertson Miller DC3. It was such an old plane that when the flight attendant asked us what we would like to drink, John in his inimitable way said, "A screwdriver." She replied, "We don't serve them on this flight", to which he said, "I don't mean a drink, I mean a Phillips head screwdriver to tighten up the screws above us that are turning around with the vibration in flight."

It was hilarious to see the look on her face as she walked back to the galley.

CHAPTER 4 A Career in the Country

After we returned to Perth, I visited Perry Lakes Stadium where the 1962 Commonwealth Games had been held. I had brought my running spikes and outfit with me in case I got a chance to run at the stadium. I introduced myself as the Captain Coach of the Colac Athletic Club and past Captain and Coach of the Kew Harriers Athletic Club and they graciously invited me to run in the 440 yards event. Amazingly I had maintained my fitness and had the pleasure of winning the race. It was a big thrill to run in the same stadium that Byron Williams had run when representing Australia in the 100 yards event in 1962.

After we left Perth, we drove south through Pemberton, Bunbury, Busselton, Albany and Esperance, up north again to Norseman and back through Port Augusta to Melbourne. When we returned, we calculated that we had driven about 6000 miles in 21 days, and agreed it was the adventure of a lifetime.

As I was living and working with senior, influential figures in the community my role as Captain and Coach of the Athletic Club enabled me to meet and mix with leading business and social people in the city. Some asked me to give a presentation on my WA trip, complete with slides to illustrate the grandeur, beauty and significance of the places we had visited.

My weekly radio program on 3CS also enabled me to 'hone my radio speaking skills' and promoted my image throughout the Western district.

I joined the Colac Golf Club and was able to win a few events because of having time after work to practise. Caltex at that time also had the rights to the official US Masters film, and I was asked by the golf clubs in the area to be their guest and show the film at their annual presentation dinners.

Ted and I had some great parties that started on the night of my birthday and often finished late on the morning of his! He had met a lady in Geelong, also named Kate, and this relationship developed with her often staying weekends in the house I shared, which gave my life a completely new social dimension!

Then the Area Representative based in Warrnambool was promoted and transferred back to Melbourne, and I was unexpectedly advised by Caltex State Office that I would be temporarily caretaking this larger area with the largest distributor in Australia. In other words, I had an area twice the size, and it wasn't long before I was permanently transferred to live in that flourishing city.

It was sad to leave my home in Colac, my friends and athletes in the Athletic Club, yet more adventures were in store for me.

I arrived in Warrnambool in the summer of 1968 and found a small one-bedroom flat near the football ground.

It was a small rear, unfurnished flat and quite basic, so I 'acquired' some furniture from an aunt in Melbourne who had to move into a retirement village and set up my home. However, I found it a lonely existence after living a busy social life in Colac, and I became somewhat depressed as I knew no-one. It was a bit like living on a desert island, but I forced myself to keep fit and healthy by running daily.

My Distributors were the infamous partners Cook & Green. Peter Cook had been a Melbourne Football Club player who moved to Warrnambool after he retired from the AFL. Maurie Green, on the other hand, had run a taxi company in Melbourne. They were the most unlikely couple. You could even say 'the odd couple' as Peter was a huge, practical, hands on affable, friendly man while Maurie was a small administrator with a financial strength who was quite introverted, thoughtful, and secretive.

Their wives were also opposites. Peter's wife, Nancy was small, pretty, sporty, and likeable, whereas Maurie's wife was tall, belligerent, loud and an alcoholic. She was a challenge for Maurie, and she would often burst into our hotel drink after work nights demanding he come home NOW and cause an almighty scene. It was interesting to learn how to cope with this, which was at times, a very awkward and volatile situation.

However, not long after I had settled in, Peter, who knew I was lonely and knew no-one, invited me to join the Warrnambool Football Club and this led me also to joining the Golf Club with a wonderful course and a gem in the Western District famous for its great layout.

I was grateful for this involvement in the local sporting society. It was very helpful, and enabled me to meet many influential business people, and great Australian sporting people like the 1960s Olympic 1500 metre champion, Herb Elliott, who one night was our guest speaker at the Sportsman's Club.

I also became friends with the 'Pic Peas' Area Representative through my group of new friends and some six months later I was invited one Saturday night to go with him and the boys to a well-known night spot, the Commodore Hotel. I wasn't one for going to hotel night spots, but I was encouraged to go and low and behold met a lovely school teacher, Joan, from Lake Bolac, who was the lone teacher at the Koroit Primary School. She was a good basketball player and golfer, and we soon became more than good friends and started seeing one another on a continuous basis.

Over a year later, on 23 August 1969 we were married at St Andrews

Church in Ballarat. In hindsight it was too soon, and Joan was too young, not even 22 years old, yet that was what happened in those years.

After our marriage, I found a brand new two-bedroom flat in a better position nearer the main city area and we shifted in to start our married life together. It was an amazing logistical experience with Joan from Lake Bolac, me from Kew, married in Ballarat and now living in Warrnambool. Whew!

Soon after, I experienced a significant event in my Caltex life. About twice a year, Caltex would send the Lubricant Engineer out to various country areas as a Sales Ambassador for the Area Representatives to take to existing industrial accounts to assist in building relationships. In addition, they encouraged us to introduce him to potential accounts as a means of gaining their business by him giving them advice or assistance.

When the engineer arrived, I met him at the Mid City Motel, the best motel in Warrnambool. I had planned some visits to a number of existing customers, and on the second day after seeing our last customer, he asked if there were any new large customers I would like to visit which would be potentially good in the future.

As it happened, we were at the time driving near Barton's Livestock Transport so I suggested we go in unannounced and see if we could set up a meeting with the owner Tom Barton. Tom was a huge man, tall and powerful and had been a footballer in his time with Warrnambool Football Club and was known to Peter Cook, yet I had never really met him, even though I had seen him often at the club.

I parked the car, and we went into his office. He was inside in a serious conversation with, we presumed, one of his customers, so we waited patiently for about 15 minutes until the conversation was over and his customer appeared happy and had departed. Tom then came over to me and the engineer and said, "So how can I help you guys?"

During the time we had been waiting, I had thought about his business and what I might say to introduce us, so I simply said, "I know we haven't got an appointment and thanks for seeing us Mr Barton. I'm George Norris the Area Representative for Caltex and I have the Senior Caltex Lubricant Engineer, here for a couple of days.

I thought we would stop by and see if we could be of any assistance to you. I realise you are a signed Esso account, but thought we would call in anyway."

Tom's eyes lit up and he forcefully and unexpectedly said, "Who said I'm a signed Esso account? They have treated me badly lately and I am not at all happy with them!"

So, I asked, "What could we do to assist you to be a Caltex customer?" He said "Well, Esso won't continue with the cartage contract I had to Murray Bridge so if you can organise a Caltex replacement cartage contract, I would consider signing over all my fuel and petroleum requirements to Caltex."

I was shocked and surprised by his frank response, so we stayed only a few minutes longer and I said I would enquire with Melbourne Office and see what opportunities were available. I thanked him for his time, we shook hands, and we immediately went back to my flat which was just around the corner and called Ric Clark, the Assistant Manager for Victoria.

I excitedly explained the situation and he quickly and enthusiastically replied that a cartage contract had just become available for a 6000-gallon aviation gasoline tanker to service the Mangalore Airport. He was happy for me to offer this to Tom to see if he was interested so they could arrange the contract.

We went back straight away and advised him of this unexpected opportunity for which he was most grateful and confirmed with me that he would be very happy to continue discussions with Caltex.

The rest is history! Caltex secured Tom Barton's Transport for all petroleum products for the whole of Australia for five years and as he owned some 60 Kenworth/Peterbilt livestock prime movers it was quite a coup for me in my new position. It really proved that courage and self-belief can take advantage of enthusiasm and opportunity, or as I later heard a Formula 1 racing driver say, "Luck is when preparation meets opportunity!"

Leadership Lessons:

1. Enjoy life doing what you love.
2. Be flexible, fluid and fearless.
3. Surround yourself with trusted friends.
4. Take a calculated risk now and again.
5. Let things happen, don't make things happen.

Chapter 5

War in the City

The year 1969 was to be a very eventful year. Man landed on the moon on 20 July. I was married for the first time on 23 August, Tom Barton's Transport account was acquired and I was promoted again, this time back to Melbourne as a Retail Area Merchandiser to look after the Chadstone to Dandenong area at the height of the vicious 'Retail Price War'.

It was during this time that I was to learn many aspects of strategic management and leadership by helping my retail service stations cope with adversity and even criminal behaviour.

One example was the Caltex service station in the main street of busy Dandenong. The proprietors, Luke and Alice Vecchiet, were trading from 6am until midnight and competing with a cut price petrol station just around the corner.

When I visited Luke one day after an urgent phone call, he explained that on the previous night after the service station had closed, some unknown irresponsible competitor had bludgeoned their price sign with an axe and wrecked the sign. He said that this had happened a number of times, was at a loss to know what to do, and asked for my advice.

I thought for a moment and simply said, "Luke if you never shut, I doubt if they will ever do that again."

He thought about my advice for a moment and said, "Sounds like a plan. I'll talk to Alice and see if we can do it! We have an employee who knows someone who wants a job so I'll interview him and if he is suitable, I'll offer him the midnight to 6am shift and see if he will do it".

He did and the service station never looked back, never got attacked again and doubled its volume the next month.

However, I learnt an interesting business and marketing lesson at the time that was hidden from normal business thinking.

The midnight to 6am shift did not double the volume in that period. It was because motorists saw the petrol station was clean, open, and with lights glowing, they came back in the day to purchase petrol. In fact, by opening 24 hours, they had inadvertently become a pioneer in the retail petrol station market. Staying open 24 hours was a massive new marketing strategy in itself, and Caltex quickly had many other service stations follow this strategy, and we won significant new volumes of business.

This strategy again proved my philosophy, 'that out of adversity comes advantage, it's just at the time of the adversity we don't yet know the advantage'.

This strategy was used by many other retail merchandisers such as my friend Ian Kent who had recently married the love of his life, the beautiful Bettine, and Caltex service stations prospered significantly during the price war in Melbourne.

Also, during this period, I was asked to host a Caltex visitor from the USA. The 'Retail Price War' had become an international phenomenon and had generated serious global interest. I picked him up from the State Office in Melbourne and we started a tour of my area to show him in person.

As we were approaching the lights at the corner of Dandenong and Warrigal Roads, Oakleigh, I thought I would have some fun with him. In answer to his comment about, "The speed of change of prices being displayed to the passing motorist", I replied tongue in cheek, "Well often while I'm stopped at the traffic lights like we are now, someone will come out with a ladder and change the price sign while you're looking." His eyes lit up and he laughed, not having really believed me.

Well unbelievably, and suddenly, a guy with a ladder came out to the front of Geisha Gas, a leading price war retail service station, and changed the price right in front of our eyes.

I couldn't believe it was really happening, and he reacted in startled shock saying, "I see what you mean." After I returned him to the State Office he dined out on the story and it became folklore for many years.

My time as a Retail Merchandiser was very enjoyable and I learnt many lessons in business development, management, strategy, time management, effective communication, relationship building, sales psychology, marketing, promotion, public relations and especially leadership and public speaking as I was often asked to relate the Geisha Gas price war story.

After a successful few years of coping with, and in many cases winning the war, I was promoted to Victorian Training Officer and later to Training Manager for Victoria and Tasmania. It was during this personal development period that I learnt many techniques and significant business knowledge to conduct training programs for staff, retailers and wholesale distributors.

In fact, on reflection, I was really 'doing an MBA' while working for Caltex. I hadn't realised it at the time, but the Caltex Management Communication course from America that I studied and implemented was also to become a significant weapon in my future business life. It is still a powerful communication skill I use to this day.

Leadership Lessons:

1. Plan logically, execute emotionally.
2. There is a stealth factor in success.
3. Draw mental pictures for people.
4. Use the element of surprise.
5. Keep learning every day.

Chapter 6

The End of an Era

This course was revolutionary because it introduced the latest business communication psychology from the USA. It had been researched and used powerfully in America for high level performance influencing and negotiating skills to gain willing action and agreement to promote progress and change.

I became a trained leader of this communication psychology in Australia. It was based on how the human brain is wired to react first or initially to perceive and visualise the key benefit or loss of an action, proposal, or idea so the person listening is then interested in the details that enable this benefit or loss to be delivered.

I became adept in its usage over time and witnessed significant positive 'willing action' results when used effectively in life, business, and sport.

After a couple of years in the Training Manager's role, I was to be promoted and planned to be shifted to a remote country area in Gippsland as a Sales Manager looking after a team of area representatives. The State Manager at the time was a very tough and autocratic man who wouldn't increase my salary in line with the promotion. In fact, I would have been on a lower salary than the area representatives who I was to manage and lead.

My Senior Training Manager, Ian Felstead, tried to reason with him but to no avail. After one of his meetings with me, he made an insightful comment that I have used many times since, "You can always tell a paranoid, except you can't tell them much." It is a great comment and one that often brings a light touch to a serious situation.

I became quite disillusioned during this stressful time as it appeared that after devoting my business life to Caltex for 16 years I was not really being recognised and rewarded for my loyalty, dedication, effort, and commitment to the company.

Then 'it' happened!

One Friday, working from home on a training project, the telephone rang, and it was Neville, the owner of a marketing and promotion company. We had been using him as a guest speaker in the Retail Training Courses to educate the service station managers on new marketing strategies. He asked me how I was doing at Caltex as he was advertising for a General Manager to run his business and wondered if I would be interested.

I replied that I was enjoying my role, yet I would be interested to talk to him.

He was free later that day, so I met with him and discussed the role and the opportunity to join his firm in Melbourne.

He wasn't aware of it, but I naturally used the Caltex negotiating course in my discussions and resulted in gaining the position at treble my then Caltex salary including a company car.

I went home and discussed the opportunity with my wife Joan and as we had a 12-month-old daughter, Nicole, and another baby on the way, we thought this was a great opportunity. So, the next Monday morning I called and agreed to accept his offer of the new General Manager for his Marketing Strategy and Promotion business.

After 16 years with Caltex this was a momentous decision to make. It was very difficult writing my resignation letter so as not to burn my bridges. Actually, the really hard part was letting the envelope fall into the mail box, as this signified the end of an era with my first employer who had developed and helped shape me and my career to date.

Leadership Lessons:

1. Be open to change.
2. Knowledge is power.
3. Paranoids are painful people.
4. Expect the unexpected.
5. Only say in negotiations what people need to know.

Chapter 7

A Clash of Cultures

I was not aware at the time of resigning that I was earmarked for a National Training role in Sydney in my future career path and I heard later that there had been many awkward phone conversations with Head Office and the Victorian State Office Manager, asking how and why my resignation had happened.

However, this was now none of my business and in June 1973 I set about the on implementation of my new role with the new company. Our clients included Rank Industries, Phillips Electronics and Brash's Stores.

My second daughter, Melinda was born on 12 April 1974 and in that time with the firm, I had not really enjoyed my new role, mainly because the business I found had been, and was poorly managed, financially. In fact, I had received four repossession notices for missed payments on my car and at least three dishonoured salary cheques, so my family's security was under threat and I was losing respect for my new employer.

It was a stressful experience I had never experienced in my previous 16 years at Caltex and I started to suffer what I guess is called 'buyer's remorse'.

I tried hard to put my anxiety to one side and soldier on, but I became more and more disenchanted and worried that my past unblemished business reputation was being tarnished.

Often in joint meetings with clients, he would promise things that I thought were not possible to be delivered and I would challenge these comments afterwards on the drive back to our office.

However, my questions were met with weird comments to 'sweep the matter under the rug'. So when I took my annual leave after the birth of our second daughter and my family travelled to Noosa Heads for a week, my head was in other places. I eventually spent the holidays searching for answers to help resurrect my future and the security for my family.

After I returned to Melbourne nothing had changed other than a new Production Manager, Gus Poskus had joined the firm from the very professional company Show Ads. He was a breath of fresh air, but he really couldn't change the management style either and I became more and more disenchanted and one day at the end of October 1974, I handed in my notice.

Neville was shocked and it made me realise that his Vision, Mission and Values were not in parallel with mine and we had a dichotomy between how he managed the business and how I wanted to manage the business. This difference, I realised would never be solved and we would never be in synergy, so the business, the team and me personally would continue to suffer.

In other words, we didn't 'fit' and there was a clash of cultures.

Initially, this wrestling with reality was very stressful and debilitating after I left the business, especially when I reflected and realised I had been in my new role for only 16 months, or a month for every year I had been working at Caltex Oil.

However, I also felt a huge weight off my shoulders. My imagination and creativity started to kick in and I realised that I might as well control my own destiny, and start my own business.

This, if it worked well, would enable me to enjoy my business life, generate a secure future for my family and achieve my own full potential, but it would be a calculated risk.

In my final months with Caltex I was introduced to Dr Abraham Maslow's famous 'Hierarchy of Needs' at a National Training Course in Sydney. I realised that by starting my own business I would actually move up from level 2, where I was anxious and angry to level 5, have the opportunity to achieve my full potential, feel happy and contented in running my own business and where I would be self-motivated to achieve my goals.

Leadership Lessons:

1. Believe and act on your sixth sense.
2. Value your own self-esteem and self-worth.
3. Only work with people who fit your values.
4. Reducing distress is therapeutic.
5. Worship your sense of well-being.

PART 2

THE INTREPID ENTREPRENEUR

CASE HISTORY 1

George D Norris
& Associates Pty Ltd

Chapter 1

A Leap of Faith

Starting my own business was exciting yet I realised, fraught with danger. So I set about writing a business plan and model, projecting cash flows and calculating the financial requirements to operate the business.

I happened to play golf with a CBA bank manager, Rod Jones, so I arranged a meeting with him and the manager of the local Westpac Bank and presented my business plan to both of them.

They were both impressed by the detail, so my business background at Caltex had paid off and they indicated that they would help me to get started.

I decided to go with my golf partner as he had been able to approve an overdraft facility to assist in the growth stages of my business.

Next I decided where I wanted to work from and after looking for offices to lease I found a suitable space, already partitioned at 44 Caroline Street, South Yarra. I bought a couple of desks and chairs, had the telephone installed and on 4 December 1974, George D Norris & Associates Pty Ltd started.

I have been asked by many people since that date, "What was it like when you made that courageous decision?" My answer is, "It was like standing on the edge of a cliff looking down into the water and seeing there was nowhere to land, yet believing there was, so I jumped."

In other words, my background, my knowledge, my strategy, my business plan, my business model, and my self-belief enabled me to raise the confidence and courage to jump off and start my own business.

As I'm writing this book my business is now over 45 years old, called Norris Management Pty Ltd and, of course, has had its ups and downs.

However, as you read my book I hope you will experience the exhilaration of being the Senior Captain of your own airliner as you navigate your way through the clouds, the turbulence and the blue sky to achieve your vision and dream of a successful business.

Interestingly, when you do jump off and start your own business, you will be amazed by how many people who know you will admire your courage. Also, if you market your business well and ethically, they will surprisingly support you and want to help your success.

The first months were difficult, yet interesting and some colleagues did support me from out of the blue.

An old school buddy who was a member of an influential supporter group for the Collingwood AFL Football Club, introduced me to the President and we created and designed a 12 month strategic player recognition and reward program to challenge the players to create a culture of team work not only on the field, but off it as well.

Leadership Lessons:

1. Ensure you start with a strategic plan.
2. Utilise your relationship circle of influence.
3. Believe in yourself and you'll succeed.
4. People love to support people with courage.
5. Develop your own point of difference.

CASE HISTORY 2

Collingwood AFL Football Club

Chapter 1

Mission Imperative

Jeff Coath had polio as a young boy, but fought on gamely at school and became quite an accomplished sportsman.

When we left school to make our way in the business world, we kept in touch and he purchased my 1926 Singer, two-seater vintage car that I had bought from the wife of the late vicar who married my parents on 2 October 1936. I bought it for 25 pounds and sold it to Jeff for the same amount.

We had a few years of fun in it and I had taken it on some car rallies with my close friend, John Robarts and our girlfriends, at the time. I called it 'Suzie' and it became an eye catcher whenever I would take it out for a drive.

One summer holiday I drove my two friends, Bruce McGinley, who I had first met in prep class at school and had taught to do up his shoe laces, and John Keeble, who I sat next to in High School from the age of 12, to Sorrento for the Christmas holidays.

Channel 9 was producing and televising the show 'Sorrento by the Sea' during the holidays with Graham Kennedy, Geoff Corke and singers, Val Ruff and Dorothy Baker, on the beach near our camp site each Saturday morning.

One Saturday the three of us returned from a late breakfast in

Sorrento in 'Suzie' only to see Dorothy walking back to her caravan. As she passed, she stopped to admire 'Suzie' and we asked her if she would pose for a photo sitting in the back. She said, "I've got a better idea, why don't you put the roof down and I'll sit up on the top of the front seat." It was a single seat tourer, so we agreed and rushed to put the old roof down. Once done, Dorothy was happy to have herself photographed sitting up top but after she had left to return to her caravan, we realised that the struts of the old roof had broken, and the roof never went up again.

I returned from Sorrento somewhat crestfallen with my dear old car's roof ruined. However, I still drove it for fun until after several fabric universal joints tore apart, I decided to sell it.

Then one Sunday, along came Jeff who joined us for a party. He fell in love with 'Suzie' and I reluctantly sold her to him.

Many years later, after I had just opened my new business, we met up again and had lunch. He had started his own business some years before and told me how courageous I was to take the risk and start mine too.

He was a member of the AFL Collingwood Football Club supporters group of businessmen called 'The Woodsmen' and one night, over a drink at my office, he mentioned that he thought there was an opportunity for me to help the club as they had just appointed their new Senior Coach, Murray Weideman, a former star Collingwood player. He went on to say that the new President, Ern Clarke, wanted to change the culture of the club playing group and suggested he could set up a meeting with Ern if I was interested.

Having just opened a new business and having no clients yet, I jumped at the opportunity. We met in the Club boardroom one

At a Caltex Car Rally with John Robarts and Jill Proctor in the 'Dickie Seat' and Pam Abrahams beside the Author at the wheel.

morning and discussed the reason for this change. Apparently, at the time there was a lack of consistent discipline among players. Some were on enormous salary packages while others were not, so the culture had become 'cliquey'.

The top player, Len Thompson, who was on a huge salary, would arrive in his Mercedes Benz, while other players would arrive in cheaper cars, by foot or pushbike. In addition, players were arriving late for training, matches and meetings, not wearing the club off-field uniform when required and were not working as a team.

Ern agreed I could design a program to motivate the players to turn around the culture. I excitedly left the boardroom having secured this rare opportunity to work with the most famous AFL Club in Australia, 'The Magpies'.

I thought a long while about the psychology that needed to be applied to the challenge and then decided on the point I had learnt from Herb Elliott when he was a guest speaker in Warrnambool, that people 'hate to lose more than they want to win' as the key strategy for the program. I then thought of a suitable name for the program and decided on 'Mission Imperative' as a play on words of the film 'Mission Impossible'.

The strategic concept was that each player would start the program and therefore the season already with a 'bank account of points' and they would lose points depending on how they were rated by the selected Collingwood judges.

The judges were to be appointed by the President and would mainly be made up of Welfare Committee members rostered to attend each match, meeting, training session and player function. They would then complete their rating score forms to be collated each week.

At the time there were some famous players at Collingwood including Len Thompson, the Richardson brothers, Terry Waters, Peter Moore, the infamous Phil Carman and champion full-forward, Peter McKenna.

Another strategic component was to erect a massive scoreboard that would be positioned inside the players' change-rooms. This board was white with all the player's names for that season painted in black. Next to their name would be the total of 5,200 points they started with.

The Player of the Month as judged would be the player who lost the least number of points and they would win a bonus of 200 points. The mother, wife or partner of each Player of the Month was also recognised and could select a merchandise prize from a list of prizes. The 20 players with the most points at the end of season would win a range of merchandise and travel prizes decreasing in value the further they were down the list.

The large scoreboard would record each player's progressive point score during the season so they could track their performance, and the program and the scoreboard became a talking point in the media and created a lot of interest among the players.

Cover of the 1975 Collingwood Mission Imperative player brochure.

It was reported to me that initially some of the high-profile players were somewhat cynical of the program but after a few weeks they were seen sneaking a look at the huge scoreboard to see how they were tracking.

The key strategic ingredient was that I had designed the scoreboard so there were no favourites with Carman under C and Thompson under T on the scoreboard which was designed for all the player's names to be alphabetical. In other words, everyone was equal as in a team.

The media, however, thought it wasn't appropriate to take down some of the old photos for a season to install the scoreboard. Even well-known ex-umpire and 3AW football host, Harry Beitzel, wasn't sure if it was appropriate either!

The program broke new ground in Australia as a corporate culture program in sport and worked well for the Club that year.

Unfortunately, 1975 saw Collingwood finish in fifth spot after being narrowly beaten by Richmond in the elimination final but the Welfare Committee could see the merit in the methodology of the program.

The following year the club decided in their wisdom, or lack of it, to design and implement their own program. Unfortunately, they finished in last place on the AFL ladder for the first time in history.

Unbeknown to anyone, I had made myself a promise that if I could conduct my business successfully for six months, I would go to the well-known men's fashion store in South Yarra, Trevor West and buy a complete window of coordinated business attire as a reward.

So, one Wednesday after running my business successfully for six months, I announced to my PA/Receptionist after lunch that I would be back in about an hour and that I was going to buy a window! She looked at me confused and perplexed about what I meant but was pleasantly surprised when I returned with the displayed coordinated clothes of one of the entire windows of Trevor West's store.

Leadership Lessons:

1. Keep in touch with old friends.
2. Luck is when preparation meets opportunity.
3. People hate to lose more than they love to win.
4. Pride is a double-edged sword.
5. A team culture has in no favorites.

CASE HISTORY 3

L'Oreal of Paris

Chapter 1

The Golden Frog

Another old school friend, Bruce McGinley, then asked me to create a recognition and reward program for his Party Plan Slipper business. He had a very tight deadline and had not realised the work involved. So again, I worked all night without sleep to create the program. He was grateful and it proved extremely successful.

Then one night after being in business only nine months, I calculated that I had equalled my previous employer's twelfth year's turnover in just nine months and had in fact found somewhere to land safely after taking the leap of my life.

A prospective client was unexpectedly happy to support my new business and as a result my company was appointed to handle the strategic marketing, communication, promotional and conference business for five years for the international firm, L'Oreal of Paris.

L'Oreal was a worldwide brand considered very high end in the female beauty business and had their Melbourne office at the 'Paris end' of Collins Street. Their Australian Managing Director at the time, John Konrads, was the 1960 Rome Olympic gold medallist, middle distance swimmer, so this gave the French cosmetic company a high image and significant clout when doing business in Australia.

Brian Lambert was the General Manager of the Hair Salon Division.

He was a pleasant, tall man with a round kind face, high business values and ethics who decided he could trust me to help his business.

Our initial performance management program was to launch the new worldwide brand positioning statement 'Because You're Worth It', throughout the hair salons of Australia.

We designed a simple program for the national salon network to achieve maximum involvement and L'Oreal was very happy with what we achieved. As a result, we were asked to assist L'Oreal in other ways to enhance their performance.

However, Brian wasn't too sure how his state workforce of salon representatives was performing in Victoria, so he suggested I do a performance audit with each Melbourne salon representative.

I must say it was very illuminating and I found a culture of conniving, convenience, and control. Even though Brian had communicated that my role was to travel with them in their car for the day and accompany them on their sales visits to their hair salon accounts, I couldn't believe the poor way they behaved in front of me. Some didn't even bother to bring their account cards with them to record comments and sales. Others made horse racing bets during the day, while others blatantly made up sales figures when they phoned in each day at 4pm.

After completing the performance audit and presenting it to Brian, he was shocked, looked at me in embarrassment and said, "Okay George, if you were me what action would you take?" I then gave him a few of my forthright thoughts.

1. You have employed the wrong profile of person.
2. There needs to be more accountability and responsibility shown by each representative.

3. By making them phone in their sales orders for the day at 4pm, I think you are putting too much pressure on them to make up figures, instead of them reporting more honestly by having the scope to create a better relationship and longer-term sales strategy with the salon owner.

He agreed with my feedback and made a number of personnel, process and procedural changes as a result. We seemed to be forging a productive, trusting, and respectful relationship.

I continued to work with him the following year and was introduced to the General Manager of the Retail Division, Kevin Charity. He was vastly different from the polished Brian Lambert. Kevin was a 'matter of fact' task-oriented manager who was very down to earth in his communication style, nonetheless, good to work with.

He had heard about our success with the Salon Division from Brian and approached me to create and co-ordinate a double conference. The plan was for the Salon Division to have their conference first, then the Retail Division would arrive, join in a total conference, and the new range of hair colours for 1977 would be launched.

The location had not been decided and he asked me for my thoughts. As they wanted a close overseas location, I suggested New Zealand, Fiji or Bali. They loved the idea of Bali especially when I suggested I possibly could arrange private villas for John Konrads and his wife Mickey, for Brian Lambert and for himself at the Sanur Bali Hotel complex.

I made a few calls to the General Manager of the Sanur Beach Hotel, Stanley Allison. He confirmed that he would make three villas available for the three L'Oreal Executives. The venue was confirmed, and wheels were put in motion for the back-to-back double conference in Bali.

It was agreed that the Salon Division would fly up first and have their own conference, then the Retail Division would fly up and join them. The new hair colours would then be launched to the total company as one family. The Managing Director, John Konrads, would also stay for both conferences to put the icing on the L'Oreal cake.

However, during a long-distance phone call with Stanley Allison, he made an important comment. He said that in view of the political paranoia in Indonesia at the time, I should inform L'Oreal management to instruct all who were travelling to Bali for the conferences to NOT write on their in-flight immigration cards that they were flying to Bali for a 'conference/product launch' and instead just indicate it was for business. He thought this would assist the accompanying hair products, and any necessary equipment, to be un-challenged by customs and allow their clearance and easy entry.

I arranged a meeting with both Brian and Kevin and told them the clear instruction Stanley, the Hotel Manager, had given me and asked them both to instruct each L'Oreal participant accordingly. They agreed this would be done and that they would advise all participants travelling to Bali.

All plans, accommodation, travel, meals, tours, function rooms were confirmed, and I travelled with John Konrads, Brian Lambert, and the Hair Salon group to set up and confirm all the details and arrangements.

Everything went extremely well for the first group conference, but when the second Retail Division group arrived with the new hair products and equipment, the photographers forgot the instruction and instead wrote on their immigration card 'product launch conference'.

The group arrived and late that afternoon I was called to a meeting with the Hotel Assistant Manager, John Konrads, Brian and

Kevin when we were informed that all the L'Oreal products and photographic equipment was being held at the airport. This was not unusual, and the customs authority often did this and virtually blackmailed visitors. That was why Stanley had given me the explicit instructions to not say 'conference/product launch'.

I asked Stanley Allison to join us in the meeting to see if he could pull any strings as he was on the board of the Garuda Indonesia Government Airlines Catering Company, Aerowisata. He indicated that in his capacity his hands were tied but suggested he could engage the negotiating services of his Food and Beverage Director, Agung who was actually a Prince in Balinese royalty.

It was a massive problem, as everyone from L'Oreal was now in Bali at the hotel, but the products they had come to launch were being held at the airport.

It was agreed that Prince Agung and John Konrads would negotiate with Indonesian Customs to release the products and equipment.

As the meeting broke up, Brian and Kevin came to me and made an astonishing confession. They had forgotten to arrange female models for the hair colour launch which was scheduled for the day after next and asked if I could help. With very little hair myself, I jokingly suggested that I wasn't suitable and after their short-lived mirth they indicated they needed several youngish females to act as models for the new hair colours to be applied and displayed.

I was astonished that they had not brought models with them in the group, so I simply said in my most professional manner, "Leave it with me and I'll talk to the Hotel General Manager and see what rabbits we can pull out of the hat for you."

Another meeting with Stanley was convened and I, rather sheepishly asked him again for his help. He handled the request in his stride and said, "There is an American/Australian social group that formed some years back so there might be some wives of the various managers living on the island who might be interested. Let me ask tonight and I will let you know tomorrow."

The next afternoon, the day before the scheduled launch, he called me and said he had acquired eight American/Australian wives of managers living in Bali who would be delighted to act as models and have their hair coloured. I was relieved and quickly let Brian know. He and Kevin were also relieved, and so the rabbits were pulled out of the hat!

The hair products and equipment were finally released that night from customs, thanks to Prince Agung and $US10,000 which I believe was paid to them by L'Oreal or by John Konrads. The launch and conference were successful and the following two days were planned to simply be for relaxation and well-earned rest.

The Indonesian press had heard on the bush telegraph that John Konrads was in Bali, so I was advised that a reporter would be flying down from Jakarta to interview him on the last day.

John was amazing to work with and simply a joy to know. However, I noticed that whenever he jumped in the pool to swim everyone from L'Oreal would get out! He swam so fast and so effortlessly. He was like a speedboat in the water.

The L'Oreal Conferences and Product Launch eventually came together and went well, but I learnt a few more life and leadership lessons along the way that were to be of value in the future.

Leadership Lessons:

1. Keep strategies simple for success.
2. Detailed planning and confirmation are critical.
3. Referrals are outcomes of consistent results.
4. Manage by fear at your peril as it stifles initiative.
5. Lead people by example and give them scope.

CASE HISTORY 4

Wurlitzer

Chapter 1

The Musical Mouseketeer

One day in early 1975 I received another call out of the blue. It was from Clarrie Pearce, the Marketing Director of Rank Industries asking if we could handle all the Marketing, Promotion and Incentive Conference work for Canon Cameras, Sansui and Patterson darkroom equipment.

He had been a client of my previous employer but had also experienced false promises. Apparently he had liked me and my creative style and wanted my business to assist the company with its future business development and performance programs.

An outcome was the Canon Cameras Incentive Conference which was to be held in Hong Kong late in 1975. This was not only one of the first major overseas conferences my fledging new business had arranged for a client, but it became a history making trip in other ways.

So, at the end of October 1975, a group of Canon retailers and their partners, together with my wife and me, departed on an older Pan Am DC-8 and flew eight hours to Jakarta where after a short stopover we departed for the final leg to Hong Kong. During this leg of the flight, and before lunch was served, I went around the cabin making sure all the group of 40 people were in good spirits, relaxed and comfortable. Suddenly I got a tap on the shoulder and turned around to find a smallish guy standing behind me.

Thinking I was blocking the aisle I apologised, then he said, "No you're fine. I have been watching you since we departed Sydney and have noticed how well you have been looking after your group and wanted to let you know that I'm extremely impressed." I replied "Thanks, I am just doing what I think is my job." He said, "Well, I haven't seen anyone look after their people on board a plane so attentively and wanted to tell you so."

He said, "Look, I'm Glenn Derringer from Wurlitzer, the organ company in America, and I've got my Australian General Manager sitting with me. Would you like to join us for lunch when it arrives as we have a spare seat between us?" I agreed and said, "Do you mind if I just speak to my wife and let her know. What seats are you in?" He told me, I went back and asked her if she would mind if I had lunch with them. She was reading and resting, didn't mind at all so I wandered back down the plane to where they were sitting.

Glen introduced me to his Australian General Manager, Hans Goeti who got up from his seat to let me pass and sit in the seat between them. Glen then proceeded to give me the background of why he was so impressed with my inflight support. He said, "At Wurlitzer we often have incentive conferences and sometimes even charter a whole ship, so I'm aware of looking after winners well."

Lunch was then served, and we kept chatting. Glen asked me about my business and my oil industry background, and after I had given him an outline he leant over and said, "Hans, when you return to Australia I want George to work with you and handle all our dealer development and performance programs.

Hans asked me when I was returning to Australia as he wanted to get together as soon as possible. I gave him my return date and asked where his office was and he said Taren Point, south of the Sydney airport.

Glen sat back and said, "That's done then." Realising the great significance of what was being proposed I then asked, "So Glen, give me your background." He replied that many years before, had been a Walt Disney TV Mouseketeer and as a young talented organist he would often play on the show. He was now the Wurlitzer Product Manager. I was impressed and asked him in amazement what area he covered? To my surprise Glen replied, "The world."

Wurlitzer went on to become a major client for us in Australia and two years later we helped them launch their new models at the Mount Buller Chalet and designed several performance management programs for their national retail network.

Two years later we were asked to create, design and co-ordinate a performance management program for the top Australian retailers and their partners to travel to the USA on a study tour of their head office in De Kalb, Illinois, then visit their factories in Corinth and Holly Springs in Mississippi, and Logan in Utah.

The program was a triumphant success and during my pre-trip to arrange and finalise all the details, I found that at each location I visited they were flying the Australian flag at the entrance, and a board in each foyer welcoming me by name.

This was an important part of my corporate education, which I have referred to for many years, and which taught me the importance of building relationships for great outcomes.

When the Wurlitzer winners arrived in Chicago, we all went out for dinner at the McCormick Inn Hotel to relax after the long flight from Australia. There was a live group playing after dinner and being by myself on the trip, one of the retailer's wives asked me for a dance. The music stopped after a couple of dances and as we were returning to our table, a young guy who was sitting nearby approached me.

As I was leaving the dance floor he said, "Hello, may I have your autograph?" I agreed and he held out the menu and a pen. As I didn't know who he thought I was, I said, "What would you like me to write?" He replied, "Just say, to David from Rod Laver." So I wrote the message and signed it. Obviously he had heard my Aussie accent and I guess at 5'7" and having similar colouring and features he thought I was Rod Laver. He raced back to his friends at his table elated saying, "I got it, I got it."

Hearing his comments and wanting to do the right thing, yet not wanting to spoil his moment of fame in front of his friends, I called him back to the dance floor and whispered in his ear, "Well done, but I'm not Rod Laver, sshhush."

Leadership Lessons:

1. Be very careful, people are watching you.
2. People are inspired by enthusiasm.
3. Your first impression is a lasting one.
4. A customer focus enables amazing results.
5. Have fun in life but value honesty.

CASE HISTORY 5

Renault (Australia) Pty Ltd

Chapter 1

The French Connection

After operating for a few months, I tried my hand at cold calling some companies after sending out some introduction letters to prospects I thought might have a need for our business. I prepared a script using the formula and techniques I had been taught at Caltex from the USA and soon had appointments and work with Electrolux and especially Renault Australia who were both clients for over five years.

The Renault story was very significant in many, many ways as I will try to explain.

The most difficult part of cold calling is the follow up phone call so the script and formula helped give me the confidence I needed to call Jerome White, the Renault Sales and Promotion Manager.

I was surprised that he was such a bright and positive person and quite interested to meet me. We set up a time, and I drove to the Renault Australia head office at West Heidelberg. I signed in at reception before Jerome arrived with a flurry of arms waving and a theatrical hello. He escorted me to a small office and arranged coffee for both of us.

After asking about my business and my background, he proceeded to give me what I would later call a brief on a project he wanted to implement for the national dealer network. We seemed to get on well and he genuinely appeared to want to support me for having the courage to start my own business from scratch. I left the meeting with the challenge of creating, developing, and administering a dealer performance management program to coincide with the launch of their new models in Australia.

When I returned a week or so later, he seemed happy with the concept strategy I presented and then said, "I'd like you to meet the senior management team and present the proposal to them."

Nick Josika, the Marketing Director was an affable and astute fellow who asked many critical questions of both of us. The Managing Director, Jacques Thoridnet also joined us. He was the French Renault Head Office representative that played the superior executive role. He had a reputation for being aloof and distant and bordered on giving a perfect impression of Inspector Jacques Clouseau straight out of a Pink Panther film. Even more amazing was the name of Nick Josika's secretary, Joy Zipfinger, a lady with immense talent who would one day become my own secretary.

My relationship with Renault, and especially Jerome blossomed, and I focused my attention on our first programs to ensure all went well. The strategy I had planned worked successfully, and they were very happy with both the Dealer Principals' reactions as well as the subsequent sales results.

At the end of the program Jerome called me to set up another meeting. This time Jacques, Nick, Jerome, and Joy taking the minutes, joined me in the briefing meeting. It appeared Renault had a problem of some consequence. France was not going to release any new models for some time, so the objective was to encourage the dealers to perform at their best without new models for the next two years and still focus on maintaining their market share.

During the meeting I was wondering about the best strategy. Then Jerome spoke to us and enthusiastically suggested that we create a trip to the 1978 Le Mans 24 hour race and take the top dealers for an exclusive tour of the prestigious Schlumpf Brother's Car Museum in Mulhouse, France as the guests of Renault.

The story of Fritz Schlumpf's passion for Bugattis is spectacular, and the narrative goes that the brothers were forced to declare bankruptcy because they put all their money into collecting and building the car museum at the expense of paying their taxes and focusing on making their textile mill financially successful. The brothers fled back to their native Switzerland and the building's vast basement houses the world's largest collection of rare automobiles and is now owned by the City of Mulhouse and a group of other French automobile organisations.

The European trip was agreed, and because I had a close relationship with the management of the Sanur Beach Hotel in Bali, it was also agreed that the Renault group would visit this idyllic island for some 'R&R', on the final leg of their return trip.

It was also agreed, due to the limit of Le Mans corporate box tickets that Jerome would escort the winning Renault dealers throughout the trip, with me joining them and welcoming them at the Sanur Beach Hotel when they arrived in Bali.

During my many visits to Renault I was introduced to a number of Renault people including one David Williams who I was destined to meet and work with 20 years later at BMW.

The Le Mans 24 hour race was spectacular in that Renault won the race for the first time in an Alpine A442, so the dealers and their partners together with the Renault Marketing Director, Nick Josika and Jerome White were over the moon when they arrived in Bali.

This performance program was a real winner and the morale of the Australian Renault dealerships was kept high even without any new models to promote the brand.

The group enjoyed a couple of days of well-deserved rest and relaxation. I had come to respect Jerome's abilities and opinions and we had become good friends, so much so that I was invited to the wedding to his second wife, Blanche.

Tragically, our friendship ended a number of years later when he passed away after a long battle with cancer.

Early the next year, Renault Head Office in France unexpectedly made a decision to close down their Australian office and distribution centre and the brand languished again for many years.

Leadership Lessons:

1. Be courteous when cold calling.
2. Mirror your market in language.
3. Think big, bold and beautiful.
4. Deliver what you promise.
5. Trust your judgment and be confident.

CASE HISTORY 6

Ansett Airlines of Australia

Chapter 1

Back to the Future

When I started my business some 12 months prior, I had been trying to negotiate with either Australian Airlines or Ansett Airlines to support me in starting my company in the incentive conference and performance management business.

Australian Airlines wouldn't give me a commercial discount arrangement which would enable me to give them preferential entre to my business clients because I didn't have a 'track record'. So I went cap in hand to Ansett for a meeting with the National Sales Manager, Gordon Ham. He was a soft, gentle but tough manager and I had come to know him through my previous dealings.
After hearing my story he was sympathetic to my cause but then sat back in his chair and said just what Australian Airlines had said. "George, I'd love to help you start your business and work with you, but you haven't got a track record yet."

I looked at him in despair, then had a light bulb moment, and with a shot of inspiration replied, "Yes, I know that Gordon, but unless you help me I won't have a track record."

He was thunderstruck, sat forward in his chair, put his hand out and said, "George, what a great comment. You're right, let's do business together and let me buy you lunch". Shocked I replied, "Thanks Gordon, yes let's have lunch, but it will be me who's buying, not you."

So started a long and profitable relationship which enabled me to buy tickets and earn a commission as a profit centre, but also to arrange free tickets for me to travel interstate and meet potential clients in order to gain their business and therefore generate the travel business for Ansett.

When I reflect on this meeting, and these negotiations, it just proves that people really want to help you in business if you conduct yourself appropriately, show courage and resilience, especially if you show persistence and explain how they will benefit from your efforts.

At about this time in my business life, I thought I should contact my old friends at Caltex again and find out if there was any possibility for me to continue to work with them in a training or performance management capacity.

I thought I would gauge the climate since I had left, so took a big breath and called the Australian Managing Director, John Landels, at their Sydney head office. I had always admired him and I found him quite amiable towards me.

To my surprise I was put straight through to him by his PA. He caught up with my progress, seemed happy that I had called, so I eventually asked the loaded question, "What opportunity would there be to continue working with Caltex in a consulting, training or performance management capacity".

To my further surprise he volunteered that I should contact the Training Department as there were many opportunities to assist in training retailers, wholesalers and staff, especially with the knowledge I had acquired while working at Caltex for so long and especially because I was a trained leader in the Caltex Management Communication program.

Caltex Star Christmas Ball. Author on left and Managing Director John Landels second from right.

He went on to say I should contact Bob Harmer, the National Retail Manager in Sydney, as there were opportunities to assist him. Also, he offered his car to pick me up at the airport and that I should advise his PA of my flight details. What a welcome!

I called Bob as requested and he was very interested in my new business. However, he indicated that the timing was not quite right and that he would get back to me in a few months when he was in a better position to know what was actually required in the retail marketplace and his new budget for the next financial year.

It was a good lesson in diplomacy in that when I resigned some 10 months prior, I made sure I simply said I was leaving to further my career and that we as a family could not make the move to the Gippsland area of Victoria as a Sales Manager for family reasons.

It proves that if you are able to control your frustrations and don't burn your bridges, you often find that 'the world is round' and you can take advantage of opportunity.

At the same time I was contacted by, Peter Maishman a previous Sales Manager of mine and now the Australian Training Manager and asked to continue training their retailers around Australia. So I commenced a further 12 years with Caltex, but this time as a speaker, trainer and management communications specialist.

The growth of the business by this time had required a shift in office location, size and the employment of more senior and junior staff to process these performance management programs. We needed to ensure we serviced the clients well so they were satisfied with the results, return on investment and remained loyal.

I initially travelled around Australia as a guest speaker for Caltex training courses where I specialised in leadership psychology, management communication and sales and marketing strategy, educating the national retail network.

Then one day out of the blue I received the call from Bob Harmer asking me to fly up to Sydney to discuss a retail performance management and customer satisfaction program for Australia.

Leadership Lessons:

1. Never burn your bridges.
2. Always be prepared to ask.
3. Listen to the hidden needs.
4. Stand for something or you'll fall for anything.
5. Be persistent but show empathy and patience.

CASE HISTORY 7

Caltex Oil (Australia) Pty Ltd

Chapter 1

A Strategy for Success

So, with my Ansett 'free of charge' must ride ticket I travelled to Sydney for a meeting that was to set in motion significant changes to my business and little did I realise would change my personal life as well.

When I arrived at the airport, John's PA true to his word, had organised his chauffeured car to take me to the Caltex Head Office in Kent Street, Sydney near The Rocks overlooking Sydney Harbour.

I was dropped off in the underground car park and made my way up to the 12th floor to meet Bob Harmer. He was a friendly, affable fellow who I had come to admire over the years and he welcomed me warmly and introduced me to his management team and support staff. He then got me a coffee and we settled down to a serious conversation in his office, which had great views of the Harbour looking west from the famous Sydney Harbour Bridge.

He outlined his thoughts and the problems the retail network was experiencing now that the national price wars had subsided. It appeared that research they had commissioned showed that their retail network's morale was poor, the presentation of the service stations was poor, the customer service was poor and therefore as a result, customer satisfaction was also poor. "We have inherited a massive problem George, and I wondered what you could do to assist, given that you know our business so well."

I explained to him the range of performance management programs we were implementing for some new clients and he was very interested. He then asked me to create a similar program for Caltex and after a long briefing meeting and lunch, I left his Sydney office feeling excited to help my previous employer and flew back to Melbourne ready to start work on creating and designing a program to achieve his objectives.

Back safely ensconced in my office in Melbourne I debriefed my General Manager, Eric Carter who had also worked for Caltex, firstly as my Sales Manager when I returned to Melbourne in the infamous 'petrol price war' and secondly as a Caltex Service Station proprietor himself for a number of years.

We set about designing a performance management program that focused on customer satisfaction through friendly, warm customer service, presentation of amenities, clean restrooms, clean sales rooms and clear, customer focused communication.

We also built into the program sales targets that were realistic in growth for each service station and a mystery shopper program to assess and rate the customer service standards of excellence.

The winning 75 service station dealerships were then to be allocated on a state-by-state proportionate basis to win trips for two for a seven-day Corporate Incentive Conference on the idyllic island of Bali.

The trip would include return airfares, transport, especially arranged tours, all meals, and a Caltex Conference Gala Dinner with special presentations by the Caltex management for the winning retailers and their wives or partners.

The program was planned to be conducted over a six month period with the trip to Bali in November 1978 and we were able to arrange some very special events through my contacts at Hotel Sanur Beach Hotel including meeting a Balinese Prince Agung, who was the Food and Beverage Manager and the Hotel General Manager, Stanley Allison, from the United Kingdom.

So, after much planning and organisation we completed our proposal, and I flew to Sydney once again and met with Bob to present our recommendations.

He was delighted with our strategy to improve the retail standards, sales, customer satisfaction and especially the morale of the retailers who had experienced a very tough, and at times, traumatic period in their business life.

However, when we discussed the budgeted figure to conduct the total program, he questioned the costings to administer the program saying that he could easily have his own staff handle this aspect.

I was stunned by his question for a few seconds, but thinking on my feet and staying confidently on the positive front foot I replied, "Well Bob, if your people will be doing all the work my people will be doing, I could save you a lot of money. From what I know in administering these intricate programs, your people be working significant overtime or, 'tongue in cheek', you have too many people employed in the first place."

He thought for a moment nonplussed, and I wasn't sure what he was going to say, then with a sheepish grin he said, "Good point George! We obviously trained you well at Caltex. I can't argue with your answer."

After more time analysing the program in further detail, he approved the program which was to be known as 'Bali Bound'.

I flew back to Melbourne happy and satisfied in the knowledge that we would both be focused on delivering a unique and historic performance management program that would change the image, standards, sales, morale, customer standards and satisfaction in the Caltex retail national network for years to come.

We worked hard as a team to make all the components work smoothly and the results were simply astounding. At the conclusion of the 6 months, Bob advised me in our final coordination meeting in Sydney, that the program had not only raised the morale, image, retail standards and customer satisfaction index throughout Australia, but that Caltex had generated in excess of an additional $12 million in sales.

Now was the time to celebrate and be 'Bali Bound'.

Leadership Lessons:

1. Rapport is critical at the start of a meeting.
2. Clarify and get agreement on all the objectives.
3. Begin any project with the end in mind.
4. Explain the benefits to overcome an objection.
5. 5.Work hard as a team to achieve great results.

Chapter 2

Bali Bound

In 1978, over 40 years ago, the world was a vastly different place. Some world events included the birth of the first test tube baby in the UK, the most popular song was Saturday Night Fever by the Bee Gees. The movies that year included Grease, Every Which Way But Loose, Superman and Heaven Can Wait.

The most famous athlete was American, Muhammad Ali, and actor, Marlon Brando was paid a record $3.7 million and 11.75% of the gross profits on Superman, and 3M invented the sticky yellow notes called 'Post-It'.

The mobile phone had only been invented by Motorola 5 years before in 1973.

The McDonnell Douglas DC 10 Series 30 jumbo was flying in competition with Boeing's 747 jumbo and for many of us the world was a simpler and happier place as social media had not been invented and people were still mainly talking to one another in person, face to face.

Many people in the world and especially Australia had never flown in an airliner at all and Airline captains frequently invited passengers into the flight deck to observe them at the plane's controls.

We were managing the largest group of people we had ever been responsible for, 165 people on behalf of my past employer Caltex and we were Bali bound!

I looked up after checking the passenger list in front of me at the special airport group check-in desk and stared blankly ahead in a tired trance.

She was walking away with a young girl and an older woman. "What great legs", I exclaimed quietly to my General Manager, Eric Carter. "Who's that, do you know?"

Other members of the group of 165 arrived to be checked in before he could answer and the moment was lost in time forever.

It was the 18 November 1978 and the day had eventually arrived to depart for the exotic, idyllic island of Bali for a group of winning retailers and their wives and partners because of a corporate performance management program.

The best performing retailers in each state had won trips for two as recognition and reward for their special efforts. The trip was to be an all-expenses paid trip for 7 days to Bali, flying with Garuda Indonesian Airways and staying at the prestigious Sanur Beach Hotel.

The group would have tours arranged to the Temple at Tampaksiring, the Monkey Forest Sanctuary, the Artist Colony and exhibitions in Ubud and then the highlight to President Suhato's summer palace near Tampaksiring, where a banquet lunch would be served after being prepared at the Hotel and transported in vans to the Palace.

In addition there would be a number of private Balinese dinners at the hotel's outdoor theatre where Balinese dances would be performed by the local, traditional dance groups.

Chapter 2   Bali Bound

The trip was to culminate in a farewell banquet on the last night, where the senior executives of Caltex would personally thank all the winning retailers and their partners for their efforts in improving the sales, service and customer satisfaction levels throughout Australia.

The night would conclude with a Balinese band playing a range of songs with the winners and their partners dancing the night away. The next day would be a day of rest prior to departing the hotel in the late evening for the Denpasar International Airport and the Garuda flight back home to Sydney and then Melbourne.

It was an exciting trip for these retailers, but also a precarious one as they needed to have made important detailed arrangements to enable their businesses to remain managed, well-staffed and financially able to continue to operate successfully.

As an extra form of thank you, and as a significant PR and company relations exercise, a number of senior Caltex management and area managers from around Australia were invited to join the group to assist as hosts during the trip. Little did they know what was in store for them in a life changing way!

The retailer group included many successful, long serving retailers including my own brother John and his then wife Erika. John had once worked for Woolworths as a trainee manager, but in 1967 was conscripted to serve in the Vietnam War for 7 RAR in Nuit Dat.

However, when he returned home he was told by Woolworths that his job was no longer available. This had been very disappointing for my brother who had entered National Service in the 'ballot system'. Shortly beforehand he had been selected as an outstanding Junior Manager and had represented Woolworths on the 'Outward Bound' executive management training course in New South Wales, who had then as its Patron, HRH the Duke of Edinburgh.

As a result I helped him join Caltex. He initially had a successful career as a Retail Area Representative but then eventually took the challenge to run his own business and leased the retail service station in Ringwood, Victoria.

His excellent management skills had then enabled him to qualify as a winning retailer in the 'Bali Bound' retailer program.

The winning retailers and their partners from Victoria, Tasmania, South Australia and Western Australia all checked in at Melbourne's International Airport, Tullamarine, joining those from New South Wales and Queensland, who had boarded the Garuda flight earlier in Sydney and so we all took off as one group from Melbourne for Bali. In those days it was planned to be the 'trip of a lifetime' and it certainly proved to be just that!

Leadership Lessons:

1. Excellence is difficult, mediocrity is easy
2. Good leaders celebrate success
3. Good leaders lead by example
4. Success in retail is in the detail
5. Good leaders recognise and reward initiative

Chapter 3

First Time Flyers

After we left Melbourne, and were at cruising altitude, my management team and I moved about the cabin to say hello to those in the group who had boarded the flight in Sydney. In addition to the Caltex management and retailers my New South Wales Manager, Kevin McNamara, an ex-Caltex employee who had co-ordinated the Sydney departure, was on board. My Victorian General Manager, Eric Carter who had also been both a Caltex Retail Sales Manager and then a Caltex retailer before the arthritis forced him to seek another job and I invited him to join my company was also on board. It certainly was an 'All Caltex' operation.

During the early part of the flight it became apparent to us that the majority of our group of 165 were first time flyers, as was usual in those days and in fact many were somewhat nervous passengers.

Many of the group had therefore never been up on the flight deck of a plane before and never on the flight deck of the world's most modern 'jumbo' at that time, the McDonnell Douglas DC 10 - Series 30.

After lunch was served, I suggested to my team that, if it was permitted, I should take as many of our group that were interested to see the flight deck and meet the captain.

They thought it was a great idea and I set off to ask the cabin manager, then known as the purser, if this would be possible.

In turn they asked the captain and he agreed provided I took up passengers in groups of four as a maximum. So, over the next few hours I must have taken nearly 40 passengers to see the flight deck of the latest jumbo aircraft in the world.

All who visited were amazed that this new huge plane, capable of seating nearly 400 passengers, was actually flying by itself on 'auto pilot'. It was also flying on an angle to our destination because of the winds at our altitude, but all was being monitored by the first officer and the captain.

All who visited the flight deck were very impressed with the flight deck and the captain's knowledge, and returned to their seats much the wiser and much more confident that the plane was in safe hands. As first time flyers they had received first class treatment and were now more relaxed and comfortable.

It's a pity this opportunity is no longer possible because of the terrorist attack on the World Trade Center on 11 September 2001.

While taking passengers to the flight deck, we passed by Ayers Rock at Uluru. It was bathed in sunshine in the distance and looked a truly majestic, impressive Australian tourist and heritage icon.

After some seven hours in the air, we could see the islands in the Bali group and the DC10 descended smoothly and landed at Bali International Airport, Denpasar.

In 1978 there were no aerobridges at the airport and after the moveable stairs were positioned next to the front and rear doors, we were able to depart.

When the door was opened, I saw Stanley Allison waiting at the stairs to greet me and my client's key executives. They followed me down the steps and I made the introductions.

Since 1975 I had brought a number of clients to Bali for conferences and Stanley had made it his practice to meet me and my client's key management at the foot of the stairs on the tarmac. This sent a wonderful message to them that they were special and that they were being treated like VIPs, which they were to both of us.

He was able to be on the tarmac because of his special clearance as General Manager of Aerowisata In-flight Catering, owned by Garuda Airways. They provided in-flight catering for all flights leaving Bali. Not only could he meet us at the foot of the plane's stairs but he was also able for PR and tourist marketing reasons, to assist me and my VIP clients through a speedy Customs and Immigration process inside the airport.

These special benefits impressed my clients and also gave me additional clout and a point of difference over my competitors who had not developed such a special relationship in this magical island.

Leadership Lessons:

1. Good leaders have high empathy.
2. Good leaders use their initiative
3. Leverage your point of difference.
4. Messages of confidence can be unspoken.
5. Good leaders make people feel special.

Chapter 4

Negotiating a Nightmare

The balance of the group followed assisted by my team and while they were clearing customs and immigration, Stanley whisked us away to the hotel in his private limousine, so we could check in and be ready to greet the group in the ballroom on their arrival.

On their arrival I introduced the Hotel General Manager, Stanley Allison to them and he in turn introduced his management team which included the Food and Beverage Manager, Prince Agun, a member of the Balinese royalty.

It had been a long day for us all and especially the first time flyers who had missed a lot of sleep prior to the flight through excitement.

The next day was at leisure and gave people an opportunity to do their own thing and explore the island or just laze around the pool or on the beach.

That evening everyone attended a traditional Balinese BBQ dinner and witnessed an impressive performance by a local Balinese dance group of the famous Kecak Dance.

The next day the group was put onto buses and taken on a tour of the Monkey Forest and Ubud and then to Seminyak where they could buy gold and silver jewellery which had been handmade by the local Balinese people.

The days were busy for me and my management team checking on travel arrangements, budgets, meal arrangements, functions, transport, children, speaking arrangements, numerous health issues and even checking on issues that arose on the tour of the Monkey Forest. It had been reported that a man had been scratched by a monkey and that a lady had had her handbag and scarf snatched from her by a monkey and she never saw them again.

The next couple of days passed without too much drama but even so, the amount of work I had to do with organisation and administration issues prohibited me from really leaving the hotel and consisted of me attending many meetings. Night time seemed to be the only time I could relax and join my team and the group.

Often a group of us would venture into the music lounge and listen to the Sanur Beach Boys, a great band who could play most of the well-known western songs. I was introduced to them on my first night and the leader would ask me each time I was there to join the band on stage to play the bongo drums, the only instrument I could play.

My favourite song to have the courage to take up his invitation was Frank Sinatra's 'Fly Me to the Moon' and each night the band would play it and ask me to come up and play the bongos and join them for a few numbers.

The second last day was planned to be very special and I had arranged with Prince Agun for the total group of 165 to travel up into the mountains and the cool air to President Suharto's summer palace after visiting the temple at Tampaksiring.

He had arranged all the food for lunch to be prepared at the Sanur Beach Hotel and taken up in refrigerated vans to ensure the meal was safe and to the highest health standards. Unlike today, 'Bali Belly' was inevitable for most travellers to Bali in the 1970s.

The day was a huge success, but I didn't have the time to go and delegated the task to my management team. Instead I worked on budgets, seating and a multitude of other things that needed attention to ensure the trip was a complete success because this was before 'event managers' were in vogue.

It was during that afternoon while taking a quick nap that I received a distressing call from the Hotel General Manager, Stanley Allison. He told me that Garuda Indonesian Airways had just informed him that the plane that had been scheduled to return our group to Australia had been allocated for the Annual Pilgrimage to Mecca for Ramadan and that they had no alternative planes for our return trip to Australia for the next four days.

Naturally I was shocked that an airline would act in such an arrogant, offhanded way and leave 165 people on a corporate conference stranded in Bali, Indonesia. I told him that it was a great problem for the businessmen and women in my group as they had already arranged to have others run their retail businesses for the planned eight day trip away and that this four day extension would put their businesses at risk and could be financially detrimental to their futures.

He explained that he was powerless to change the situation but that he would negotiate with Garuda Airways to pay for the accommodation and meals for the four extra days. I told him I thought this was the least they could do but in view of not giving me or our group any notice of the four day extension they would also need to cover all drinks and liquor as well!

After much discussion Stanley agreed, and I then had the dubious duty of advising the Caltex management team of the situation in which the airline had placed us.

Of course this major delay was a real headache for most in the group as they had not planned for an event such as we were about to experience. They had arranged for their businesses to run without them for eight days and had put deputy managers in charge and many had utilised friends, family and relations who could cope with running a retail business short term. They had only given these temporary managers limited authority for important duties to enable the business to continue to trade.

So there began a stressful stream of international telephone calls from the exotic island of Bali to the busy cities and towns scattered around Australia delivering news that nobody really wanted to hear.

Little did I know that this was just the first crisis these 'winning' business people would have to endure on this trip. However, during the next few days everything seemed to settle down and in fact the group started to really relax and enjoy Bali and turn off from thinking about their business.

Leadership Lessons:

1. People love pomp and ceremony
2. Leaders focus on detailed planning
3. Always show respect to your customers
4. Stay strong in negotiating a crisis
5. Work for a win/win outcome.

Chapter 5

Beauty and the Banquet

The second last day of the delayed trip was fast approaching, and the organisation for the official Bali Bound Banquet began in earnest. It had been an interesting logistical exercise to seat all 165 people in the most appropriate areas, and at the most appropriate tables, as many had made new friends during the past 12 days and wanted to sit with them.

It was also important to allocate Caltex management to sit and act as hosts during the evening and also to sit the two families that were in the group together, so the children felt comfortable and at ease.

We had many meetings debating a number of issues and trying to cater for all their culinary needs and finally after many hours the seating plan was agreed and given to the Food & Beverage Manager.

The meetings finished that day about 4pm and I decided that I couldn't go any longer without having a relaxing swim in the hotel pool to cool off.

Somewhat exhausted I changed from my working outfit into my swim togs and set off and plunged into the hotel's large and inviting pool. Wow, it felt good after all those days inside!

After a while, a group of children started to play 'pool ball' and it would often finish near me. I started to throw the ball back and they enjoyed my involvement and got into it throwing the beach ball back with some enthusiasm.

All of a sudden they quietened down and I heard a voice behind me ask, "Do you often play ball with children?"

I looked around somewhat startled to see a dark haired beauty sitting on the seat near the edge of the pool.

"Oh yes", I said. "I enjoy being with children. In fact I coach about 70 children at my athletics club back in Melbourne".

She seemed impressed and replied, "I don't know many men who would enjoy that!"

"Thanks for the compliment", I said. "Are you enjoying your holiday?"

"I'm not really on holiday", she said. "I am here with a conference group from Australia."

I asked if she was with the Caltex Oil group and she said, "Yes, I am here with my daughter and mother."

"Oh", I said. "You must be Susan from Corowa, that's your daughter Sarah in the pool and your mother, Dawn is travelling with you too from New Zealand."

She was taken aback and said, "How do you know all that?"

I replied, "I'm the person in charge of the Caltex group and it's my business to know the details of who is here."

"Are you enjoying Bali so far", I asked. "Yes, it's been great so far, except the Monkey Forest."

"Oh, you must be the lady who had her bag and scarf taken by the monkey."

"Yes, but how did you know that?"

"Well, I get briefed every day by Caltex management and it's my job to know these things in case there is an emergency and if we need to take any action."

I then asked her, "Are you going to the banquet tonight? I have seated you, your mother and your daughter at the table with the other family from Geelong."

She looked at me reservedly, "I'm not sure if I'll go yet. I'm thinking about it."

"Well, if you go I'll ask you for a dance as long as I don't get a knock back."

"Okay. I'll think about it", she said, and with that I got out of the pool and made my way back to my room.

Time was running out and I had lots still to do in putting the finishing touches to the banquet night's activities, but I couldn't help being somewhat interested to meet the lady from the pool again in more formal surroundings, that is if she decided to attend at all.

I acted as the MC for the night and introduced the Senior Caltex Oil executive to the group. He spoke in glowing terms of the professional skills of the winning business owners and proprietors and how the customer research had shown a marked improvement across Australia in both standards and consistency. He handed out awards to all the winners to loud applause, thanked me and my firm for all the arrangements that had gone so far without a hitch and then the band started playing and the dancing started.

As my official duties had concluded for the night, I looked across at the table of families and saw that the lady from the pool was sitting with her mother and daughter, so true to my word I wandered over and asked her mother, "May I have the pleasure of dancing with your daughter?" to which she replied, "Yes", and we danced the night away.

It was during the dancing that I looked down and realised the lady from the pool was the lady with the great legs that I had seen at the airport. Wow, what a night we had on the dance floor!

Leadership Lessons:

1. Keep focused on your priorities.
2. Stay the journey with commitment.
3. Let your hair down and relax sometimes.
4. Maintain a professional presence at presentations.
5. Show respect to older people and you'll usually win.

Chapter 6

A Birthday Surprise

The day before our scheduled departure I received a call from the hotel General Manager to urgently meet him in his office.

I finished some bookwork quickly and walked down to his office. When I got there he had a solemn look on his face and I became concerned.

Stanley Allison was a very amiable Englishman but on this occasion he became very serious.

"George", he said, "I have received advice that security will be tighter than normal tomorrow tonight when your group checks in at the airport for their departure and it has come to my attention that some of your group may have been unfortunately involved in purchasing drugs. I thought I should warn you that they will be arrested if they are caught by Customs and Immigration. What do you think you should do?"

This discussion was to be the unexpected start of one of the most dramatic, exhausting and nerve racking four days of my business life!

"Well", I said, "tomorrow is the final group dinner and it just happens to also be my 38th birthday, so I could address the group over dinner, thank them for their co-operation over the past 12 days and remind them of the details of times of our departure from the hotel, our flight number, departure time and arrival time in Sydney.

I could then mention that tonight I have been advised that the airport security will be very tight and to make sure they check their luggage to ensure they are not carrying anything they shouldn't be carrying before they leave the hotel.

He agreed and we left the meeting feeling that my strategy was the best way of handling a very sensitive and serious issue.

The final day was one of relaxation and celebrating my birthday and that evening we all gathered for the final group dinner before departure.

The band on this last night in beautiful Bali, played 'Fly Me to the Moon' as a farewell tune! How appropriate but even more special was the entrance of the hotel waiters with a monster birthday cake for yours truly, to the tune of 'Happy Birthday'.

Pieces of cake were handed out to all 165 people which was an amazing spectacle and this gave me the opportunity to thank the group. I then mentioned the airport security issue without making it too obvious that I suspected that some passengers could have placed themselves in serious trouble with the security police at the airport.

The celebrations concluded, the group members departed for their rooms for late check out and no doubt anyone who had done something illegal quickly repacked their luggage.

The hotel departure went smoothly as did the airport departure check-in, so my message must have been heard and heeded by anyone who had a guilty conscience.

Our Garuda DC10 Series 30 flight departed on time and at last the 165 Caltex business owners and support management staff were on their way home to Australia. At least that's what they thought!

Some 30 minutes after take-off from Denpasar airport, I was cleared to go up on the flight deck to meet the captain and ask him if I could bring up some passengers to the flight deck in my group, just like I had done on the flight to Bali, to see the cockpit in action for their first time, especially as many of the group were first time flyers.

The purser was most obliging and introduced me to Senior Captain John Miller who was on loan from McDonnell Douglas where he was the Chief Test Pilot for the new DC10 Series 30. He was a middle aged Englishman from Lancashire, with an engaging personality, a calm understated disposition, a lovely wide smile a beautiful refined English speaking voice and a very senior professional presence.

He mentioned that he was training the Garuda first officers to fly these exciting new jumbo planes, and that his wife was on board and they were planning some R&R for a few days in Sydney.

We spent about 20 minutes together discussing his role and my request and developing, I hoped a trustful relationship. At the end of our meeting he said, "Yes George, that's okay to bring them up in groups of four provided you accompany them but wait until after dinner has been served."

As I prepared to leave I thanked him for his time and agreement and he asked if there was anything else he could help me with. During my 20 minutes on the flight deck I had observed him continually swivel around from looking at me in the 'jump seat' and adjust the settings on three dials on the instrument panel in front of him.

Each dial had the ability to show 100:00 and he would make 'very small' adjustments on a tiny wheel next to each dial to always make the three dials show the same readout, e.g. 100:00, 100:00, 100:00 or 99.6, 99.6, 99.6 and he would do this every couple of minutes.

This intrigued me, so I asked him what he was doing with these dials and what was achieved by his actions.

His answer, which I didn't know at the time would be one of the most profound lessons of my business life, was simply that he was adjusting the speed of the fans in each of the three massive jet engines.

When I asked him why he did this he said, "So there is no cabin noise or vibration, and 300 people back there have a comfortable flight!"

I thanked him and left the flight deck in awe of the attention to detail of a chief test pilot in flying this massive aircraft and with the realisation that is why he was the chief test pilot!

I returned to my seat in business class, as I had been upgraded on departure with my two general managers and as dinner had just been served I sat back in my seat and quickly finished my meal.

However, the purser approached me a few minutes later with a request that the captain wanted to see me now! I was naturally surprised as he had indicated that I should bring up the groups in about an hour after the meal had been finished, but I got up and walked to the flight deck feeling that something had happened.

Perhaps it was, as they say, a sixth sense!

When I entered the cock pit, Captain Miller spun around slowly in his seat and said, "George, shut the door and take a seat please."

I immediately started to realise that something was wrong as this is the instruction a manager usually gives to a person when he or she wants to give them some bad or serious news.

My heart skipped a beat!

I asked if there was any problem, and he calmly stated, "Well George, about five minutes after you left, the tail engine oil seal failed and we have had to shut it down, so it is idling and not really in use."

I looked at the tail engine control arm in the console and he showed me that it had been pushed back to 5%. He went on to say that if he shut it down completely it would act as a brake and possibly break the tail off the plane. Wow!

My heart then skipped two beats!

I then thought to myself, this is what every airline flyer dreads, an in-flight emergency that you are helpless to do anything about.

I looked over at the two other engine controls and noticed that they were now at a higher power output setting, just as Captain Miller mentioned, "So we are now flying on only two engines."

I probably at that time went into some form of shock as I realised we had only departed Bali approximately 90 minutes before and we had another six hours to fly.

However, I tried to remain calm and said to the Captain, "Okay John", we are on first terms names now, "what options do we have?"

"Well", he said in a matter of fact style, "I'm not authorised to fly over Australia for six hours on only two engines with so many passengers so we have investigated a number of options. Firstly, we can return to Bali but there is no accommodation and no parts to repair the engine. Secondly, we can land at Darwin where there is possible accommodation and no spare parts. Thirdly, we can land at Surabaya, but there is not enough accommodation and no parts or fourthly, we can land at Jakarta where there is ample accommodation and spare parts."

In my shocked, naïve state I said, "So what is your decision?" He laughed and replied, "George, we are going to Jakarta and I have already turned the plane around about 30 minutes ago and we are on our way!"

My heart skipped three beats!

"Wow John", I said, "all in my group are expecting to be landing in Sydney and Melbourne in six to eight hours and they will be very shocked and distressed as they have already been delayed four days and they have businesses to run and families expecting to meet them". He said, "I realise there will be problems, and you have already mentioned, many of your group are first time flyers."

"So as the captain I am swearing you to secrecy about the current situation, and we will not be telling any passengers that we have diverted to Jakarta because they could panic as they could think we have been hijacked. Therefore, I am instructing you not to tell any passengers in your group, not even in your management team."

"In fact George, when we land in Jakarta in about four hours it will be about 4am and the airport will be closed as it has a midnight curfew. We will have to park the plane on the runway away from the airport building as there will be no air bridges in operation."

"When we land, I will need your help to explain the situation to the passengers. When we come to a stop, please come up to the flight deck area and use the internal telephone and speak to them to explain the situation and ask them to remain calm, as I and my crew will have a lot of operational things to do at that time."

Then, as a casual afterthought he said, "By the way George, we will be flying through a tropical storm on the way to Jakarta so it could be quite bumpy too! The purser will call you to the internal phone just outside the flight deck when we land. Sorry George for the circumstances you are in, but there is nothing more we can do now except cope with the situation and manage it with your help."

I returned to my seat trying not to look shocked, worried or emotional and sat down to collect my thoughts. The flight attendant had served me a glass of port while I was on the flight deck and had left it on my tray. I picked it up to take a sip, but found my hand shaking so much that I had to put quickly put it down, so I wasn't telegraphing any message.

Just then my General Managers, Eric and Kevin looked over at me and said "Hi, everything alright", to which I replied, "Yes fine thanks", and gave them a wink. They looked at me with puzzled stares and I got up from my seat and started to walk about the cabin to mingle and talk with my group of passengers, so I wouldn't have to field any more of their questions.

Just as I proceeded about halfway through the economy section, we heard thunder, saw lightning and the DC10 lurched and pitched with the turbulence so I was forced to sit down in an empty seat for a few minutes to collect my thoughts, thinking to myself, "And we are only on two engines now."

I then continued to move throughout the cabin, chatting to my fellow passengers, including Susan and her mother and daughter, and making strained small talk while looking as cool, calm and relaxed as possible.

Interestingly, six of the male passengers in the Caltex group were light aircraft private pilots and as I approached two of them sitting together, one said to me, "George, why hasn't the sun come up yet on the horizon?" I knew they were on to something significant, so I laughed and made some pathetic reply like, "It must be late today", and then stared at him achieving direct eye contact as if to tell him something without telling him anything!

Leadership Lessons:

1. Small adjustments have a massive impact on change.
2. Customer service enables customer satisfaction.
3. Leaders need to be proactive and assertive.
4. Leaders must calmly evaluate options.
5. Your eyes can talk and send messages.

Chapter 7

Attitude and Aptitude at Altitude

I eventually returned to my seat shaken and, I hoped, looking calm and tried to relax, knowing everything but saying nothing and just thinking and planning what I would say when the plane landed in Jakarta in a few hours' time.

The passenger sitting next to me was Jim Chang, the Vice President of the Chase Manhattan Bank, New York and we started up some sort of conversation about what I was doing, how large was my group, who was my client and what we had been doing in Bali.

I engaged him in the conversation, all the while wanting to tell him that he wouldn't be connecting with his flight back home to America and instead trying to appear interested in his story. Little did he realise we were about to go through an arduous adventure neither of us had ever dreamed would happen.

It seemed like an eternity but eventually, the plane started to descend and the purser, not Captain Miller came on the intercom saying, "Soon we will be landing", but not saying where, "so please return to your seats, stow any bags under your seat or the seat in front of you and fasten your seatbelts."

On our final approach we again hit some turbulence but thankfully only briefly and then descended slowly towards the airport runway.

Just before we landed, I felt prepared, as I would ever be, to speak to our 165 shocked and scared passengers aboard. Then I realised that there were another 30 private passengers who would also be shocked and distressed, making my audience a total of 195 people I would have to speak to, reassure, help them be calm and assist.

We glided towards the runway smoothly and just as the wheels were about to touch down, two delightful elderly ladies sitting to my left had what I believe to be an amazing moment in their lives when the one sitting nearest the window said, "Look there's the Sydney International Airport sign", only for her friend to exclaim in a shocked state, "No it's not, its Jakarta International Airport. Why are we here?"

After the plane had come to a complete stop, and amid the screaming and yelling of the 195 shocked and scared passengers, I proceeded to the area next to the flight deck, was given the public address telephone by the purser, gathered my composure and thoughts and said, "Ladies and gentlemen, as you can see, we are in Jakarta and not Sydney!"

The reason for this is that the oil seal in the tail engine failed about 90 minutes after we left Bali. We are lucky that Captain John Miller, the chief test pilot for McDonnell Douglas is flying our DC 10 aircraft and in the interests of your safety made the decision to fly to Jakarta as he was not allowed by air traffic authorities to fly across Australia to Sydney on two engines with 195 passengers on board.

I know you are all as shocked and distressed as I am and have been for the last four hours after being advised of the situation, but not being able to tell you at the captain's directions for safety reasons. However, I would now ask all the Caltex business winners to remember why you won your trip for business management excellence and put these attributes into practice to help us all cope and manage the situation. I will advise you of further details as soon as I am told. At present the airport is closed, but please stay seated and calm while we have the airport opened so we can cater for your needs."

Just then I was approached by some passengers yelling that a lady was possibly having a heart attack and asking could I get a doctor. I quickly told Captain Miller of the serious situation and he suggested I go to the rooms under the airport building where the first aid nurses are located. Some passengers attended to her while the captain lowered the planes inbuilt stairs for me to walk down some 10 metres to the ground.

My athletic background kicked in and I ran as fast as I could, some 400 metres to the airport building while the Captain radioed the control tower for an ambulance. I luckily found two nurses at the first-aid centre at the base of the airport and made frantic sign language to them to come quickly with me to the plane to help a passenger who was having a suspected heart attack or going into shock. Fortunately they were able to decipher my sign language and English charade, picked up their first aid kits and followed me as fast as they could back to our crippled aircraft.

At this stage passengers were starting to realise the affects that whilst we had flown the planned elapsed time of 6-7 hours we were actually in Jakarta at 4.30am instead of Sydney at 6.30am.

Leadership Lessons:

1. Information of trust must be kept in a vault.
2. Show courage and confidence in a crisis.
3. People will surprise you in a crisis.
4. Keep calm, cool and collected in crisis.
5. Communication is 93% visual and 7% words.

Chapter 8

Teamwork in Action

When we arrived back at the plane, which was parked on the runway some 400 metres from the main airport building, we carefully and tentatively climbed up the steps some 10 metres to the plane's door and entered a new world of pandemonium.

Passengers close to the lady had removed some of her clothing to help her breath easier and the nurses set to work to assist her. As it turned out she had experienced a severe anxiety attack, and this had caused her to hyper-ventilate after she realised she was in Jakarta and not in her home town of Sydney. The nurses gave her some medication and she started to recover slowly. Thank goodness it wasn't more serious!

The cabin staff in my absence had given all the passengers who needed them, a blanket to keep them warm as even though it was very hot and humid outside the plane, the plane's air-conditioning and the stress of the ordeal had put many into a state of shock and they were in need of warmth to help them cope and recover.

I then checked again with Captain John Miller to plan the next stage of the process and he informed me that the airport manager was on his way from home and that he would arrange airport buses to ferry the passengers from the plane to the airport terminal and lounge as soon as he arrived.

We waited together for another 30 minutes or so and he then informed me that the airport manager had arrived, and that Garuda Airlines senior management wanted to meet me in the airport manager's office to discuss the necessary arrangements for the passengers' stay in Jakarta.

I went in the first bus with the first group of passengers to the airport terminal at about 5.30am and was then escorted to the Garuda airport manager's office in the main airport building.

After introductions, the Senior Garuda Indonesian Customer Relations Manager set out the detailed plans for the day.

The first news she gave me was that apparently it would only take the engineers two or three hours to repair the damaged oil seal in the tail engine, but because the captain and crew had flown the same elapsed time they would have flown if we had arrived in Sydney, they had exceeded their regulation flying time. As a result, they could not crew the flight until 7pm that evening and therefore all the passengers and crew had to be accommodated in Jakarta for the day.

They advised me that, in view of the situation, they had booked everyone into the Intercontinental Borobudur Hotel in Jakarta.

We then negotiated for some time about meals, drinks, and liquor for all the passengers and Garuda finally agreed to provide these free of charge. I then negotiated with them for passengers who wanted to see the city to go on an arranged tour of the city and environs and Garuda agreed, provided the passengers stayed on the coaches.

This brought up a major issue that had to be resolved quickly. None of the passengers had current visas to enter Indonesia as they had been cancelled and their passports stamped by immigration officials when they departed Denpasar Airport, Bali.

After much discussion it appeared that the only solution was to arrange for all the passengers to give their passports to me and hand them to Garuda for safe keeping for the day. These were then to be given back to me for return to the passengers as they arrived back at the airport that night.

They then asked me how I could do this for the total of 195 passengers. I thought for a moment, and then had a light bulb moment. I replied that I would delegate the task to the team of Caltex managers and my managers who had travelled with the group to provide support and assistance if required. Now it was their time to shine!

I was then asked one of the most difficult questions I would ever be asked in my business life. As the plane was still 400 metres from the airport terminal and as it was now nearly 8am, three hours since we had started our meeting, what did I want to do regarding the passengers' luggage on board the DC10 parked on the runway?

To help consider my decision I asked how long it would take to have the luggage brought into the airport terminal so the passengers could claim it and have it cleared by customs and immigration then loaded on the coaches.

When I was told about a further two hours, because of all the logistics of starting up the plane, parking it at a gate, removing the luggage, putting it on the conveyors to reach the luggage carousels so it could be claimed and then cleared through customs, I made the decision to leave the entire luggage on board the plane.

I wanted the shocked, scared and stressed passengers to be transferred to the Hotel Borobudur as soon as possible so they could rest and recover or we would have more serious problems.

After nearly four hours I left the Garuda manager's office, tired, and wearily entered the main lounge in the airport. What a sight I saw! People everywhere, blankets being used liberally by passengers to keep warm, and scared, stressed faces, in other words, people in shock and in fear for their life, their business, their wellbeing and wanting leadership and direction of what to do.

I hastily called the Caltex management and my management team together and briefed them on the visa issue, what I had been able to negotiate, and what role they had to play in the important logistical exercise. Each one of the managers would be responsible for collecting passports in alphabetical segments, ie A–C, D–F, and so on, and that they should spread out near the check-in counters so that passengers could form orderly queues.

They wearily agreed, and then I thought how do I ask the passengers to co-operate and give someone else their own passport so they can enter Indonesia and leave for the hotel? My answer was simple yet effective, I would stand on the check-in counter up above the group so people could see and hear me easily, explain the situation and ask them to form a queue in front of each manager. It was to be a true test of their trust in me, and my ability to communicate clearly.

I guess I'm lucky with a loud voice, so I mounted the check-in counter, stood up straight and gave it my best effort with my loudest, clearest, slowest communication possible.

To my amazement and relief, they all understood, formed their orderly queues, and handed their passports over to virtual strangers for safe keeping for the day. I was relieved and astounded!

After this exercise was completed, I then had the daunting task of informing all 195 passengers that as it would take a further two hours to arrange for their luggage to be off-loaded and clear customs, I had made the decision, in their best interests, to leave all passenger luggage on board the plane.

There were some murmurs and random comments, yet all strangely seemed in agreement with my decision except Jim Chan, the Vice President of the Chase Manhattan Bank. He loudly exclaimed, "But George, I'll be in the clothes I'm wearing now when I board tonight." I replied, "So will I Jim, and if I can cope with you, I hope you will cope with me!"

To my relief the coaches arrived and all the passengers, to their credit, made their way in methodical fashion to board their respective coaches and set out for the Hotel Borobudur.

Leadership Lessons:

1. Leaders encourage teamwork in times of crisis.
2. Anger makes blood leave your brain for poor decisions.
3. Think outside the square for solutions in a crisis.
4. When communicating difficult issues speak slowly.
5. Decisive decisions give people confidence.

Chapter 9

Sleepless in Jakarta

There were a lot of tired and distressed passengers on the coaches, yet to their credit they behaved wonderfully well and co-operated with amazing patience and resilience.

The hotel reception staff had been briefed thoroughly by Garuda management, checked the passengers in quickly and efficiently, and went out of their way to make them welcome and feel safe again.

All passengers were given meal and drink vouchers and then made their way to their rooms for a well-earned rest and, if possible, some sleep. After checking with Caltex Oil management, I too went to my room to try and get some rest and, if possible, some sleep.

I opened my brief case to check all details, went to the bathroom and then phoned my family in Melbourne to explain the situation and let them know we had been diverted and delayed. My wife understood well and said she would tell the children that Daddy would be home a day or two late.

I put my head down on the pillow and tried to get some sleep as it had been over 24 hours since I last slept in Bali. No sooner had my head hit the pillow when my mind started to wander and reflect on the past 24 hours and the events and dramas that had unfolded.

I found it hard to believe that I was in Jakarta and not home in

Melbourne and my mind wouldn't turn off and let me sleep. One thing that I found somewhat overwhelming was the fact that I had been totally trusted by the captain to speak to all 195 passengers in view of the stressful situation, when he could have easily spoken to them himself.

It wasn't until later that I realised the potential disaster he was dealing with, and the workload he was experiencing on the flight deck in handling the engine, flight logistics, thunder storms, airport safety and security issues to enable us to land safely.

I kept re-living the key aspects of the flight and the various tasks, management issues, communication challenges, health and well-being concerns, organisational and logistical issues. I had handled the negotiation and organisational issues well, and was happy with my performance, when in fact I'd never done this before at this level.

Just as I felt myself at last drifting off to sleep, the bedside telephone rang and I wearily reached over and picked up the receiver.

"Hi, it's Ray Taylor here George." Ray was the senior Caltex manager on the trip, so I knew his call was important. "George, I'm worried about the mental state of many of the passengers, as a lot of them are scared and worried about their safety, their families and the flight home tonight. What do you think we can do to help the situation and calm them down?"

I thought for a moment and replied, "Well Ray, do you have your company credit card with you?" He replied, "Yes". I then said, "I suggest you buy each female a bottle of perfume and each male a bottle of after-shave to give them with Caltex's compliments. They haven't got a change of clothes remember."

I then had another idea "Ray, I will also ask the captain and his flight crew to introduce themselves to all the passengers when they are in the airport lounge prior to departure tonight. I'll ask Captain Miller if he will speak to them to reassure them of a safe flight, why we were diverted to Jakarta and give them some confidence to help them enjoy their flight home to Australia."

He thought these were great ideas, especially having the captain speak personally to the passengers as many he said were quite scared.

He ended the call happy, but little did he realise I wasn't sure if I could carry out my part of the solution, as I had never before asked an airline captain to address 195 passengers before their flight.

I put my head down on the pillow again to collect my thoughts and work out a strategy to achieve this presumptuous initiative.

Just as I was about to drift off to sleep, the telephone rang again. This time it was Garuda management. I listened patiently to what they were saying, but was perplexed with the arrogance of their suggestion. "Mr Norris", she said, "As you will be departing at 7.30pm tonight we would like to make it a scheduled flight and land at Bali to pick up more passengers."

A lack of sleep and latent assertion skills kicked in and I let her know, in no uncertain terms, that the flight tonight was definitely not a scheduled flight as we were in Jakarta instead of Sydney and that we had a lot of scared, tired and distressed people in our passenger group. If we again landed in Bali, they would be reminded of the drama we had just survived, it would delay our arrival even more in Sydney and put them through further distress.

My comments appeared to be falling on deaf ears and the manager went on to say, "Well Mr Norris, there is a curfew in Sydney, we can't land until after 6am and we will therefore arrive early." I replied, "Well if that is the case, ask the captain to fly slower and land after the curfew because if you don't, I can tell you I will let the media in Australia know what we have been through and I'll bet you never have a group fly on Garuda Airlines again!"

I was greeted by silence. She then replied, "Okay Mr Norris, I understand the situation. I'll discuss the issue with the airline and let you know."

My room was quiet again, and I put my head back down on the pillow only to be interrupted some 15 minutes later by the Garuda manager again on the phone.

"Mr Norris, I have discussed your request with the airline and they have agreed to over-fly Bali and take a slower route to Sydney so they don't break the curfew of 6am".

I thanked her sincerely and hung up.

My head hit the pillow again and I actually started to doze off when the bedside telephone rang again.

This time it was the Garuda flight co-ordinator. She was a delightful lady, but her comments again raised my hackles.

"Mr Norris, as the flight to Jakarta was the same elapsed time that would have taken the plane to travel to Sydney, the plane's entertainment system would have been viewed by passengers and they will now see the same programs again tonight. I just thought I would alert you to this problem."

"Well", I said, "If I were you, and you wanted the passengers to be happy and fly with Garuda again, I wouldn't do that and instead install a new entertainment program for the flight."

My comment was again met with silence. She then said, "I understand your point Mr Norris. I will change over the entertainment program." I again said, "Thank you for your understanding."

Before we ended the phone call, I thought as this manager had a more understanding disposition, I would ask her if she could have Captain John Miller telephone me as I had an idea to run by him to help put the scared and tired passengers' minds to rest before we departed. She left me with the hopeful comment, "I will ask him when he wakes up as he is sleeping at present."

My head again returned to the pillow but now it was just impossible to sleep as my mind was cluttered with landing issues, negotiations, entertainment systems, scared passengers and what and how I would say to Captain Miller, if in fact he ever called me.

I got up, resigned myself to the fact that I would not get any sleep that afternoon and made a cup of coffee and ordered some room service by the way of a 'club sandwich'! When it arrived, I just sat down, relaxed, and stared into space totally exhausted yet knowing that this crisis of unexpected consequences was only part way through, and there were nearly two more days to go.

Leadership Lessons:

1. All people have latent talent.
2. Speakers must match their audience.
3. Keep your hand on the mental health button.
4. To negotiate difficult issues explain the benefits.
5. People with pride always excel in a crisis.

Chapter 10

A Calming Influence

I had just finished my coffee when the room telephone rang, again. This time I wondered who it would be and hoped it was Captain Miller. It was, thank goodness. He calmly said that the tail engine had been repaired in two hours and all was in readiness for our evening departure.

He then asked me what I would like him to do at the airport and I explained that the passengers were quite scared, in shock and very apprehensive about being in Jakarta instead of Sydney and the unknown issue with the plane's engine which caused the diversion.

He immediately understood my concern that many of the passengers would be suffering from delayed shock and he agreed to put their minds at ease and talk to them all prior to boarding, in the airport lounge.

We worked out a format where I would get all the passengers together, introduce him and mention importantly that he was the Chief Test Pilot for McDonnell Douglas, the manufacturer of the DC-10 Series 30. He would then explain to them in layman's terms what had happened to the engine, why he had to divert to Jakarta for such an emergency to ensure their safety, and all was now well.

I was impressed with his empathy and willingness to co-operate with me. I really did not hold any power to enforce such a special performance. It was however, during my phone call with Captain Miller that I realised that I had earned a serious position of trust with him during the flight and after the plane had landed. I had a degree of influence as a leader that I hadn't previously realised or recognised.

I had, I now realise, been exhibiting high performance traits of emotional intelligence, right brain soft skills, that had enabled me to create a relationship of trust and respect with him and by association the Garuda Airlines management.

However, I was to realise many years later that I only 'fragile power' which could be fractured at any time if I ever lost the emotional intelligence in my leadership style.

At about 4pm the telephone rang again and it was Ray Taylor from Caltex to inform me that he and his managers had purchased the perfume and after-shave. They had delivered them to every passengers' room, and all of them were surprised and grateful that Caltex had thought about them in such a kind way.

We all checked out of our rooms at 4.30pm and the fleet of coaches started the convoy back to the international airport.

I signed off all the room documentation, checked that the passengers' passports had been released from the hotel safe and went in the first coach so I could control their safe return to the passengers with the management team.

After arriving I asked the Caltex managers and my managers that I would again need their help when the passengers all reached the airport check-in area. I suggested that the passengers again form alphabetical queues so their passports could be returned to them before clearing immigration and customs.

Chapter 10 A Calming Influence

This mammoth communication went very well again and it showed me the power of clear communication and teamwork to achieve a desired goal.

All passengers calmly cleared immigration and customs and assembled in a group in the airport lounge, as I had asked the Caltex managers to instruct the passengers when they returned their passports.

At about 6.30pm, some 30 minutes prior to boarding, I met with Captain John Miller at the prearranged location.

We confirmed our agreed format and I introduced him, his first officer and cabin manager to all 195 passengers. They were quite taken aback as I don't think they had ever experienced such an event, even in the movies, and I know they had never seen Captain Miller in person since we had all departed Bali the evening of the day before.

Captain Miller in his laconic, humble, understated, quiet, matter of fact manner introduced his senior flight crew and then proceeded to explain what had happened to the oil seal on the tail engine, why they had to virtually shut the engine down, why he was not allowed by air traffic authorities to fly across Australia (the width of North America) with 195 passengers on only two engines and why he had made the decision, in their interests to divert the plane to Jakarta.

After his formal presentation he wished everyone an enjoyable flight and assured the passengers that he would do everything in his power to make the flight enjoyable, and stress free.

The airport lounge erupted in applause and I thanked Captain Miller for his comments and leadership.

He and his senior flight crew then departed to board our plane. At the time I did not realise I would never be so influenced and see such leadership at that senior level again.

Leadership Lessons:

1. Empathy is walking in another's shoes.
2. To gain acceptance explain why.
3. Co-operation shows maturity.
4. Leaders must have emotional intelligence.
5. Leaders must be visible in a crisis.

Chapter 11

He ain't Heavy

The plane departed on time for Sydney and the flight was as 'smooth as silk' but all on board were so tired, including me, that no-one was remotely interested in visiting the flight deck to watch the captain in action flying this new plane. He mentioned, as we flew over Bali, that we should look down and see the lights of the island. I don't think many, if any, passengers were interested.

I wandered around the plane periodically during the flight back to Sydney and chatted briefly with any passengers who were awake and not watching the in-flight entertainment. However, I was really exhausted and chose to try and relax and sleep as often as I could but my mind was too active and so I gave up and decided to watch a movie, just like most of the passengers.

The flight back to Australia so far had been uneventful and gave everyone a chance to unwind and mentally recover from the distress they had suffered over the past 36 hours.

It wasn't long before it was time to land in Sydney and I checked my watch to realise that it was just about 6am and the airport curfew was about to be lifted.

At 6.15am Captain John Miller was on his final approach on the east-west runway and everyone without exception was wide awake after being served a light breakfast about an hour prior.

We all waited for the 'big bird' to touch down but to the Captain's credit, he again excelled and in airline parlance, Captain Miller 'painted it on'. This is airline speak for the Captain painting the landing on like a paint brush making a smooth stroke and no-one felt a jolt or bump of any sort.

It was then that the emotion of all 195 people erupted and all clapped the Captain for making such a wonderful landing of excellence and bringing them home safely.

I then realised why Captain John Miller was the Chief Test Pilot in the world for the manufacturers of the plane, McDonnell Douglas.
The huge plane taxied to the gate at Sydney International Airport and all passengers disembarked. The Sydney passengers moved quickly to go through immigration and customs while those going on to Melbourne and further cities like Adelaide and Perth went to the transit lounge to wait to be called to continue their journey.

It was in the transit lounge that I was to experience my final test of leadership, patience and communication skills.

After waiting for over an hour, the passengers started to naturally become tired, frustrated and impatient. Many had not slept for 48 hours and were worried about their business and were looking forward to being reunited with their families.

I could sense the anxiety mounting so I sought out the Garuda airport manager to ask why we had not been called yet to board the plane for our on-going journey to Melbourne. He looked at me sheepishly and then stated that Sydney was the originating port for the scheduled flight to Bali and as such the plane was not able to depart until the advertised and designated time slot which, due to our early arrival necessitated another hour and a half wait so the plane was back on its scheduled service timetable.

I understood as the person dealing with the airline logistics of the group's flights, but was not sure if the other passengers who were tired and distressed would understand so easily. So I braved the situation and called the waiting passengers together to explain the sensitive situation.

When I finished my best slow, sensitive, clear explanation, one of the male Caltex retailers couldn't cope any longer. He yelled, "What an unbelievable situation. It's a wonder they are in business." I replied with unexpected calmness, "And so Sir, I expect you run the perfect business and never have any customer issues.

Please be reasonable and give the airline a chance to get back on schedule. I had forgotten that because I requested them to over fly Bali that we would arrive nearly two hours early, so it's my mistake and it didn't cross my mind to advise you."

The transit lounge fell quiet and I felt I had squashed any further unrest so I decided to visit the men's room. As I went inside another passenger bumped into me and apologised. "Well done George, you certainly put that guy back in his box." I quietly replied, "Thanks, that was John, he's my brother."

Leadership Lessons:

1. Keep people engaged in a crisis and show you care.
2. Leaders must visibly show respect by listening.
3. Icing on the cake of success makes it memorable.
4. Tiredness creates anxiety, frustration and distress.
5. Help distressed people understand why and be patient.

Chapter 12

Home on AutoPilot

After what seemed an eternity we were finally given the call to board the plane for Melbourne, the final leg for me but not for the passengers from South and Western Australia who still had a day's travel ahead of them.

After an uneventful take off the plane was hit by significant and unexpected turbulence and there were a few audible outpourings of anxiety and fear from some passengers.

I wandered around the cabin again when the turbulence had passed and the seat belt sign had been turned off, to reassure my group that all was okay and to try and put their minds at ease.

This seemed to help them, but I could tell they were scared and unsettled from the ill-fated flight to Jakarta.

Eventually the plane touched down at Tullamarine International Airport in Melbourne, but the landing was a bit bumpy. It was not Captain Miller now at the controls. He had stopped off in Sydney with his wife who had been with us for the entire flight from Bali to Jakarta and back to Sydney.

It then occurred to me how professional and motivated Captain Miller had been, because it must have also been extremely stressful for him to handle the decision on the plane, with his wife as a passenger, in such a serious predicament.

The Melbourne passengers disembarked, said their goodbyes to the interstate passengers in the Caltex group and proceeded through immigration and eventually through customs.

As I was exiting customs, Susan and her daughter Sarah were close by and we waved goodbye and departed.

I had parked my car at the long term car park expecting to be home five days earlier so I was expecting a hefty charge for the long stay. I wasn't surprised by the charge, paid it quickly and drove home to a family I had not seen, it seemed, for a lifetime.

It was a tough drive and on reflection it was totally irresponsible to even consider driving my car, as I hadn't slept for a combined total of three full days, or 72 hours!

However, I arrived in one piece and wearily made my way up the driveway.

My wife, Joan was busy inside with the children who were only six, four and our son who was 10 months old and they looked like they had seen a ghost.

Hugs and kisses were given and then I gave them a quick update before unpacking and climbing into bed for a well-earned sleep.

I slept the first night for 16 hours, the second night for 14 hours and the third night for 12 hours. It just shows what the human body and brain can experience before it stops and shuts down.

Adrenalin is an amazing thing and can enable a human being to achieve feats of endurance and mental gymnastics often not considered achievable by people thinking rationally and logically.

*My three children about that time.
Melinda on left, Campbell and Nicole.*

I had been exposed for the first time to something I would later learn in life, the effects of eu - stress or good stress as well as di - stress or bad stress. It was eu - stress that had helped me function in a leadership capacity that I had never knowingly exhibited before in my life.

It also made me realise then, and many more times later, that out of adversity comes advantage! It's just that at the time of the adversity you don't have the ability to know what the advantage will be.

The result of experiencing this near disaster, and its complexities, proved to me then, and time and time again in my future business life, that you really don't do business with companies, you do business with people who work for companies, and creating business relationships is an investment not a cost.
The airline adventure also created for me a formula for excellence:
Your Attitude + Your Aptitude = Your Altitude

In other words, to be a success in life, business and sport you need high performance leadership skills, but just remember it only gives you 'fragile power'.

Leadership Lessons:

1. Be prepared to expect the unexpected.
2. Tiredness can contribute to poor decision making.
3. Remember to turn off and recharge your batteries.
4. Understand the difference between Distress and Eustress.
5. Self-talk reinforces your self-worth and self-esteem levels.

CASE HISTORY 8

Tooth Hotels Pty Ltd

Chapter 1

The Horse's Mouth

After returning to family and business life, I settled into my role of developing business for my company.

I had appointed Kevin McNamara as the New South Wales Representative for my company and while he was trying his best to open doors and business, he called one Friday for our regular Friday conference call. "How's the week been?" I asked him. "Well", he said, "it's been busy but not as successful as I'd like. Do you mind if I suggest an idea that I think will help me get through doors so I can engage with the decision makers better?" "No", I said "what do you suggest?"

"Well, I suggest we change my title from New South Wales Representative to New South Wales Manager." "Why?" I said. "Well that title, I believe, will enable me to get over the drawbridge and into the castle."

"Okay", I said, "do it."

Within two weeks I received a phone call from Kevin to say he had gained an appointment for us both to meet with Wayne Gilbert, the General Manager of Tooth Hotels. They had 550 traditional hotels that they supplied their beer and allied products to, and due to new government legislation they were going to be prohibited from supplying them on an exclusive basis in the future.
Kevin mentioned that Wayne had liked the fact that he and I worked

for Caltex in the past as this enabled us both to better understand the problems Tooth Hotels would be facing in the future with their 550 licensees or hotel keepers.

We worked out a mutually acceptable date and time and the meeting was confirmed. Kevin picked me up from the Sydney airport and we duly arrived at the hallowed head office of the nearly 100-year-old company that was steeped in history and tradition.

We were ushered into Wayne's office and asked if we would like tea, coffee or a beer. We sensibly reneged on the beer and instead settled on coffee.

Wayne Gilbert started the conversation off by asking me about my background with Caltex and I then asked him to tell us what his current needs were and what objectives he wanted to achieve.

Wayne was a small, dark haired man who sat behind this enormous desk, and it became apparent to me as he outlined his needs that he personally needed to be respected more as the General Manager, and that there was a major communication problem between the company and their 550 hotel keepers.

The meeting progressed very well, and I suggested a number of options that could work to promote loyalty between Tooth Hotels and their hotel keepers.

I then suggested that there could be a need for a Tooth Hotels magazine to stop the confusion in the communication between Tooth Hotels and both their hotel keepers and the marketplace.

However, suddenly Wayne stopped this dialogue and asked several pointed questions.

"How often should this magazine be published? What would it look like? What content would it have? What would it cost to produce and administer? What about distribution, who should it be sent to?"

I quickly focused on the answers, as I saw it at short notice and when I suggested that the content should include at the start a section headed 'From the General Manager's Desk', Wayne stopped the discussion with the comment, "I like this idea a lot as it will help us communicate more accurately, and virtually straight from the horse's mouth!"

He wrapped up the meeting saying he loved the recognition program concept and especially the magazine idea. I asked him when he wanted the proposal and investment budget so it could be considered for approval. He mentioned a date within two weeks and so we left Tooth Hotels having learnt three valuable lessons: 1, that a title is important so prospects can perceive the power and authority of the person they are talking with; 2, small men often need to be perceived to be larger than life, e.g. 'small man syndrome' and 3, clear communication is a critical component of corporate culture.

We debriefed the meeting on the way to the airport, and inside the Ansett Golden Wing Club lounge, and I then boarded my flight to Melbourne excited that my fledging business had taken some more steps towards success.

When I arrived back in Melbourne I met with my management team and we explored the options to include in the proposal to Wayne Gilbert so that Tooth Hotels could achieve their objectives.

To enable the 550 hotels to improve their relationship with Tooth, we created a recognition and reward program which recognised the Top 50 hotel keepers based on a pro rata allocation on the various

Area Manager territories and taking into account metropolitan and country locations.

We then decided that the criteria for becoming a member of the Club 50 program should be based on a combination of Tooth product purchases, percentage improvement and the best results out of 100% for a mystery customer program based on criteria of five areas; (i) Service, (ii) Cleanliness, (iii) Attitude, (iv) Facilities and (v) Customer Experience.

The best 50 hotel keepers would then win a trip for two to a selected destination where they would be educated and entertained at a Club 50 conference with selected guest speakers on topics to assist their business acumen and development.

At the conference they each would be awarded a Club 50 plaque to display in their hotel, a Club 50 tie for the men showing the year they won their membership and a Club 50 scarf for the ladies.

It was suggested that the first Club 50 conference would be to New Zealand for a study tour of the Lion Brewery hotels, who had shown leadership in pioneering an initiative of restaurants to make their hotels more appealing to families and females.

This concept was included in our initial proposal, as was the new magazine which we suggested be called 'The Horse's Mouth'. The Tooth Hotel's logo was 'Invicta' the horse. The problem of secondhand inconsistent communication would be addressed through a section near the beginning of the magazine entitled 'From the General Manager's Desk.'

In addition, there would be sections including 'From the Managing Director', 'Industry News', 'Stop Press' and a cartoon to add humour and light relief. Also included in the centre-spread would be photographs and a list of the Club 50 winners and on the front and back covers, interior and exterior photographs and management and staff from a hotel which was selected as the 'Hotel of the Quarter'.

This feature proved very powerful in welding the 550 hoteliers into a tight group of loyal hotels with many hotel keepers contacting us personally to nominate their hotel for the Hotel of the Quarter.

The Horse's Mouth, while somewhat of an afterthought in the initial meeting with the General Manager actually turned out to be the strategic strength of the Club 50 program.

In the second year of the program, Club 50 winners travelled to Singapore and Bali. In Singapore they visited the Tiger Brewery on a study tour and then to Bali for the Club 50 conference.

The keynote speakers we arranged were a hotel management consultant from England and Phillip Ruthven, the well-known founder and Managing Director of IBISWorld. Phillip had established himself as one of Australia's foremost keynote speakers on business data, strategies, trends and future predictions.

The Club 50 conference was a huge success and gave the Hotel keepers the knowledge and confidence to continue their strategy of fine tuning their businesses more towards the family as the trend had moved to more dining out than in.

The third year the Club 50 winners travelled to Tahiti for the Club 50 conference and Phillip Ruthven had proved so popular and informative that he was again invited to be the keynote speaker.

The Award's Dinner was held at the amazing Hotel Intercontinental located on the cliffs above Matavai Bay where Captain Cook first anchored when he arrived in Tahiti. The main function room was designed and fitted out as an exact replica of the dimensions of the deck of his ship the 'Endeavour' and was simply breathtaking in its ambience, splendour and authenticity.

Matavai Bay has a unique black sand beach and is one of the main tourist attractions in Tahiti so, this last night of pomp and ceremony was a significant final event for the Club 50 conference.

During this stay in Tahiti I was fortunate to meet Jimmy Taylor, the step brother of the Hollywood actor Robert Taylor. His wife Bella was our tour director for Tahiti Nui Travel. After a few days of getting to know her, she introduced me to Jimmy who joined us for a surveillance tour of the main island to investigate the logistics of the Club 50 winners visiting the most prominent Captain Cook landmarks and attractions.

During our discussion on the journey he told me his story of how he met Bella and married her. At the time, Jimmy was married with children and living in Los Angeles. However he accepted a position to work in Tahiti on the 1962 film 'Mutiny on the Bounty' starring Marlon Brando, Trevor Howard and Richard Harris. Jimmy Taylor had previously worked as a costume director for the 1953 film 'The Robe' and his Tahitian wife Bella was a seamstress making the costumes for the film in Tahiti.

After the film, Jimmy stayed in Tahiti and married Bella. He showed us the sewing machine and some of the costumes the actors wore in the film and a painting of the Bounty given to them to commemorate the film.

The Club 50 fourth year winners travelled to Hawaii where they had their conference at the Hawaiian University of Hospitality. This was to be the last year of Club 50 which had achieved its objectives and protected Tooth Hotels from the new open trading legislation and the Victorian hotel brewery predator, Carlton and United.

The Horse's Mouth continued for another year and we were also asked to write and produce a hotel training manual.

Our five year involvement then concluded when the General Manager, Wayne Gilbert left Tooth Hotels and joined a company in Brisbane. However, in the second last year of our association, the Marketing Director, Jim Boyce asked me to help the company celebrate its centenary. Tooth Hotels was a company steeped in tradition and it had a rich heritage which was exhibited in the Tooth Museum at their head office.

We had already worked with the Shirley Brothers in designing and producing large 10 metre rear projection presentations to support each year's launch of the Club 50 program and to focus on various political and corporate aspects that needed to be mentioned.

By this stage we had opened our Sydney office in Liverpool Street and appointed Jill Newton, the Sydney Manager as Kevin McNamara had retired.

After many hours of discussion our creative team came up with a concept of a film showing the history of Tooth through the ages using archive footage and the current film presentations we had shown. I created the title, which Tooth accepted immediately, 'Heritage and Destiny'.

It was then produced by the Shirley Brothers in conjunction with us and was shown at the centenary celebrations.

At this time Tooth was also concerned about becoming a more visible corporate community champion and creating a culture to give the Club 50 strategy some longevity.

Based on this brief, I created with our Sydney Manager, the Tooth Corporate Cup Golf Tournament.

These golf days were to be ahead of their time and the concept we designed of having a hotel keeper play in a four with a supplier, a Tooth Hotels' manager or employee and an Australian PGA Tour golfer was seen to be breaking new ground.

PGA golfers came from far and wide to play; even from the Japan tour, Asian tour and Australian tour and the prize money was larger than the New South Wales Open.

All of the 1st and 10th tee groups were filmed, and the contestants hitting off were shown during the corporate dinner afterwards.

The well-known PGA Champion of Australia, Stewart Ginn, became the resident professional for the event and conducted golf coaching clinics prior to the participants hitting off. He then was guest speaker at the Presentation Dinner and presented the awards together with the Managing Director of Tooth, George Haines, to the winners of each category.

These golf days were extremely successful and were conducted at The Lakes Golf Course and The Manly Golf Course.

Our association with Tooth Hotels then concluded and both parties were happy that their association with the hotels was cemented.

Then Adsteam and the infamous John Spalvins, bought them all!

Chapter 1   The Horse's Mouth

Leadership Lessons:

1. Business titles give people self-esteem.
2. Business titles open doors in business.
3. Listen carefully for the key need.
4. Give clients what they want.
5. Deliver what you promise.

CASE HISTORY 9

Indian Tourism Board

Chapter 1

Incredible India

In 1983, I was approached by Air India's head office in Melbourne to travel to India as their guest and as the guest of the Indian Tourist Board.

It appeared that my company's reputation was such that they saw us breaking new ground in the incentive conference and education market and believed that we could help pioneer conference and incentive travel programs to increase tourism in India.

The trip co-incidentally coincided with my second marriage to Susan, the lady with the great legs at Melbourne Airport in 1978, in the Bali Bound Chapter.

Fate is an amazing thing, and who could have imagined that this would have ever happened, let alone be possible? So, as I had been invited to bring a partner, my new wife and I made the business trip double as our honeymoon.

It was a significant milestone for my business as we had obviously been put through a due diligence check and had passed with flying colours for an overseas government and the government's airline to be prepared to take the initiative to invite me.

We had only been operating as a business for nine years, yet I was proud that our reputation for innovation, quality, reliability, strategy, and client service had made such a mark on the Australian conference travel industry. So, in April 1983 we set off for 'Incredible India'.

The government had communicated with us through their preferred ground operator in Bombay (Mumbai) and we had been provided with a car, driver, accommodation, meals, visits and return business class airfares flying with Air India direct from Melbourne to Bombay.

Our itinerary included visiting and staying at The Taj Mahal Palace Hotel in Bombay, The Lake Palace in Udaipur, The Rambagh Palace in Jaipur, The Sheraton Hotel in Agra – the home of one of the modern seven wonders of the world, the Taj Mahal and a luxury houseboat with resident houseboy in Srinagar on the Dal Lake in the Kashmir region. We would then fly back to the capital, New Delhi for a government reception and dinner where I was to give an address to the Department of Tourism government officials.

The flight to India went without a hitch and we arrived in Bombay to a milling throng of Indian people, all in a great hurry to meet passengers and impress them with their enthusiasm and endeavor to please.

We met our host and driver who collected our luggage and whisked us away to the Taj Mahal Palace Hotel. It is a heritage listed, five star hotel which was built in the Saracenic revival style and opened in 1903. It is situated next to the famous Gateway of India and overlooks the Arabian Sea. The one word that came to mind to describe it was 'opulent'. It was quite awe inspiring to arrive in the exquisite and vast reception, be checked in like VIPs and escorted to our beautiful suite in the Taj Mahal Palace which looked over the Arabian Sea.

Our stay in Bombay was unfortunately all too brief and 48 hours later our driver arrived in a 'Morris Oxford limousine', which at the time was perceived to be quite upmarket in India, and chauffeured us to the airport for our flight to the majestic marble Taj Lake Palace situated on Lake Pichola.

The hotel was significant in that it played a central part in the 1983 James Bond film, Octopussy, starring Roger Moore. We were told on arrival that the film crew dredged the lake before the film and found a submerged lake boat which was restored and later used in the film.

After travelling across the lake by 'Indian water taxi', we were shown to our rooms; the very same vast suite that had previously been allocated to Malcolm Fraser, the Prime Minister and his wife Tammy on their official tour of India in 1979.

The hotel was built in 1746 of marble by Maharana Jegat Singh in the majestic Rajput style and stands on a four acre island.

We were fortunate to stay at the Lake Palace for two nights and taken to dinner on the second night, by our driver, to a restaurant in the city of Udaipur after he had driven the 1034 kilometers from Mumbai.

Leadership Lessons:

1. Appreciate how others perceive your success.
2. Realise country cultures and customs matter.
3. Be gracious in accepting hospitality.
4. Act with responsibility and accountability.
5. Pride in oneself enables excellence.

Chapter 2

Forbidden Fruit

The next day we were again ferried back to the mainland by water taxi and our chauffer drove us in the Morris Oxford limousine 400 km to the 'orange city' of Jaipur.

The trip was an adventure in itself as it took some eight hours over mainly unmarked rough roads littered with rocks, piles of cow dung, holes and rubble.

We eventually made it safely and were welcomed into another palace built by the Maharajah of Jaipur in 1925. In 1957, the Maharajah converted it into a plush hotel and it became a member of the Taj Hotel group.

Our arrival was amazing with elaborately dressed elephants parading around the majestic and manicured grounds, as were the many beautifully colourful peacocks.

After checking in to our magnificently appointed suite, we were escorted to dinner in the main restaurant.

During dinner, our chauffer mentioned that a Hollywood film crew was staying in the hotel and using the grounds for some scenes for a new film 'The Far Pavilions' starring Ben Cross of 'Chariots of Fire' fame. The film was being directed by well-known Hollywood director, David Lean.

After the sumptuous main course, I took a visit to the gents, and lo and behold, stood next to Ben Cross at the urinal. I looked over at Ben's face and said, "Hi Ben", to which he pleasantly replied in his English accent, "Hello Mate", obviously picking up quickly that I was an Australian.

The next morning Susan decided to go for a stroll and look at the shops. I decided to stay in our suite and attend to some business reports I needed to write of our visit so far. After writing some pages I thought I would try some of the unique looking fruit from our complimentary fruit basket. Now I was in a quandary, as before leaving Australia, some well-meaning friends mentioned, "Don't eat any fruit unless it is cooked."

However, the fruit looked so good that I thought it would be safe to eat. So I reached over and selected a couple of small white fleshed pieces and ate them. They tasted delicious, but little did I know they would become the 'forbidden fruit' of my visit and proved to be my downfall as they gave me food poisoning and I was incapacitated for the next three days!

The trip to Agra to visit the Taj Mahal was eventful, and the rough surface through the suspension of the Morris Oxford, I am sure, contributed to my stomach upset when we arrived.

I don't really know how I managed, but our chauffer stopped at a number of heritage listed historic sites like the Fatehpur Sikri, the city of Victory built in 1583 by Emperor Akbar and the Agra Fort which is built in stunning red sandstone. The Agra Fort includes the Moti Mahal and Musamman Burj where Shah Jahan, the Mughal Emporer who built the Taj Mahal in 1654 in the memory of his wife, Mumtaz Mahal, was imprisoned and died.

We finally arrived at the Taj Mahal and I marvelled at its splendour, but suddenly and without warning I found that it's difficult being on the manicured lawns of the Taj Mahal, one of the seven ancient wonders of the world, when you have food poisoning and you 'have to go NOW' because you can't control your bowel.

Agra was to be the highlight of our trip, but unfortunately, I was very ill and confined to my hotel bed and we never really got to see its other attractions.

The next day after taking numerous pills to help my condition, we flew to Srinagar, the largest city and the summer capital of Kashmir. It lies in the Kashmir Valley on the banks of the Jhelum River.

After arriving at the Srinagar Military Airport we were taken by our chauffer in another Morris Oxford limousine to our houseboat on the Dal Lake.

The houseboats were incredibly ornate and came with a houseboy/cook to prepare your meals and generally assist. The houseboats included a relaxing outdoor area complete with couches and cushions, a lounge/dining room and one, two or three bedrooms, all with ensuites.

The reflections in the Dal Lake were spectacular and it was possible from one area to see the reflection of Mt Everest some 1,333 kilometres to the North West, in the still waters.

On the morning of our departure we visited the local carpet weaving factories where the art is handed down from father to son. We bought a pair of rugs identical in quality and design, small enough to carry back in our luggage but large enough to make a statement on the floor or wall of our home.

Later that day we boarded our flight to New Delhi where the next day we were to be given a formal Government reception and dinner and where I was to make a keynote address and presentation to the Indian Department of Tourism.

My preparation for my address was very difficult as I had been awestruck by both the squalor and the opulence of people's living conditions in the areas we had visited. So, in a diplomatic strategy, I decided to save face for our Indian hosts and focus on the breathtaking beauty, heritage and architectural significance of the hotels, venues and cultural attractions we had experienced.

There was no doubt that at that time in 1983 the country was ripe for an increase in Australian tourism particularly in the conference market.

The dinner went very well as I had by then recovered from food poisoning and we both left feeling exhausted but excited about a new vibrant opportunity for my business.

The next day we flew back to Bombay (Mumbai) for our last night at the fabulous Taj Mahal Palace Hotel.

The Indian Tourism Board had gone out of their way to make us welcome and help us experience the amazing tourist and hospitality treasures of India, which we could now tell and sell to others in Australia.

Prior to our departure the next afternoon, I went shopping in the Hotel's shopping arcade and fell in love with a superb Sitar, the plucked string Indian instrument that was invented in the 13th century and used in Hindustani classical music. It was a beautiful memento of a time like no other I will ever experience.

The flight home was smooth and uneventful. While Susan slept I wrote a report for the management of Air India in Australia. The only problem or challenge I had was thinking up adjectives to described India. Nevertheless I completed it in flight using the adrenalin I had stored up in my body and the command of the English language that I never knew I had retained from school and which was lying latent in my brain.

Since then I have come to understand that many people, if not all people, have talent lying latent in them waiting to get out if only they are given a chance. That's why the art and power of delegation is so important for managers and leaders to understand and implement in order to grow their people.

In fact I've come to realise that the real role of managers is to become leaders and be responsible not only for the 'bottom line' but also for how many people they have grown to use their full potential.

We arrived home exhausted and in a state of shock, in that we had been the guests of a country so steeped in heritage and history, a country that housed one of the ancient wonders of the world and yet our country, Australia was so young and innocent in the eyes of the world.

The management of Air India was grateful for my report but even happier with the confirmation of the potential business that was possible in 'Incredible India'.

Leadership Lessons:

1. It's important to keep learning.
2. Be yourself abroad but show respect.
3. Stay with your health plan overseas.
4. Time management is a key for success.
5. Talent is lying latent in us all.

CASE HISTORY 10

Operation 84, America's Cup Conferences

Chapter 1

Sailing into the Future

In 1983, Australia was starting to come through the deepest post-war recession, mainly because it coincided with one of the most severe droughts in history.

So, buoyed by my experience in India, and excited to keep 'the pedal down' for my business, I started to think more and more in a creative, innovative way with a strong feeling of self-confidence.

India had motivated me to realise that you can achieve the impossible if you try hard enough with enough self-belief.

The America's Cup campaign had become a major national pride event and was commanding considerable attention across all forms of media.

After our tour of India my company, and I as the Managing Director, was appointed by the shipping company P&O as their incentive conference consultants. Their Marketing Manager, Jeff Lynch was a similar age and personality to me and we both had a love of the game of golf. His goal was to increase the incentive conference business on their group of ships making Sydney their home port.

Their flagship, the SS Oriana, was the focus of this strategy. Launched in December 1960, she was the largest and fastest P&O ship ever built and perfect for incentive corporate conferences as she plied her way between Australia and New Zealand.

We had several strategic meetings after my return from India and I included P&O in many proposals to clients as a means of an innovative incentive conference concept and venue. They had also agreed to sponsor an innovative event that was appropriate, and that would help develop their cruising brand in Australia.

It was about this time that Australia's challenge for the 1983 America's Cup started to gain traction and media focus. It was being seen as a positive and uplifting event to raise the spirits and endeavor of the Australian people after the recession.

Still influenced by my incredible Indian experience, I continued to think creatively, and I became obsessed with the idea of conducting two conferences with the code name Operation '84, to motivate Australian business people to 'think outside the square' and take risks again. P&O thought it was a great opportunity to sponsor the conferences to lift their profile.

I would watch television with my wife and really not be focused on the program but on how I could make the conferences special enough with speakers who could communicate, educate and motivate people and inspire them again to succeed after experiencing a recession.

During this time I was also invited by Cathay Pacific to fly with them to Hong Kong and Vancouver in an airline study group to promote their airline and experience their first class service with a view to increasing business in the lucrative incentive and performance management market.

Our company was becoming one of the leaders in incentive conferences in Australia, and I was so proud of my management team and 30 staff in achieving this position.

The Cathay Pacific trip was to depart on 28 September, my mother's birthday, and I would be joining a group of 12 other owners and managers of similar companies to mine in Australia.

The more I thought about the idea of motivating Australian business people the more excited and creative I became. Over the next weeks of late August and September of 1983, I called, visited and confirmed a range of influential speakers that could educate and motivate Australian business people. In Sydney I visited Dr Tony Kidman, Nicole Kidman's father at his clinic, focusing on men's health and psychology at the Sydney University of Technology and confirmed him as a speaker. I then visited and confirmed Allan Pease, the Australian world authority on body language whose books were sweeping the world.

The next speaker I was recommended to visit was Wilfred Jarvis, a behavioral scientist living in North Sydney. I hired a car and drove out to his beautiful, quiet and secluded townhouse with some apprehension as I had heard he was a very private consultant who was somewhat surrounded by mystery. After introducing myself, he made me most welcome and we discussed a range of topics he suggested that could be suitable and relevant for the focus of the attendees at the conference.

He then mentioned the problem of managing stress in managers and business men and women and the fact that he was seeing a spike in this issue in Australia. I asked him what his main point would be. He sat forward in his chair and gave me one of the most important pieces of performance psychology I have ever received in my life.

"Well," he said, "most people I consult with don't know that there are only two types of stress we encounter while we are alive. One is Di-Stress or bad stress we experience when something happens that hurts us both mentally or physically, the other is Eu-Stress or good stress we experience when something happens that excites us or we enjoy both mentally or physically. The only time we don't suffer stress is when we are deceased."

I was spellbound by his comments and insights and immediately could see the subject being not only suitable but very relevant as managers had been experiencing a bad recession and were now trying to come out the other side and restart, re-enthuse and motivate themselves and their staff.

"That's great Wilfred," I said, "I'd love you to be a speaker" and he agreed.

Leadership Lessons:

1. Self-belief can achieve the impossible.
2. Continually think creatively to grow.
3. It's great to think outside the square.
4. Make sure you set SMART goals.
5. Learning is like eating your favourite meal.

Chapter 2

A Light Bulb Moment

I flew back to Melbourne very satisfied with myself that the keynote speakers were taking shape, but now that I was starting to consider how I would create the conferences, so they at least became cost revenue neutral for P&O Cruises.

Australia II, skippered by John Bertrand, was racing against Dennis Conner and the yacht, Liberty, in the waters off Newport, Rhode Island, just north of New York. The USA had achieved a 3 to 1 lead over Australia and the result again started to look like America would defend the Cup again after 132 years.

However, Australia II fought back and had levelled the score at 3 to 3 with the final race to decide the America's Cup due on 25 September 1983.

As I was watching television with my wife on the night of 25 September my brain was working overtime and all of a sudden, I had a 'light bulb moment'. Could I possibly get John Bertrand to be the 'Guest of Honour and Speaker' for the conferences I had planned?

I excused myself, got up and went to my study and phoned OTC. At the time, OTC or Overseas Telecommunication Commission, was Australia's overseas telephone network. It had been established in August 1946, but had recently been updated in August 1983, so it was prominent in the media and on my mind.

I asked to be connected to the New York Yacht Club and within a few seconds the call was answered by a female American voice saying, "Hello, this is the New York Yacht Club. How may I help you?"

Having travelled to America a number of times previously I remembered that I should speak a little slower than I do in Australia so I would be more easily understood, so in a slow and clear voice I replied, "I am calling from Melbourne, Australia. My name is George Norris and I wanted to know if you could give me the telephone number of the Australian team for the America's Cup in Newport."

Without any hesitation she replied "Mr Norris, I have three telephone numbers, the America's Cup number, the Australia II team number and the direct phone number to the Executive Director, Warren Jones. Would you like me to connect you to Warren Jones?"

I was nearly speechless. Here I was in the study in my house in Melbourne, my wife was in another room watching Dallas on television and I was about to be connected to the direct telephone line of the Australia II America's Cup syndicate at race headquarters in Newport, Rhode Island.

I slowly and calmly swallowed and replied, "Yes please, and thank you for your kind assistance!"

The telephone rang for a very short time and then I heard the loud, aggressive voice of Warren Jones saying, "Hello, Warren Jones!"

I took a big breath and calmly and slowly said, "Hello Warren, I am calling from Melbourne, Australia, and I wanted to know if and when it would be possible to talk with John Bertrand." I quickly went on, 'I'm running two conferences in Sydney and Melbourne in October, which are being sponsored by P&O Cruises and I wanted to ask him if he could be our guest of honour. I realise he hasn't won yet, but we would like him to inspire and motivate Australia's business people even if he doesn't win tomorrow."

There was a deathly silence and then Warren barked down the phone line, "Don't you know we are trying to win an America's Cup. We are all busy at the moment, so call back after tomorrow and I'll try and get him for you."

I thanked him slowly and calmly and hung up the phone stunned. I had done what most people would not do in a lifetime, and had found the courage, inspiration or even the gall to actually call and talk directly to the person in charge of the Australian II team for the 1983 America's Cup.

I made a note of the details of the conversation and wandered back to watch TV. Dallas was still playing, and Susan casually asked, "Where have you been?" I replied, "I have been in the study on the phone to the New York Yacht Club and the Australia II Team's Executive Director, Warren Jones." "Why did you do that?" I replied, "I was trying to ask John Bertrand to be the guest of honour and keynote speaker for the conferences. I've been thinking, I've got some really good speakers but we need a powerful person to promote the conferences and act as the keynote speaker". "How did you go?" she said. I replied, "I don't know yet. He asked me to call back after the last deciding race is run the tomorrow. "Well good luck with that", she said and we continued watching Dallas, or more to the point, she did!

The next day I confirmed two more well-known speakers from Melbourne in Ron Barassi and Phil Ruthven. Ron, the high profile AFL player from Melbourne and successful Coach of Carlton, North Melbourne and to a lesser degree, Sydney Swans, was a great motivator and recognised as one of the top business speakers in Australia. He was keen to be involved.

Phillip, as founder and Managing Director of IBIS World, on the other hand had become the best known and in demand futurist in Australia and was delighted to be invited to give the participants some insights to help them plan for the year ahead.

When I mentioned that I was trying to procure John Bertrand, they relished the opportunity to speak.

The next day was unfortunately called off as a 'lay day', due to the weather conditions and the final race was rescheduled for 26 September. The next night I couldn't sleep, and instead watched the final race on TV all night in bed while my wife tried to sleep.

When we won, I was over the moon, and to her annoyance, woke her up.

It was an amazing race with Australia II coming from behind to win by 41 seconds. The race was seen from a purist's point of view to have been won by a master stroke of skill, strategy, determination and resilience by the Australia II skipper, John Bertram, and his crew.

The Australian media dined out on the story for days as did Bob Hawke, the Prime Minister of the day, when he famously and exuberantly told Australians, in answer to a journalist's question that, "Any boss who sacks a worker for not turning up today is a bum!"

The next day I was exhausted but exhilarated to know that I could have the opportunity of a lifetime with the skipper of Australia II as the guest of honour and keynote speaker, if only I was able to locate him to invite him.

Leadership Lessons:

1. Light bulb moments are exciting.
2. Match your communication style to your marketplace.
3. Silence can be powerful.
4. Show courage and you get rewarded.
5. Think big and ride the wave.

Chapter 3

Needle in a Haystack

Since Australia is almost a day ahead of America due to the date line and the time zone difference, I realised sadly that I would not be able to call back as Warren Jones had suggested, for several reasons. It would be a futile exercise as the race team would be completely tied up in formal celebrations and in party mode, and John Bertrand if they won or not, would be inundated with the world media. Anyway I had to prepare for a trip leaving the day after with Cathay Pacific on a tour to promote their new longest flight from Hong Kong to Vancouver.

On the day of my departure it was mentioned in the media that John Bertrand was about to leave Newport and vanish to Hawaii for a well-earned rest with his wife and family. As I prepared to leave the office for the airport I met with my Business Development Manager, Peter Dunn and asked him to use all his contacts he had in Hawaii to find John and to keep me informed at the hotels I was to stay in on the trip. We both knew it was to be a classified search and one that needed to be achieved with the utmost secrecy and urgency.

The Cathay flight took off from Melbourne and I had to keep myself together with the knowledge that this search could be one of the most difficult we would ever undertake.

The flight to Hong Kong was uneventful and we were looked after superbly by Cathay Pacific. I mingled with the others in our group and made conversation, all the while wondering if Peter had been successful in his search.

Eventually we landed in Hong Kong and were transferred to our hotel near the airport to freshen up and rest before we departed for Vancouver on what was at the time the longest over water flight by a commercial airliner in the world. It was to take some 17 hours in their new Boeing 747-300 and this was a flight to promote the launch of this new service.

When I checked into the hotel I asked if there were any messages for me and was handed an envelope. Inside was a note: No luck yet, Peter.

I put the envelope in my attaché case and lay down for a quick nap after arranging with the front desk to wake me at the prescribed time so I could shower before being collected to return to the airport. It was just as well I'd booked a wakeup call as I quickly fell into a sound sleep. No doubt the excitement and lack of sleep in the previous few days had caught up with me.

We all arrived at the airport with a degree of expectation and trepidation. This plane, we were told, was the heaviest jumbo in the world because of the extended fuel tanks to take the extra fuel that was needed to fly to Vancouver.

Our flight took us north, close to the South Korean peninsula, then to the west of Japan on the great upper circle flight path to Vancouver.

After about seven hours we hit considerable, consistent turbulence, and as we were over water there started to appear a few white faces in our group and some interesting scary comments from those brave enough to make them. However, after a further three hours the flight became smooth, and we eventually landed safely at Vancouver.

Sleep and rest were the order of the day, or was it night, and we assembled mid-morning to take in the various Vancouver sights. The most impressive structure I saw was BC Place which had only opened in June 1983, with an air-filled roof which at the time of our visit was the largest of its kind in the world. We took in many other sights and then met at the revolving restaurant on the top floor of our hotel which had views of the Pacific Ocean in the distance.

That night, before returning to my room, I checked with reception to see if I had any messages. To my delight I was handed a sealed envelope. I decided not to open it there, but to wait and open it in my room. I was glad because inside was a note which just said: 'Found him – Halekulani Hotel, Peter.'

Excited, I sat down and called the hotel and asked to be put through to John Bertrand. "I am sorry sir, but Mr Bertrand is not taking calls until after 7.30am." I thanked the operator and checked the time difference so I could make my call in the morning. It would be tight as we were being picked up around 11.30am to go to the airport for my personal trip extension to New York for two days as I had planned to meet with the General Manager of the famous Winged Foot Golf Club, in Mamaroneck.

The 1984 US Open Golf Championship was to be played there in June and I had planned to meet with the General Manager to discuss how he was planning the event. Since conducting the Tooth Hotel Pro Am Golf Tournaments, I had become interested in learning more about the finer points of the organisation of events and thought this knowledge could assist me in conducting the forthcoming conferences in Australia.

I set my alarm for 10.45am as I figured this would be 7.45am in Honolulu.

Leadership Lessons:

1. Plan ahead for confidence.
2. Keep confidential plans close to your chest.
3. Use your connections wisely.
4. Leave no stone unturned.
5. Tell people what country you're calling from.

Chapter 4

Catching a Marlin

I packed as much as I could before I went to bed so that in the morning I would be able to shower, meet and have breakfast with the group and then return to my room to call Honolulu. That evening I slept well knowing I was close to achieving my goal.

The next morning, I had breakfast with the group and as I was about to leave for my room one of the guys who I had befriended said he would call by my room at 11am and come down to the foyer with me. Not wanting to make a fuss, I simply agreed that was fine, and left the group knowing we all would meet up again in Vancouver in three days' time after my trip to New York.

Back in my room I brushed my teeth and packed my remaining things. I sat down at the desk with my diary, notepad and pen and thought what I'd say to John Bertrand, if he would talk to me.

Finally I called the Halekulani Hotel at 10.45am when my alarm jolted me into action. Just then my friend knocked on the door and I invited him in and asked him to please be quiet as I was on an international call. The operator at the Halekulani Hotel answered and I simply said, "Could you connect me to John Bertrand's room please?" Without any hesitation she put me through, and a young voice answered, "Hello", to which I replied "Hello, can I speak to Dad please?" The young boy called out, "Dad, it's for you."

I had just used a communication technique to build relationships called 'mirroring' which I hadn't studied at that time, but which I learnt 10 years later when training Jetset Travel Consultants throughout Australia.

John came to the phone and said, "Hello, John Bertrand." I replied, "Hello John, thanks for taking my call. I'm calling from Vancouver, Canada. My name is George Norris and I live in Melbourne, Australia. I am planning two conferences in Sydney and Melbourne in late October to inspire Australian business men and women to be positive and get Australia back on track again after the recession. I have confirmed some top speakers and P&O Cruises have agreed to sponsor the conferences and I would be honoured to invite you to be the guest of honour and the keynote speaker."

There was a deathly silence then he replied, "I'd love to, but it's a pity you didn't call yesterday as last night I signed a contract with IMG and each time I speak they will charge a fee of $5000." I replied, "I don't have a problem with that and would be happy to pay it if you'll agree to the invitation." "Okay", he said, "Let's get together in Melbourne when we both return and discuss the dates and details." He gave me his Melbourne business address and phone number and we both agreed to get together in about a week's time and I hung up.

My friend, still sitting in my room, was stunned and with a look of bewilderment said, "Was that who I think it was, John Bertrand?" I replied, "Yes, but you can't say a word to anyone please. Firstly, they won't believe you, and secondly they'll think I am kidding you!"

We departed a couple of minutes after 11am and took the elevator down to the lobby, with him all the while shaking his head in disbelief.

I arrived at the airport, caught my flight to New York and sat back in my seat in a state of either 'eustress', something I didn't know about before meeting Wilfred Jarvis, and with a smile on my face 'like I'd caught a prized marlin'.

On arriving in New York, I retrieved my luggage and took a cab to the city and my hotel. The cab driver was a pleasant young black guy and we struck up a conversation on the way. When we finally arrived at my hotel I thought the driver had shown enough evidence to be trusted and would perhaps appreciate some extra work the next day. So I took a calculated risk and asked him if knew Winged Foot Golf Club in Mamaroneck and would he like to pick me up in the morning and take me there. He replied, "Yes, it will take about an hour to get there." So I agreed to meet him at 7.30am as my meeting with the Manager was scheduled in his busy day for 9am and the traffic would be heavy at that time.

The next morning I was ready in the foyer at 7.30am and my driver arrived on time. He put my luggage in the trunk and we set off. However, just after we neared Central Park he stopped and went over to speak to another cab driver lined up outside a hotel. I wasn't sure what was going on, but soon found out.

We made our way through the heavy traffic and I was glad we had allowed 90 minutes to drive the 25 miles. After about 55 minutes I started to become worried we would be late so I asked the driver how we were going for time. He said he thought we were okay and I reminded him that my meeting was at 9am.

Soon we arrived at a tollway pay station and I heard him say to the attendant, "How far to Winged Foot Golf Club from here?" The attendant asked, "Where have you come from?" The driver replied "Manhattan", and the attendant looked down at the driver and said in a dismissive manner, "Well driver you have driven south instead of north. It's going to take you at least 45 minutes to turn around and get there." I was furious, as that meant I would miss my appointment with the Manager, and I had flown all the way from Vancouver to meet him.

I called the golf club from the driver's two way radio phone to alert them to the fact I had been delayed, to which the receptionist said she would give the Manager the message.

You could have 'cut the air with a knife' in the cab and I stayed silent all the way until we arrived and pulled up at the entrance portico.

I waited until the driver had unloaded my luggage out of the trunk and I had given it to the 'bag boy' who had come over to greet me. The driver then said to me, "That will be $90", to which I replied, "No it won't, I will give you $50 and that's it because you lied to me about knowing where the golf club was, and you've made me miss my appointment." He looked sheepishly at me and I turned around and proceeded with my bags with the 'bag boy' to the reception area inside.

I'm sure the driver wasn't happy, but guess I did him a favour he will never forget. I won't either, because I now always make sure I know the way to my destinations.

The Manager was most gracious, understood my predicament and allocated the young guy who had helped me with my bags to show me around the golf club.

I was really disappointed I didn't have time to meet with the Manager, but I took in as much of this world famous golf course and bought a memento putting hole commemorating the 1984 US Open. I still have it today to remind me of a lesson in life I'll never forget.

Leadership Lessons:

1. Mirror other's communication style.
2. Explaining clearly why is critical.
3. Use empathy in phone calls.
4. Eustress allows confidence.
5. Always know the location of meetings.

Chapter 5

Syncing with the Skipper

When back in Vancouver, I reconnected with the group, and we boarded our Cathay Pacific flight to return to Hong Kong and then Melbourne.

My friend sat next to me all the way, and had a perpetual smile on his face, as did I.

When I arrived back in Melbourne I waited a couple of days and then phoned John as planned. He invited me to meet with him at his sail making factory in St Kilda Road, just up the hill from the St Kilda junction. When I arrived I found him sitting between the sails they were making. Here, it could be argued, was the most famous America's Cup skipper in 132 years, just going about his business in the most unaffected manner you could imagine.

He asked me to sit down with him and we chatted about all things America's Cup. I asked him what he had learnt about winning, teamwork and about himself. His answers were enlightening, riveting and very insightful. He mentioned that his focus on the job at hand was the key to winning. He mentioned that teamwork and physical fitness and especially mental toughness enabled all the dots to be joined. He finally mentioned that he learnt that his self-belief, calmness, judgment, and decision-making enabled him to show the leadership required to win.

He went on to say that how he communicated with the team, and how they reviewed each race without fear or favour of each other, before Alan Bond arrived with the grog on the 'Black Swan', enabled them to agree on a strategy for each future race.

I asked him how much influence Alan had on each race, to which he replied, "Very little! We had reviewed each race, agreed on ways to be better and our future strategy, before he arrived, yet he was helpful on some occasions."

We discussed the conferences or seminar format and I gave him the list of confirmed speakers and their topics, to which he seemed impressed.

I informed him that I had booked the Hilton Hotels in Sydney and Melbourne and that I was in the process of asking the two state premiers if they would host a cocktail party after the seminar in their state. He agreed to be the final speaker at the conclusion of each conference and to take questions for about 20 minutes after speaking for about 40 minutes.

I left the meeting 'between the sails' feeling very pleased with the outcome, and that we had a recipe for success to help Australian business.

When I returned to my office we confirmed our arrangements with John and all the other speakers and discussed all other final arrangements with the Hilton Hotels. We had selected these hotels because I knew the Manager of the Melbourne Hilton and he was a proactive, professional manager who was happy to assist me and my company in these seminars by donating the ballroom area required and the cocktail party reception areas. He was also able to influence the Manager of the Sydney Hilton to provide the same room and areas for our America's Cup seminars.

We then set about asking the premiers of each state to host a cocktail party, which we would pay for and to join the speakers, including John Bertrand and to present to him with some special and priceless mementos of his victory.

Neville Wran, the Liberal Premier of New South Wales immediately replied and offered to close 'The America's Cup Bar' at the Sydney Hilton and pay for the cocktail party. John Cain, the Labor Premier of Victoria, the home state of John Bertrand, never replied to our invitation in spite of numerous follow up phone calls and never attended. Simply amazing!

Our next task was to decide what mementos to give to a person who had created history by taking the America's Cup from the Americans for the first time since the race began 132 years ago.

We thought and scratched our heads and many suggestions were put forward. Someone had the bright suggestion that if possible we could give him the cartoons the political cartoonist for the Herald, George Haddon, had drawn for each race. There were obviously seven of them and they were all humorous, and brilliant in their detail.

He had also drawn a magnificent final cartoon to celebrate the Australia II win, and this we thought would be great to present to John if George would agree. Before we could ask him, George suggested it.

I knew George well, as he was working afternoons in our building in St Kilda Road as a freelancer, and had been doing a lot of work for our clients, especially Tooth Hotels and the Ford Motor Company.

We arranged a meeting with him and to our surprise he offered to give us all his original black and white drawings so we could have them framed. It was a magnificent and selfless gesture and typified the character of this very talented man.

The planning for these historic seminars had gone better than expected, but now that we had the skipper of Australia II we thought the seminars needed the final finishing professional touch. We needed an MC to introduce the speakers and link them together in a strategic way, so we maintained the focus and meaning of these business seminars.

Lots of names were suggested and then Mike Shirley, the Principal of Shirley Spectra who had confirmed he would be a speaker on Business Theatre and provide the visual support for the speakers, thought of Bobby Limb. I had met Bobby in Sydney to discuss a potential role in performing the narration for the Tooth Hotels film we had produced called 'Heritage and Destiny'.

He had recently called to ask me to help the Graeme Lyall Orchestra in its future as 'The Don Lane Show' on Channel GTV 9 Melbourne was due to finish in November and there was great uncertainty as to what direction they should take. I had already met with Graeme and his lead trumpet player, Norm Harris, in an initial planning meeting. So, I called Bobby Limb and he at once agreed to act as the MC in both Sydney and Melbourne. At last, all the components were in place, and we now put the marketing strategy into action to promote the seminars.

The first conference/seminar in Sydney went very well. The speakers were excellent, as was John's keynote presentation. Premier Neville Wran was very gracious and played the perfect host afterwards in the America's Cup Bar at the Hilton. John was quite humbled by the original cartoon mementos the Premier presented to him.

Melbourne was also a success, and Jeff Lynch from P&O Cruises complimented my company in his presentation. As the Premier had failed to show at the cocktail party, I asked George Haddon, the cartoonist, to personally present John with the special final cartoon he had drawn and which had been a feature of the story in the Herald. John was again surprised by George's generosity and thanked him accordingly.

It was then that Ron Barassi, the AFL legend, approached me quietly and said, "How did you ever get John Bertrand to be part of these seminars?" I told Ron an abbreviated version of the story to which he replied, "George, you'll have plenty of people saying you were lucky, but mate, luck had nothing to do with it!"

John's presentations in Sydney and Melbourne were extremely insightful, inspirational, motivational and enlightening. He mentioned 10 very significant leadership key traits that were very relevant in achieving a winning culture and result.

1. Visualisation: He mentioned that all the team on Australia II mentally thought they were Jonathan Livingston Seagull flying and swooping over the water.
2. Honesty: They all were prepared to be honest with one another in giving feedback after each race without fear or favour.
3. Clarity: They all spoke clearly and specifically in setting out the goals to be achieved.
4. Self-Belief: They all had to have total self-belief in their roles.
5. Communication: He especially made sure he listened actively to others, and spoke with conviction saying, why strategies were needed.
6. Resilience: They all had to be able to bounce back from failure and defeat and show one another they were committed and resilient.

7. Silence: They all were disciplined and had a pact of not talking to others and to the press about anything, allowing John and Warren Jones to be the spokesmen.
8. Mystery: They kept an air of mystery surrounding the winged keel that Ben Lexcen had secretly designed.
9. Decision Making: He and his key people on board made sure they weighed up the data and information and then made clear, incisive decisions for action.
10. Focus: He thought this was the key for success and actually, I think tongue in cheek, said that he didn't think he won the race, but that Dennis Conner lost it by not focusing and covering Australia II on the final leg when they tacked wide to get the wind that he saw, but Dennis Conner didn't, and that they were lucky to win!

Leadership Lessons:

1. Try to be in sync with others.
2. Empathy is a powerful tool.
3. Give honest feedback without fear or favour.
4. Leverage contacts for assistance.
5. Luck is when preparation meets opportunity.

CASE HISTORY 11

Australian Motor Industries Ltd: TOYOTA

Chapter 1

Trust comes by Foot

There is no doubt that the game of golf enables people to form opinions about character and trust, and therefore, forge relationships.

After playing golf a few times with a senior divisional manager of Toyota, Norm Iddles, he said to me in late 1983, as we walked from the 7th green to the 8th tee, "Call me Monday!" I replied, "Why?" To which he answered, "Because Alan Hingston is joining us from Ford, and he will need you!"

I guess the impact we were making in the marketplace with the John Bertrand seminars, together with our relationship on the golf course, had been responsible for him to trust that I could and would assist his company.

After our game of golf, I reflected and realised the potential missing link of why I had been asked to call him. Alan in his previous role in marketing with Ford had been, no doubt, able to witness our retail dealership program in 1981 to help lift the customer service standards, product knowledge and sales with our performance management program, 'Lift off to Paradise'.

It was a very special program. The program had been conducted from July to September 1981 with the 40 winning dealer principals and their partners spending 10 days on the big island of Hawaii and the last night in Honolulu. We had booked all the business class seats on two Boeing 747 Qantas jumbos on non-stop return flights from Sydney and Melbourne exclusively for the Ford winners and management.

On arrival in Honolulu we met up and flew to the island of Hawaii to stay at the brand new Sheraton Royal Waikoloa Hotel on the Kona coast. In fact the Ford people were the very first people to stay at this new stunning hotel. As well as relaxing we had flown in performers for a New Orleans Jazz and Casino Night and had helicopters drop frangipani flowers over the group during an Hawaiian style barbeque on the beach.

The final night would see the group staying at the world famous Sheraton Waikiki after a spectacular special afternoon boat tour of Pearl Harbour. The evening included dinner at the Kahala Hilton near Diamond Head, served on 22 carat gold edged plates and would include a performance of specially selected music by the Royal Hawaiian Police Band.

It was acknowledged by Ford that the program broke new ground in creativity, education and excellence.

Again, I learnt another valuable lesson during the Pearl Harbour cruise regarding communication. We were cruising on a majestic all aluminum hulled high profile cruiser that was frequently booked by actors, entertainers, celebrities and politicians. Around mid-day the staff started serving lunch to the Ford group.

I was busy checking the itinerary details when Max Gransden, the Ford Director of Sales and Marketing came up to me in an agitated, angry state. "George, have you seen the lunch they are serving to my Ford people?" I replied that I hadn't yet, and asked, "Why, what is the problem, Max?" He replied, "They are serving open sandwiches on paper plates, not china, with plastic knives and forks. We can't have this standard for our Ford winners!"

I immediately spoke to my Manager, Peter Dunn and his counterpart at Ford, Peter McGinnity, who had both travelled to Hawaii at our expense months earlier and put all the detailed arrangements together. I explained the situation to them and instructed them to stop the lunch. Then I asked them both the question, "When you briefed and negotiated with the cruise company, what lunch did you ask for?" They sheepishly replied, "We told them we wanted a good lunch!" I asked them what they thought 'a good lunch' meant, and they were unable to give me a definitive answer.

After the serving of the lunch was stopped, I called the Sheraton Waikiki Sales Director from the ship's radio telephone on the bridge and we sped at 18 knots towards shore to enable the Ford group to eat a 'good Ford standard lunch' in the hotel's ballroom.

It was a lesson I will never forget and I often ask the question, "What is a good lunch?" in a seminar or workshop to illustrate clear communication.

On Monday I called Toyota as requested and arranged to meet with Alan that week. At the meeting he mentioned that Toyota was at that time, No 5 in the market place in Australia and their goal was to become No 1. He also mentioned the first challenge was to head off Nissan and Mitsubishi as competitors, and they wanted to capture both their market shares as soon as possible.

So, we set up a task force and worked over the Christmas break to be able to launch the 'Toyota Attack Pack' range of strategies in the first weeks of January 1984 to catch Nissan and Mitsubishi off guard with the element of surprise. Our strategy included using our political cartoonist and friend, George Haddon, to weave a humorous military theme throughout the printed material to give the message impact and help its focus and memorability.

The program was designed in military camouflage and all the 'Battle Plans' were contained in a filing system in a special 'Attack Pack Satchel'. The highlight of the strategy was to take the top 15 dealers and their partners to the Los Angeles Olympics which were being held in August 1984 and then on to Tahiti for five days of R&R. We had organised that they stay on 'Toyota Island,' an off the hotel coast man-made island, in opulent over water, thatched bungalows, or as the Tahitians called them, 'fares'.

We arranged tickets to the Olympic hockey, gymnastics, athletics and closing ceremony followed by a day at Disneyland, a visit to the majestic Queen Mary and famous Spruce Goose (Howard Hughes' monster aeroplane), both located together at Long Beach. The final night in Los Angeles was to be a Toyota Banquet in Beverly Hills at the Beverley Wilshire Hotel. This auspicious event was the icing on the Olympic cake of success which had culminated in the Toyota group witnessing one of the most spectacular closing ceremonies ever performed at an Olympic Games.

The next day I set off on an earlier flight for Tahiti to check on all the arrangements for the group's accommodation and transport from the airport to the hotel.

We had arranged with the local Toyota dealership to collect the 15 winning couples and management team from the airport in 16 Toyota Hilux vehicles and drive them in a convoy to the Beachcomber Hotel Resort then over the bridge to the island that we had renamed 'Toyota Island' with the overwater grass thatched 'fares The Toyota group of 15 winners, partners and management were then to be welcomed to Toyota Island with a complimentary drink and given their 'fare' key and registration form to complete. After the long flight from Los Angeles they rubbed their eyes at what they saw in disbelief.

The first day was a leisure day after a 'silver service' breakfast brought to them by hotel staff on an outrigger.

The next was our last day in Tahiti and in the morning before the gala dinner we had planned something very different for the Toyota group. We were sailing to Moorea for a tour, then Toyota had asked me to present an 'In Search of Excellence' business seminar. I was to show the film, based on the book, which contained 10 American case histories and give my thoughts after each case history, about the importance of 'creating excellence' in everything a car dealership did in the interests of the customer. The focus was 'success all comes from people'.

The case histories included Disneyland and it's University, Stew Leonard's Dairy Supermarket, 3M and how the yellow post-it notes were created, the Dana Manufacturing Corporation, IBM and the caring culture they created for their employees and McDonalds staff training in product knowledge and product presentation.

The seminar was divided into two segments, and after each case history I answered questions from dealers and their partners. It seemed to go really well and I felt comfortable and confident in presenting the knowledge I had gained after meeting one of the authors of the book, Bob Waterman Jnr in San Francisco earlier in the year when planning the Toyota Olympic Games/Tahiti trip.

On the walk to our boat to return to Pape´ete, I was spoken to by several dealer principals who thanked me for the presentation.

One of the more influential dealers looked me in the eye and said, "George, I can see you giving those seminars and helping lots of companies in Australia with that film. It's really insightful and excellent."

Little did I know how right he was in predicting my future?

I had been planning the Gala Farewell Dinner for that night to be a 'Bounty Banquet' and had arranged for Bella (Elizabeth) and Jimmy Taylor to be our Guests of Honour and for her to create a display from the 1962 film 'Mutiny on the Bounty'. This would include her sewing machine and the shirts she had made, and were worn, by Marlon Brando, Trevor Howard and Richard Harris together with the painting they had been given of the ship by the director as a memento for their roles in the film.

Jimmy then gave me some amazing news. He mentioned that the Tahitian girl who played Princess Maimiti in the film, Tarita Teriipaia, was in fact working in our hotel as the Restaurant Manager.

I asked him if she would mind being introduced to the Toyota group during the banquet. He asked and she graciously agreed. What a coup!

The 'Bounty Banquet' Gala dinner was brilliant and brought the trip to a fitting finale!

Leadership Lessons:

1. Golf is a game to form relationships.
2. Remember, people are always watching you.
3. Qualify the meaning of a 'good lunch'.
4. Utilise the element of surprise for position.
5. Use the 'check twice, measure once' carpenter's mantra.

Chapter 2

The Cook from Essex

After the group departed for their flight back to Australia, I arranged to stay on with my wife for a much needed three days break to wind down after a hectic 12 months with Toyota.

The hotel upgraded us to an over-water fare, so we kicked back and enjoyed being pampered in a magnificent setting which included the silver service breakfast delivered to us by outrigger to our verandah and the glass floor porthole giving us the opportunity to watch the colourful fish swimming below in the crystal-clear waters.

On the first morning of our extended stay, we decided to have our breakfast in the restaurant where Tarita Teriipaia, Princess Maimiti was the manager. It was good to see her and thank her for agreeing to make our 'Bounty Banquet' so authentic and special.

On our walk back to our room, past the swimming pool, my wife saw a dark-haired guy lying on a sun lounge reading a book and whispered to me, "Do you know who that is?" "No", I replied, "I don't have a clue." "I think its David Essex, the English singer", she whispered. "Wow", I replied, "If it is, I wonder what he's doing here so far from home."

Back at our fare, I noticed the message light was illuminated on the room phone, so I phoned reception who said there was a telex waiting for me.

During the six months prior to the Olympic Games, I had been secretly in negotiations with Michael Edgely and Michael Linnit, the manager of Torvill & Dean, the Olympic ice-skating stars, for them to perform in Adelaide the following year to help launch the new front wheel drive Corolla, on ice.

This had never been done before in the car industry, and I had been continually in discussions with them. In the Telex was the complete proposal, and their actual acceptance of the project. I had pulled off the unthinkable!

Walking back, I again passed the dark-haired man and having gained confidence after my successful recent negotiations, I said, "Hi David, are you enjoying a well-earned rest?"

He looked up smiled and said, "Yes but I'm working on a project while I'm here." "Well," I said, "what a great place to work on a project."

He then asked, "Why are you here?" I replied, "I have just organised a trip for a group of Toyota dealers to the LA Olympics, including a stopover for a few days on the island in the overwater fares." "Oh, that's interesting, I saw the sign at the little bridge saying Toyota Island and wondered what was happening. How did the trip go and what was Los Angeles like?" "It was non-stop activity, yet exciting to be part of," I replied.

We seemed to connect and chatted for a few moments then he surprised me by saying, "Have you got a few minutes? I'd like to show you the project I'm working on." "Yes that's fine," I replied and we set off for a walk to his room, an executive suite way up on the top floor of the hotel which had spectacular views out over the sea. He opened the door and there was a range of instruments, books and notes set up all around the suite. "Wow", I said, "you certainly have a lot of gear here. Are you writing a new song?" "Well," he said, "I'm actually not writing a new song, but a whole stage show to premier next year in the West End." "That sounds fabulous, can I ask what it's about?"

He looked at me with an earnest expression and replied, "Well, it's a stage show called 'The Bounty' and I am in Tahiti to also research it, and the travels of Captain Cook as part of the visit." I quietly replied, "Why is Captain Cook important? I don't think he was involved in the mutiny on the Bounty."

He again looked at me earnestly, took a long breath and said, "Well as it turns out George, my name isn't David Essex, its David Cook and I am a descendent of Captain Cook. My manager didn't think David Cook was a good stage name, so he suggested we change it to Essex as that's where I lived."

I was stunned as he had taken me into his confidence, and I realised I had a great responsibility to keep this information private unless he chose to make it public. Our conversation continued and I asked him how he was getting on with his research for The Bounty. He replied that he had only just arrived and was still also planning on finding out more about Captain Cook's visit to Tahiti.

Suddenly I had an idea and I told him that I knew Jimmy and Bella Taylor who had worked on the costumes for the 1962 film 'Mutiny on the Bounty' and that they lived in Pape'ete. I asked him if he would like to meet them as I was sure they could assist him with his research and possibly give him some direction on where to go and who to ask.

He agreed that this would be most valuable and asked if I could arrange for him to meet them. I then left and wandered back to my room with my feet hardly touching the ground. I phoned Jimmy and filled him in on David Essex and his Tahitian project. Jimmy accepted my invitation to meet David. We arranged for him, Bella, David, Susan and I to have dinner the next night as the following day was to be our last in Tahiti and we were flying out that evening. Jimmy suggested a well-known Chinese restaurant in Pape´ete and said that he would make the booking for 7pm. I sent the details on to David and then Susan and I spend the rest of the day and the following day relaxing by ourselves.

The dinner went exceptionally well. After making the introductions I watched and was privy to an intriguing and interesting discussion. We left after a beautiful meal of various dishes and went our own separate ways to digest the night and sleep, but only after we had a couple of night caps at the bar!

The next morning, I woke up a bit 'second hand' due no doubt to the night caps. After breakfast I wandered over to the office, past the pool, to check our account as we were departing that evening.

Walking back I saw David had arrived so I sat at the end of his pool lounge and asked him how he felt about the evening and especially how he felt after the two night caps. "Well," he said, "I can't thank you enough. It was great to meet Jimmy and Bella and they are going to arrange to show me around so I can learn more about the mutiny on the Bounty and Captain Cook's visit.

George, I want you and your wife to know that you are welcome to stay in my apartment in New York anytime you are there and I will send you both an invitation to attend a performance of the stage show in London which should premier in early 1986."

He then grabbed a napkin and wrote down his name, address, phone

Napkin given to me by singer David Essex with his PA's contact details.

number and the name of his personal secretary, Madge Godwin. We then parted company to get packed to leave Tahiti with some wonderful memories of meeting David Cook!

Leadership Lessons:

1. Create opportunities to stretch yourself.
2. Be a very good, 'active listener'.
3. Be your authentic self.
4. Be inquisitive about other people.
5. Be 'the broker' often and just sit back.

Chapter 3

A Path to Perfection

We arrived back in Melbourne from Tahiti feeling exhausted, yet at the same time excited after a memorable experience, and rubbing shoulders with world famous stars.

Since walking off the 7th green at Yarra Yarra, my company's experience with Toyota had grown at a rapid rate. It seemed like every time I visited head office to attend the meeting on the progress of a strategic performance management program, the manager I was meeting with would say to me on arrival, "By the way the Manager of Toyota Parts and Accessories, or the Manager of Air Conditioning, or the Manager of Toyota Finance wants to see you about a project before you leave."

Early April 1984, before we had even thought of shifting or buying a building, Jeff Martin, my client contact at Toyota, arrived for a meeting with me in our St Kilda Road office. This was most unusual as I always visited him at his office.

I welcomed him into my office, and before taking his seat he said, "Do you mind if I close the door? Of course, I replied "No", but immediately, perhaps because of my upbringing and formative years, thought was there a problem of some sort and worriedly replied, "What's the problem?" He replied "Oh, there's no problem, I just want to ask you to launch a car!

This discussion is classified top secret, but in April 1985 Toyota will be the last of the five major car companies to launch a front wheel drive car, and it will be the new Corolla. It's going to be the biggest marketing event we have ever undertaken in Australia, and Doctor Toyoda, the Managing Director, will be visiting Australia for the first time to host the event."

Initially I was rendered speechless and then replied, "I'm flattered Jeff, but I have never launched a new car before." "I know that", he replied, "but we like the way you think. We have confidence that you can do it." I was amazed. He went on to say that the launch would take place on 16 April 1985 in Adelaide, and it would be held at the Festival Centre.

I sat quietly, listening, trying to take in his comments, and digest the enormity of the project. We discussed a number of other issues and then as he left, he turned around, smiled and said, "The launch should be a lot of fun, very exciting and I know you'll come up with a great concept, but remember it's confidential at present."

I thanked him and he departed. I went back to my desk and sat for a few more minutes before calling in my General Manager, Eric Carter, and my Program Manager, Meredith Ashton, who was the lead executive working on the Toyota account.

I relayed the news to them and they were naturally very excited, but realised that it was strictly confidential and they must at all costs 'keep a lid on it' until we had the final approval to proceed.

I went home elated, but also knowing I couldn't tell anyone for the time being about the project. My wife could tell there was something on my mind and asked me what it was. After dinner I decided to take her into my confidence and told her about the meeting, the launch planned for 1985, and that she must keep what I had told her strictly confidential. She was happy for us but not as excited as I was.

Jeff had asked me to come back to him with a concept idea within a week and on the Friday night, Susan and I went to a gala performance by ice-skaters Torvill & Dean at the Melbourne Entertainment Centre, which had been the venue for the swimming events for the 1956 Melbourne Olympics.

The show was breathtaking, and the skaters were glamorous, exhilarating and moved with exquisite grace and poise.

Torvill & Dean, the gold medallists at the 1984 Winter Olympic Games in Sarajevo and who were by now world celebrities, gave a short exhibition prior to interval after the Australian ice-skaters had performed.

The lights came on and I just sat there in a trance. Susan looked over at me and asked, "Where are you, you don't seem to be here with me tonight?" I looked at her and quietly replied, "I know how I'm going to launch the new front wheel drive Corolla. We will launch it on ice and I'll get them to perform as the main act to reveal the car. The car can move and dance like a skater because of its front wheel drive and the back can sway and move like an ice-skater."

She looked at me and just said, "Let's get an ice cream.'

After interval I was convinced that the ice concept would work. That week we subtly investigated whether the stage at the Festival Centre could be converted into an ice-rink without letting them know why we were interested.

I had arranged a meeting with Jeff at Toyota for 3.30pm that Friday and I was interested to know how he would react to my concept.

He made me a cup of coffee and we sat down in his office. He looked at me and asked, "Okay, what have you got to tell me?" I took a big breath and said, "Well Jeff, last Friday night I went to see Torvill & Dean and believe the way to launch the Corolla is on ice with Australian ice-skaters and Torvill & Dean being the major attraction. As the cars are front wheel drive they should be able to turn and dance across the ice like ice-skaters and I think it would be amazing."

He sat there with a blank look on his face and with a blank note pad in front of him. The only words he wrote in our meeting which lasted an hour or so, were the words 'on ice' which he circled. He then asked me if it was possible for an ice-rink to be constructed at the venue and I informed him that we had subtly contacted the Festival Centre and they had informed us that it was possible to lay an ice-rink over the main stage.

His eyes lit up and he then smiled and said, "Good luck getting them. That would be amazing if you could pull it off."

He gave me his blessing and I left. I had gained agreement from him that Toyota, as was their normal way, would cover any research and planning costs for me and my team, and we continued with this ground-breaking project.

We agreed that I would keep Jeff updated on progress. He also mentioned that we had a budget of $150,000 to cover the concept, development and administration of the Australian launch, and Toyota would cover all the dealers' travel, accommodation and meals.

After making the necessary conference notes of the meeting for my team, I set off home for the weekend.

I was in the office bright and early on Monday and called a meeting of what I called the 'Corolla Launch Taskforce' and put Meredith in charge of all the logistics. She would work directly with me to find out who were the managing agents of Torvill & Dean, what was necessary to negotiate their availability, who in Australia built ice-rinks and the Australian agents for ice-skaters.

Meredith also started discussions and arrangements for air travel, ground transport and accommodation options for the Australian dealers to travel to and from Adelaide, and the logistics with the Adelaide Festival Centre.

It wasn't long before Meredith was able to inform me that I would have to discuss their availability with Michael Edgley International, Michael himself, his Australian Manager, Andrew Guild and Michael Linnit, their London Manager. She continued focusing on sourcing contacts for ice-rinks and Australian skaters while I focused on contacting Michael Edgley.

I finally broke through and gained a meeting with Andrew Guild who, at the outset seemed very interested in the project. He eventually gave me Michael's unlisted direct telephone number in Sydney and thus we began an interesting relationship.

Michael indicated that Torvill & Dean were planning to launch 'Ice Planet' in London about the same time as the Corolla launch. However, performing in Adelaide wouldn't prove too much of a problem as they could take a week off from their London performance, for which Her Majesty Queen Elizabeth II, was a patron.

Our negotiations had eventually enabled us to gain two extra parts of the overall contract, additional promotional and trade appearances and their use in another five countries in the world if Toyota agreed to the proposal for the launch which had turned out to be named 'A Path to Perfection'.

The Corolla car launch Ice Planet proposal which confirmed that Torvill & Dean could perform at the launch in Adelaide.

Leadership Lessons:

1. Be careful of doing too much at once.
2. Creative thinking happens in a quiet cocoon.
3. Always think on the bright side of life.
4. Aim for the stars for brilliance.
5. Remember, nothing is ever perfection.

Chapter 4

A Golden World

At the end of 1984 we were working in one strategic way or another for every single department of Toyota in Australia. I had been very pleased with our growth, but the constant business had necessitated employing additional people to handle the business and this had made it necessary to lease additional space. So in late 1984, I made the decision to buy a building that I knew was for sale by a competitor in a similar business to mine.

This would have the benefit of gaining an asset instead of paying dead rent money and enable all the staff, now totalling over 30 people, to have more room and designated work areas to accommodate the travel department, the administration department and the executive management, over three different levels

The building was a heritage listed four storey former tea house with a Baltic pine lined attic in Queensbridge Street, South Melbourne which had been beautifully restored at great expense by the previous owner.

It gave us a new home of which we were very proud and at the same time enabled the staff to increase their productivity with better communication and higher morale.

Prior to the Los Angeles 1984 Olympic Games in August, my wife and I had travelled in July 1984 to Europe to set up a special Toyota Performance Management Program for the Gold Toyota Dealers of

1984. This award was for the dealers who had performed best from 1 June to 30 September 1984.

To maintain the growth in market share, and their position in the marketplace, we were asked to design a special travel itinerary that would generally not be available.

I had already created a concept for such a special trip and had kept it under wraps for such an occasion

We called it 'Golden World' and it included such opulent highlights as flying business class from Melbourne to London on British Airways, visiting the International Motor Show in Birmingham, flying to Paris and enjoying a dinner cruise on the river Seine, visiting the famous Cite de l'automobile Schlumpf Brothers vintage car museum in Mulhouse.

The dealers would then spend a night on the town at the Moulin Rouge before embarking on the highlight of the trip, travelling in black tie on the Venice Simplon Orient Express to Venice and staying at the world renowned Hotel Chipriani which was the scene for many feature movies.

The Toyota Golden World Group would then fly to Vienna where they would visit the Schoenbrunn Palace and as a finale, attend a dinner at the Alsberg Palace complete with a chorale presentation by the Mozart Boys Choir before returning to London and flying back in business class to Australia.

As you can imagine, this performance management travel award for the Gold Dealers was not only very difficult to imaginatively create, but just as difficult to arrange. So, in the spirit of excellence, we test drove the trip to make sure every small detail was planned and confirmed so it would in fact be a golden world experience.
The highlight of our pre-trip was to be the journey on the Venice

Chapter 4   A Golden World

Simplon Orient Express. We arrived at the Paris Gare de l'Est railway station about 7pm for the trip overnight to Venice. In keeping with the elegance of the occasion we dressed in black tie and on arrival were welcomed on the red carpet to the special waiting lounge

The train was 17 carriages long, and sitting at the station it protruded out so far it crossed over two other platform lines.

After the boarding call we were greeted by our carriage attendant who took our main luggage for stowing and our overnight luggage which he said he would place in our suite.

He then asked us what we would like for breakfast and at what time. He collected our passports and escorted us to the dining car where I had booked a table for two for dinner with a view out of the panoramic window.

The dinner experience was amazing and afterwards we retired to the club car where a pianist played on a glossy white grand piano. We stayed and listened to the music for some time, met several other guests and then retired to bed. As I left, I asked the pianist how long he played each day, to which he replied, "Sir, I play from 7pm until there is no one left in the club car."

Arriving back at our suite we found the bed folded down and our bags on the floor ready for us

The evening was interesting as it was a different experience and unusual trying to sleep on a moving train as it rocked gently from side to side. We stopped abruptly however when we reached the Italian border so the two locomotives could be replaced.

The next morning, we woke up, opened the blinds, and watched the Italian landscape pass by before arriving in Venice at the Santa

Lucia station

However, during the morning as we travelled through Innsbruck, I decided to go for a wander through the carriages. Along the way I was met by James Sherwood, Founder and Chairman of Belmont Ltd who had recently purchased the train and had restored many of its historical carriages. Travelling with him was his wife Dr Shirley Sherwood.

He asked me how I was enjoying my journey and I told him I was very impressed and that I was planning to bring a group of Australian Toyota Gold World Dealers on the train later in November

He was very grateful as he had recently re-launched the train's image in its new current state. While we were talking, his wife was busy, clipboard in hand, checking every small detail of the cleanliness and conditions of the carriages.

Although I had no idea at the time, this experience was to gain me an amazing opportunity to manage a similar train in the future and to learn what was required for it to be successful in Australia.

We arrived in magnificent Venice, a vision to behold.

We collected our luggage and made our way with some trepidation to the other side of the station where the water taxis were lined up waiting for passengers. This was an unforgettable trip. We motored down the canals of Venice and the scenery was just stunning.

By this stage my wife had become frustrated with me being consumed in the detail of the trip and grabbed my camera from me saying, it's about time I use that. She then proceeded to take as many shots as she could before looking up at me sheepishly and said, "What does it mean when the counter reads 43?" I replied in an equally frustrated way, "It means that you haven't put a film in it."

There was a strained silence in the water taxi until we reached our hotel, checked in and had a rather subdued dinner.

Next morning, after breakfast we took a ride on one of the many gondolas around the canals taking in, among other things, the famous Grande Canal.

Venice was a captivating place and our stay, while short, was truly memorable.

After checking out the next morning, we caught one of the many water taxis to the airport for a flight to Vienna, the home of Mozart

As we left we were warned by the hotel that the water taxi could be expensive and it was best to agree on a price before setting off. I did, but the price we agreed used up our remaining Italian lira so when the taxi driver/captain asked for more money before giving us our luggage I was surprised and not happy. I told him so, got our luggage and left.

The flight to Vienna was uneventful. On arrival we checked into the Vienna InterContinental Hotel which was just opposite the botanic gardens with the famous statue of Mozart prominently situated in the centre.

That night we visited the Schoenbrunn Palace and watched a performance by a chamber group orchestra in one of the magnificently ornate drawing rooms.

The next day was a work day for me, and I met the ground travel agent who was arranging for our group to have the Palais Auersperg opened especially for them for a grand dinner and a special choral presentation by the Mozart Boys Choir.

Our short stay in Vienna was nearly over. That night was our last night, however while we were sleeping I was awoken by my mobile phone ringing in the middle of the night. I was worried something was wrong back in Australia, but it was Torvill & Dean's Manager, Michael Linnit calling me from London about the details for the Corolla launch due to be held in April 1985.

It was a positive conversation and becoming more likely that they would agree to be part of the launch I had started working on before we had left Australia. I didn't sleep much after we concluded our conversation. My wife slept peacefully.

After finalising everything for the Golden World Dealers trip that would include London, Paris, Venice and Vienna, we flew back home to Australia, at the end of July, to quickly prepare for the Toyota group trip which was planned for late August to the Los Angeles 1984 Olympics

My life was very busy, the business was growing, I now realise probably too fast and with too many eggs in one basket with Toyota. Yet at the time I was 'on a roll' running on adrenaline, and experiencing what I now know as a good dose of eustress or good stress.

We had also gained other smaller clients including Elders Pastoral, NEC, Dunlop Pacific, and life was becoming very, very, very busy!

Leadership Lessons:

1. Referrals are the best form of marketing.
2. Customer satisfaction is gold.
3. Draw on unique experiences for the future.
4. Frustrations can cause oversights.
5. You're vulnerable with all your eggs in one basket.

Chapter 5

Rabbits in the Hat

After returning from the Los Angeles Olympics and Tahiti it became apparent that the negotiations and discussions regarding the Corolla car launch were taking more of my time than I had planned.

It was critical for our young company, so I decided in late September not to go on the Golden World Toyota group trip departing on 26 October and instead stay in Australia and focus on the Corolla launch.

My General Manager, Eric Carter, and his wife Lesley agreed to go and manage the Toyota group, so I briefed them fully on all the details and nuances of the trip. Eric was now well experienced in his role and was most reliable in his attention to detail and responsibility.

My mind was at peace knowing our large client would be well looked after, and I now had the time to concentrate my energies on the launch.

During the day I caught up with Jeff Martin, the National Sales/Promotion Manager and confidentially told him the good news that I had received the Proposal from Michael Edgley confirming the opportunity of Torvill & Dean performing at the Corolla launch. He beamed as he didn't think I could pull the deal off!

However, the opportunity to engage them became conditional on Toyota paying £2.5 million to sponsor the initial 'Ice Planet' production in London. Toyota's head office in Japan was approached by Jeff at Toyota Australia, but by him having to approach them, I had lost my ability to influence the agreement as it was really in Jeff's hands.

Toyota Japan, I was informed, was not interested in funding the London production. Surprisingly, I was then asked by Jeff to call the Toyota UK Managing Director and discuss the opportunity directly with him. I duly arranged the call, but as I had never met him or spoken with him before, and therefore had not been able to develop any relationship, it proved too difficult to convince him at short notice of the value and the opportunity for the Toyota brand worldwide.

So Toyota lost the Torvill & Dean opportunity, which not only included the Corolla launch, but also the retail promotion, advertising and public relations opportunities for the rest of the world which I had worked hard to achieve for them over nearly nine months of protracted and difficult negotiations.

We were now back to square one, but Toyota loved the idea of launching the Corolla on ice so we continued with that strategy and decided to include other well-known Australian artists to support the launch.

Jeff Martin had been an entertainer and singer in his home state of South Australia and suggested the singer and actress, Debbie Byrne. I suggested the singer and pianist, Simon Gallaher who was at the time very popular on Australian television.

Jeff then engaged Disc Image Productions to produce and direct the car launch stage show we had suggested. Many creative meetings were held, and finally the launch format was agreed.

Australian ice-skaters would start the launch on stage, on the rink we would have specially built. Then Debbie Byrne would be lowered from the ceiling in a space ship and once landed she would then sing a number of songs with Simon Gallaher who would be dressed in a white suit and playing his special 'see-through' Sony grand piano.

Ice mountains would then be detonated to reveal the new front wheel drive Corolla cars which would be driven by special stunt drivers, just like I had visualised while watching Torvill & Dean 12 months earlier, swaying and dancing on the ice-rink to music.

The finale would include a speech by the Toyota Chairman, Dr Toyoda, thanking the dealers and their partners for their performance and attendance at the launch. Food and refreshments would then be served outside the Festival Centre.

I couldn't believe it was finally going to happen, and with such an exciting launch concept that I had created.

I then got another interesting call a few days later from Jeff to say Toyota wanted to entertain the dealers at the Adelaide Hilton the night before the launch, and did I have any ideas on how we could do that, and the costs involved. On completing the call, I thought for a while then called in Meredith as well as Eric, who had now settled back in the office after hosting the successful Toyota Golden World European trip.

We brainstormed a number of ideas and finally agreed that I should call the Hilton Hotel and ask them what they could also suggest. I called the Manager and found out to my surprise, that the American superstars, Dionne Warwick and Jack Jones, were due to perform a series of shows starting on the night of the launch. The Hilton gave me their agent's contact details and phone number in Las Vegas and suggested I call them to see if they would perform for Toyota one night earlier than their start date and ascertain their fee.

I duly called their agent and explained the situation and opportunity. They contacted us two days later to say they would perform exclusively for Toyota and that the fee for themselves and their orchestra would be AU$42,000 for the performance.

I called Jeff Martin with the news and he immediately agreed for us to confirm the booking. Unfortunately at the time, I never realised or established that their fee would be coming out of the $150,000 launch budget that had been confirmed initially. I assumed it would be an additional budget allocation in view of the additional late request.

A couple of days later Jeff called me again for another 'rabbit to be pulled out of the hat'. As Dr Toyoda would be visiting Australia for the first time, and had never been to Adelaide, he asked could I contact the City of Adelaide and negotiate what they could do to honour his visit in view of the launch at the Festival Theatre of the new Corolla and the publicity it would generate for Adelaide.

At this stage the launch details were being kept highly secret and classified in terms of letting the dealer network, or any other outside people or suppliers, know when and how the launch would take place.

I called the Mayor of the City of Adelaide and explained to her personal assistant what was planned and asked what they could do to honour Dr Toyoda. I received a call a few days later. The Mayor would agree to present Dr Toyoda with the keys to the city. Also, they would close William Street for security and safety reasons and hold a Mayoral reception over lunch in the Adelaide Town Hall in his honour. This would be held the day prior to the launch and before the Dionne Warwick and Jack Jones show that evening.

We were elated. We asked them to confirm all the details, timing, and logistics in writing so we could present the invitation to Dr Toyoda for his acceptance.

I called Jeff Martin at Toyota. He couldn't believe what we had been able to negotiate and was ecstatic that he could present this to the Toyota directors.

Our taskforce, headed by myself and with Meredith in charge of logistics, had now pulled a 'number of rabbits out of the hat' for Toyota. As Christmas 1984 was approaching I thought it would be a good idea to celebrate our year with Toyota by inviting their key executives and their partners to a night on George Norris Marketing to say thank you and consolidate our business relationship.

Tina Turner was visiting Australia for a series of cabaret concerts at the Hilton Hotels and as we now knew the Manager of the Melbourne Hilton very well, we arranged for two tables of 10 in prime positions.

The plan was to meet downstairs for pre-dinner drinks in Juliana's Nightclub and then move upstairs for dinner and the Tina Turner cabaret show.

We arranged for one of Australia's Walkley Award winning cartoonists, George Haddon, who was doing a lot of work for us and our clients' performance management programs, to design the invitation. I think it was one of his best creations and showed Tina Turner holding her microphone aloft whilst sitting on my lap, legs askew in fishnet stockings.

It brought a true touch of self-deprecating humour to the event and gave him the opportunity to show why he had won so many Gold Walkley's for his creative work.

We also arranged for a presentation tape of the latest Tina Turner album to be placed on the table in front of each Toyota couple.

The evening was a triumphant success. After dinner had been served, Jeff Martin came over to me and said, "George, you have done a super job tonight. Thanks for a great year's work." I replied, "Jeff, it is not all me. I have a superb team that works well together, can think big, and with great detail."

Leadership Lessons:

1. Always get budgets confirmed in writing.
2. Delegate and 'throw to grow' latent talent.
3. Realise it is ok to be ok with yourself.
4. Be patient and detailed in negotiating.
5. Use empathy and celebrate success.

Chapter 6

Trust leaves by Horse Power

January 1985 started with a bang and was to teach me several serious lessons in leadership and life.

Since April 1983, it had been a ride of a lifetime, and it seemed if I had been a surfer, my board was forever on top of a wave of new business.

We maintained our focus, enjoyed the facilities, and working from our own new building. Then early in 1985 a new senior manager came on the scene at Toyota from Mitsubishi.

To try and build a relationship with him I went out of my way and invited him to visit our new office for a tour and to meet our people.

Then late one night a week or so later, just before leaving my office, I received a phone call from Jeff saying that the budget he had confirmed to me for all the work to be done for the launch had been cut from $150,000 to $100,000.

I was in shock and protested strongly to him that we had worked for nearly 12 months believing the launch budget we had been told by him, and that we would lose money as we couldn't recover the costs. He seemed upset and nervous and just said his hands were tied and there was nothing he could do about it.

I was stunned and shocked and called the divisional manager, Norm

Iddles, who I played golf with, and who three years earlier had asked me to work with Toyota. We seriously discussed the ethics of the situation and he agreed as a compromise to pay any shortfall we would suffer as a consequence.

I left for home feeling shocked yet feeling somewhat pleased that we would at least be able to get paid for the work we had been asked to perform.

We regrouped the next day, had a taskforce crisis meeting and agreed we had too much to lose and decided to press on, albeit with some trepidation.

From that moment on I started having problems with our relationship with Toyota, and I never let my 'sixth sense' take over when I should have!

The launch lead up was hectic and we were juggling a lot of 'client balls in the air'. The final piece of the logistical jigsaw came together when we successfully negotiated with Ansett Airlines to arrange charter flights from Sydney, Brisbane, and Melbourne to enable all the dealers to arrive at about the same time.

The 'after launch banquet' was finalised to be held in the Festival Centre Banquet Room and we arranged all the people power required for the event.

The launch night was sensational. We were told Dr Toyoda was thrilled with the launch, the ice concept, and the Adelaide Mayor's hospitality. Apparently, we had as a team, set a new benchmark for a car launch in the motor industry in the world.

However, the world changed after the launch on 16 April 1985 for me, my company and my family.

We worked with the new clients in NEC, Elders Pastoral, BBC Hardware and continued to work for Toyota, but it wasn't the same as we were suffering long delays in payment of invoices for the shortfall on the launch and some other department projects.

Jeff Martin was then promoted, and we were asked by another executive who was to be our new contact at Toyota, to meet with him so he could introduce himself. We met off-site at a coffee shop he had suggested, and my first impression was he wouldn't be easy to work with in the future.

However, he briefed me on the next Toyota Dealer Performance Management program for 1986, and we created the concept of Casino Royale which would take the Golden World Dealers for 1986 to the Formula 1 race in Monaco. We duly blocked off the necessary accommodation at the famous Loews Hotel, which overlooked the race track and started putting the necessary arrangements in place.

Apparently, this new executive had personal problems, went out one morning to buy a packet of cigarettes, was said to be missing in action, and never returned to Toyota. He eventually was found to be living in Hawaii!

1986 became the year from Hell. As the year progressed we were starting to suffer financially from late payments and we had still not been paid for the balance owing for the Corolla launch on ice. Our other clients were paying regularly, but I realised this was giving me a false sense of security. However, our bank overdraft was escalating and I finally phoned Toyota to bring the issue to a head.

By this time, they owed us approximately AU$180,000 and we were working for every division of the company in Australia – New Imported Vehicles, Fleet Vehicles, Parts and Accessories, Finance,

Air Conditioning, and complete built-up vehicles in Altona. Too many eggs in one basket!

I called Norm Iddles, my golfing mate, and made an appointment to meet him to discuss the issue. After explaining the precarious financial situation Toyota had put me in, he said it was out of his hands and that he couldn't over-rule the new senior manager they had appointed.

I then met with the new senior manager and he said, "George, you're the most creative person I've ever dealt with, but we won't be paying your account in full, especially the shortfall for the launch in Adelaide." I was shocked beyond belief!

I broke down in his office and explained that unless he paid what was owing to us I would be forced to close my business. He said that was my business to decide!

I left their office feeling totally distraught, betrayed and shocked as I couldn't understand why Toyota wouldn't fulfill our agreement and pay what they owed.

I returned to the office and met with Eric Carter and Meredith Ashton and we discussed the situation. It was agreed that I should meet with the Toyota Australia Managing Director, Norman Itaya, and that I should let him know that we had agreed to work with Toyota on an exclusive basis and believed we were not being treated honourably.

I subsequently arranged a meeting with him, and we met in their boardroom. He would not budge or override the decision by the new senior manager. It seemed that this would have belittled his decision and that this was not the Japanese way!

It was now September 1985, and after a number of meetings with my accountant and bank manager I decided, on their advice, to close my business after 12 wonderful years, sell the building I had recently bought, sell my house, sell the six Toyota company cars, put off all my staff and management and pay them out with my superannuation and then put my business into administration with a firm of accountants, lick my wounds and get a job.

Leadership Lessons:

1. Be careful when you're on a wave because it breaks.
2. Trust your sixth sense and act on it quickly.
3. Sometimes culture takes place over logic.
4. If you don't hold the right cards, quit.
5. Leadership is going down with the ship.

Chapter 7

Hitting the Canvas

It was very difficult for me to come to terms with this crisis in my life and I couldn't believe that the client we had worked so hard and creatively with on an exclusive basis for nearly five years would treat us so shabbily, with such contempt and a complete lack of respect and dignity.

However, in hindsight it taught me a valuable lesson in that we never do business with the company, but always and only ever with the key people who work for the company. It is also critically important to build strong relationships, but to hedge yourself and never have 'all your eggs in one basket'.

It was like a death in the family, losing my business, but I tried to stay calm and composed and draw on the many experiences I had learnt in leadership and developing resilience especially from the DC10 Bali airline crisis in 1978.

I was grieving, and so depressed after selling the building and closing the business, that I couldn't bring myself to empty the building and throw out 12 years of work into the dump masters that arrived every few days.

The next step was to sell our beautiful home and that really brought the situation to a head and put our lives into perspective.

We leased another home in Mont Albert, further away from

Canterbury, to enable us to take a breath, regroup and work out a strategy for the future to get our lives back on track.

After paying my management and staff totally some 30 people with my superannuation we had nothing left and selling the building, house and company cars had paid out the bank debt and most of our creditors.

It had been important for me at the time to make the decision to 'stop the train and get off' as they say, so that my company and my own reputation was not trashed after 12 great years.

Not long after, I received a call from the owner of a similar business in Sydney who I had known in a competitive nature and who had been involved with me and a group of like-minded owners in forming an association for our profession.

His business was more of a sales promotional business, yet one with some synergy with mine. We talked about my situation and eventually negotiated a business plan for me to open a new business 'Performance Management', with an office in the Clemenger Advertising building in St Kilda Road, Melbourne.

The deal we agreed was that I would give him the current clients and programs I was working on with NEC, Elders, and BBC Hardware, before I was forced to close, and would introduce him to Toyota. He would pay me a salary package, provide me with office space and cover any travel costs to and from Sydney.

I was in no position to negotiate so in my family's interest I accepted his offer. Wrong! It didn't take many months to realise that he just wanted my remaining clients and was not interested in my welfare as he kept riding me day after day for new business, even though I was working hard and diligently trying to develop relationships with new clients, something that takes time to create.

One day after returning from a prospective new client meeting, he rang me and again badgered me about new business in his usual belligerent manner. I at last had the strength to take a stand, make a decision, and not endure his attitude any more. After giving him my progress report, he again belittled me, so I simply took a big breath and said, "John, I resign of this minute. Thanks for the opportunity of trying to work with you. Good luck and goodbye!"

I packed up my desk and office things and drove home to tell my wife the news. I knew she would not be happy, but it was a load off my shoulders to be free again to fly and be the best I could be by believing in myself again. I then knuckled down, spent every minute of the day either keeping fit with walking, putting a CV together, and looking for a job that I would love.

I also considered starting afresh in a consulting business, with just myself and a PA in a serviced office in one of the new office towers. I then saw an article regarding an opportunity to visit serviced offices in the new Rialto Towers in Collins Street, Melbourne on the 44th floor. I arranged a tour and was given an attractive, unusually large, colour brochure to take away with me. I took it home and stood it in front of my desk, on a bookshelf in the den of our leased house, to motivate me every day so that one day I might work again and possibly even in this magnificent building.

Leadership Lessons:

1. Always treat people with dignity and respect.
2. You never do business with companies, only people.
3. Leadership is making the tough decisions.
4. Protect your IP and reputation fiercely.
5. Stand up to people who try to bully you.

CASE HISTORY 12

Australian Vintage Travel

Chapter 1

Bouncing back Up

I never did sign a lease to run my own consultancy in the Rialto, yet it was to be valuable to see the building and store the experience in my brain for the future.

Then one day I saw an advertisement for a general manager for a tourism venture, and having such in-depth experience in the industry, I applied and asked to meet them. It was with some trepidation that I went for my first interview in 30 years, and somewhat confronting to be on the 'other side of the desk', yet thought I handled the challenge well.

The first interview was to check out if my application and the person matched, but the interviewer wouldn't tell me what the tourism venture was that I was to manage. However, I must have impressed them as I was asked to attend a second interview. At this next interview they felt comfortable enough to say what the tourism venture was. I was excited to learn it was the restored 'Melbourne Limited Train'.

When asked what experience I had with a similar product, I was able to draw on my experience and journey on the Venice Simplon Orient Express that travelled between London, Paris, Milan and Venice. I was able to explain how it operated, what level of opulence it exceeded, who owned it, the fact that I had met the owners, James Sherwood and his wife, Dr Shirley Sherwood, its high standard of service and how it was staffed and designed for the target market.

I was considered a fit with knowledge too good to be true and was asked to meet the new owner and his team at his offices in Newcastle. I made the journey the next week and was introduced to who I thought must be Australia's version of Howard Hughes, Michael Wansey and his team.

This was not his only venture, he also owned the television station, NBN 3 and I also learnt in the briefing meeting that he had purchased the SS South Steyne Manly ferry, which was now moored at Ballina and was currently being refurbished.

After an intense day of meetings and a grilling by Michael's legal adviser, a high-powered lawyer called Peter Cleaves, I had learnt that they had gained a $5 million loan from the Victorian Government's VEDC investment fund. As the meeting progressed, I was finally told that they were satisfied with my business acumen and I was appointed General Manager.

However, when asked where in Melbourne I thought the new office could be located, I found I could pull another 'rabbit out of a hat', opened my attaché case and pulled out the beautiful, elegant brochure of the Rialto Towers and replied, "We should initially lease some serviced offices on the 44th floor until we are established." They were impressed with the brochure, the location and position, and that I'd had enough foresight to think ahead and bring the brochure with me to the meeting.

A discussion then took place regarding the trading name of the venture and when it was decided to include a restored DC 3 plane from Sydney, I suggested we call the business Australian Vintage Travel and it was agreed on the spot.

I also pointed out that all three travel products could be seen from our prospective offices, high up in the Rialto Tower in Collins Street as North Wharf where the SS South Steyne would be moored, the Spencer Street railway yards where the Melbourne Limited Train would be parked and the Essendon Aerodrome where the DC 3 would be based, were all visible from the offices. This seemed to cement the negotiations, Australian Vintage Travel was born, and they agreed to my salary package and contract there and then.

I flew back to Melbourne and was excited to be part of a new tourism venture for the State of Victoria and thought my wife would be happy too!

Another supporting benefit for my appointment was that in the preceding year I had been asked to stand as a Board Member for the Melbourne Tourism Authority. I had been elected for three years and this gave me the opportunity to leverage my contacts and my tourism and conference knowledge. I had also been on the Board of the Melbourne Convention Bureau for three years.

Life was starting to take shape again and I was able to move through the grief cycle's five stages, to accept that one part of my career had closed, however difficult that had been, and I had used the past, not as a rear view mirror but as a spring board for the future and I had bounced back up on my feet.

Leadership Lessons:

1. Visualisation is an extremely powerful tool.
2. You never know how important your past is.
3. Always try to plan and think ahead.
4. Believe in yourself and your judgement.
5. To heal you must pass through the 5 stages of the grief cycle.

Chapter 2

A Vintage Year

It was adrenalin time. Events moved very quickly, then the following week, Peter Cleaves arrived in Melbourne and wanted to meet for lunch. He had mentioned in passing in Newcastle, that I had been appointed as General Manager instead of Simon Galbally, the youngest son of the well-known QC, Frank Galbally, yet he could be useful to assist in opening government and other doors for the new business.

We met outside his hotel in Collins Street, and he introduced me to Simon who would be joining us for lunch and who had booked us in at The Australian Club. Our owner, entrepreneur and visionary, Michael Wansey then also appeared from the hotel and we all set off for lunch. Walking along Collins Street, suddenly Simon stopped outside Henry Bucks men's wear store and said quite loudly, as was his way, "Michael you won't be allowed into The Australian Club without a tie and a jacket. Perhaps you should duck in and buy them here before we move on."

This was to be the first time I would witness the Howard Hughes element in Michael as he came out of Henry Bucks looking very smart in his new, very expensive jacket and tie. An interesting event for us all to experience on the footpath that day in Melbourne!

Lunch was very enjoyable, and the conversation lively. It was agreed that Simon would be employed as Commercial Operations Manager. After lunch I showed Michael, Peter, and Simon the suite of offices I had been able to lease in the Rialto Tower and they were in awe of the view, especially of the sites where the train, the plane and the SS South Steyne would be based.

It was a valuable day in many ways, and one that made me realise I needed to watch Simon closely as he had a presence larger than life, and a voice to match!

We moved into the offices within the week, and I started to think who else we needed to employ to enable the business to hit the ground running. A couple of people came to mind. The first was Joel McGlynn as the Marketing Manager, the second, John Taaff, of radio fame as Sales Manager and lastly Edward Howard as Marketing Services Manager. Joel had 15 years' experience as General Manager for the successful Colonial Tramcar Restaurant. John had a sales background in radio and had been responsible for the initial sales development of The Melbourne Limited train. Edward was an interesting catch as he had previously been the Australian Manager for the Venice Simplon Orient Express for five years and had been acknowledged for booking the highest number of passengers per capita of any market in the world.

So I had a team, or thought I did, of experienced, travel product, tourism industry professionals and a great foundation to enable Australian Vintage Travel to start moving forward.

There were many balls to juggle as the leader of this embryonic business, and I soon became engrossed in keeping them all in the air.

The biggest challenge for me was to chair the group of 'experts' involved in restoring the SS South Steyne which was moored on the river at Ballina. I travelled up to Ballina each month to chair the meetings and to ensure progress was being made in line with its scheduled date of completion and arrival at its new home in Melbourne, planned for September 1987.

The ex-Rebel Air DC 3, owned by Michael Wansey, was relocated to Melbourne and at a strategy meeting, after its arrival, we brainstormed a new name for it to fit into the suite of Vintage Travel products. There were many suggestions and finally we decided on my suggestion of 'The Spirit of Melbourne'. It could seat 30 passengers, travel at 170 mph and with two foot wide windows offered brilliant, unequalled views.

The Melbourne Limited Train was proving to be a challenge to sell and market. It was, at the time, only available for charter, had no regular timetable, could only travel to Albury or Swan Hill because of the width of the train lines and had no sleeping cars in its configuration or as is correctly known, its 'consist'. This presented an enormous cost/benefit analysis issue. I could now see why the train had experienced financial trouble and was bought by Michael with the $5 million loan from the VEDC. My assessment, and that of my team, was that it was not going to be commercially viable unless we were able to acquire some sleeping carriages from the same era.

We started to make enquiries and one day Joel McGlynn came into my office with a broad smile on his face. I said, "Why are you so happy Joel?" He replied, "I've found six sleeping carriages stored away in the Spencer Street railway yards. They match The Melbourne Limited carriages in style and design." He excitedly and quickly arranged for us all to visit and view them at the Spencer Street yard.

He was right, they were authentic, and in fairly good condition considering their age, but would need significant work to restore them to match the existing Melbourne Limited Carriages in the same style and ornateness.

Simon, as the Commercial Operations Manager was given the responsibility to negotiate with the Victorian Railways to purchase or lease the carriages. We also started discussions with interior decorator, Michael Knight, who Joel had previously engaged to refurbish the Colonial Tramcar Restaurant interior, to see if the carriages could be refurbished and to ascertain the cost to complete this restoration successfully to the level required.

While this feasibility study was in progress the team met regularly for strategic planning sessions to enable the train to be financially viable. We had decided that no-one in their right mind would regularly pay to travel in a 'seat only' carriage all the way to Sydney eating only scones, jam, and cream.

The concept had to be changed. We would need sleeping cars and the train to travel perhaps to Sydney. For this to happen the train's bogie axles would have to be made wider to fit the rail gauge in both Victoria and in New South Wales.

Leadership Lessons:

1. Deal with perception not sight.
2. Surround yourself with a very good team.
3. Beware the loud mouth manager.
4. Put yourself in your customer's shoes.
5. Delegate tasks to enable the multiplier effect.

Chapter 3

A Vintage Betrayal

By now AVT was taking up an enormous amount of my time. My wife and I had purchased a small delicatessen in Maling Road, Canterbury, which she was running. Between the two of us, we were flat out working and trying to recover our financial situation.

About this time, I needed to draw breath again, and celebrate my rebirth. So one afternoon on the way home, I again visited the well-known menswear store in South Yarra called Trevor West.

Back in 1975, six months after I had started my business George D Norris Associates, I had promised myself that if I lasted six months I would go to the store and 'buy a window of clothes'. The store was unique in that one window would display a matching coat, trousers, shirt, belt, shoes, and socks and one lunchtime I went out and bought a window as a celebration of success.

Then in 1987, 12 years later, I walked into the store again and the same salesman greeted me. "Hello", he said, "and what window does sir want to buy today?" I needed a blue suit so I said "the window nearest the main door in Toorak Road, thank you". He replied, "Certainly sir and are we still a 36 short?" "Yes", I replied proudly, and bought my second window consisting of a suit, shirt, tie, belt, shoes and socks. I had done it again 12 years later!

In 1985, a company called Dollar Sweets, who became famous for making hundreds and thousands, the main ingredient for fairy bread, took on a militant union in a dispute, survived a 143-day picket and won a Supreme Court battle that changed the face of industrial relations in Australia. In doing this it helped shape the career of a young barrister, Peter Costello, and he went on to become the Federal Treasurer for Australia in the coalition government.

I had the pleasure of meeting Fred Stauder, founder of the Dollar Sweets company, in November 1986, at a Pursuit of Excellence Awards presentation, where I was one of four keynote speakers, alongside Andrew Hay, Hugh Morgan and Dr Bob Montgomery. Coincidentally, Fred's wife Judith had opened a Dollar Sweets shop next to our Maling Road deli and my wife, Susan became friends with her. It wasn't long before they were 'bosom buddies' and we would often visit their home for Friday night drinks and a BBQ.

One night, after we had arrived back home, Susan mentioned that Judith had suggested they go into business together and asked me what I thought of the opportunity. I was somewhat surprised that this relationship had developed so soon after they had met. The Deli was still in its infancy and both of us were trying so hard to get back on our financial feet.

I thought for a moment and said I had some concerns because we were vulnerable, the delicatessen needed her focus to be successful, and if we did enter into a partnership then both of us would be jointly and severally liable for the debts of both businesses. Susan was not happy at all and argued the case strongly with me. I listened and replied that if she didn't believe me, she should consult a solicitor or our accountant, Bob Brown, for their opinion and advice.

I didn't have long to find out what she had concluded, and decided. One Wednesday about a month later, I came home from Australian Vintage Travel about 7pm to find she had moved out of the house and into the apartment above the deli, taking most of the furniture and the car I have given her.

I was devastated and completely blindsided by her actions. I called her and asked why she had moved out as I didn't feel I had done anything to warrant it. She said that she had found me controlling and that I wouldn't let her make her own decisions. I tried, unsuccessfully, to explain that her decision to go into business with Judith Stauder put me at risk too, but she didn't want to accept this.

I tried very hard to sort out our problems, but to no avail, so I packed up the house we had leased and shifted in with my mother who was still living in the house I had grown up in, at North Kew.

Again I found myself going through the grief cycle and found myself for quite a while stuck in level 3, 'bargaining'.

Susan eventually agreed to meet with me and specialist relationship consulting psychologist, Dr Bob Montgomery. She described my behaviour, as she saw it, and asked me to explain why I was concerned. Yet when I became serious and passionate, and explained the legal implications, she interrupted by saying to Dr Montgomery, you can now see how controlling he is.

He was surprised by her reaction and explained to her that I wasn't being controlling or angry, but just passionate and concerned about possible repercussions. She seemed set in her beliefs and did not want to believe him, so we made a follow up appointment for two weeks later.

I arrived early, waited and waited, but Susan didn't show. So I met with Dr Montgomery alone. In the following weeks he contacted her on several occasions, but she never met with me. She seemingly had another agenda I wasn't aware of.

I tried to focus and work hard at AVT but was very depressed. My mind wandered, worrying about my life, my marriage, my three children, her two children, who I had co-parented for seven years, and my ageing mother, who unbeknown to me, was losing her sight. My brother had also been admitted to the Cairns Base Hospital to recover after a head on collision with an American tourist who had forgotten which side of the road we drive on in Australia. My world was turning upside down again, and it was a difficult time.

After a couple of difficult weeks we started to plan the strategies to launch The Melbourne Limited Train on a scheduled service to Sydney and put in place the purchase of the six sleeping carriages with the loan monies from the VEDC.

Barry Beattie, General Manager of the VEDC, announced on 2 December 1986 they would provide the loan funds to enable the additional carriages to be purchased so the train could operate interstate.

To celebrate the achievement, we agreed to change the name of the train so that it would be embraced more easily by the New South Wales population. We decided that when it operated interstate using a diesel locomotive and the sleeping carriages, it would be known as 'The Southern Cross'. It was an exciting moment in our lives.

Then came the news that Michael Wansey's American girlfriend was coming to Australia for a visit and was going to visit all the Australian casinos to promote the business.

She and Michael spent about 12 days travelling around Australia and at the end of the time visited us in our Melbourne office to debrief their trip. At the meeting I invited all our team and after hearing the report they left, gave their expenses to Simon Galbally and flew back to Newcastle. We all sat around the boardroom table with whimsical looks on our faces until I broke the silence, "Well, what do you all think of that?"

The first to speak was Joel, who really stated what everyone was thinking, "Well that sounded to me like a trip to show his girlfriend a good time, and isn't promoting the business what John and I are employed to do anyway?" I replied, "You are right, and they are using VEDC loan funds which I am responsible and accountable for in the process." Simon just smiled and nodded his head. The next few days were busy, and we focused on the tasks at hand.

On the Monday of the following week, I arrived at my office only to receive a call from Newcastle from the Chief Financial Officer, Stephen Browne. I could tell he was very stressed and worried, "George, we are not happy with your current performance and we would like you to leave our employment today." "What is the problem," I asked, to which he said, "I won't go into that, but I have been asked to tell you to pack up your desk and other things and leave now."

I was shocked and angry with myself for making the comments with the team about the VEDC and Michael's trip. However, in shock I packed up my desk and instead of calling a solicitor, I simply drove home to break the news to my ageing mother, who I was now living with again and reflect on what had just happened.

Leadership Lessons:

1. Enthusiasm can be a double-edged sword.
2. It's okay to celebrate your success in life.
3. Beneath the iceberg of the bully is self-doubt.
4. Be courageous, responsible and accountable.
5. When you're bullied consider calling a solicitor quickly.

CASE HISTORY 13

The Australian Bicentennial

Chapter 1

Living a Dream

Like most mothers, mine was very supportive and understanding, and wisely counselled me to take a big break and try and think rationally about what I should do about the issue and my future. It seemed at the time that the world was falling in on me, and that I was worrying about what I couldn't control instead of focusing on what I could control. This philosophy has proven to be a powerful strategy that I have since shared with many people to help them cope.

Shock is a debilitating condition, and I needed rest and recuperation. It was like waking up in a permanent fog each day.

However, what I had suspected turned out to be true and Simon Galbally, I was told by Joel, was sitting in my chair the very next day. It made me wonder why he said nothing in the boardroom after the debrief with Michael and just smiled. After some tough months, the fog began to lift, and I began to regain some of my self-confidence and self-esteem.

Eventually I was strong enough to see a solicitor to find out my legal position and was advised that I may have a case for wrongful dismissal in view of the evidence I was able to provide. However, the legal process often turns slowly and by the time we were in a position to start proceedings, it was announced in the media that Australian Vintage Travel had gone into liquidation owing, not just $5 million to the VEDC but a whopping $10 million in debts to the VEDC and many other suppliers. Unfortunately, the business

I started enthusiastically had failed to be a financially successful venture.

The SS South Steyne had been restored and launched at North Wharf, The Spirit of Melbourne DC-3 had been relocated to Essendon airport as planned, but 'The Melbourne Limited' train had proven it wasn't the right product, as I had predicted and 'The Southern Cross' interstate sleeping version was never completed as we had planned. So, if Simon had said, "I will bring you down and take your place", he also had the dubious honour of losing all that money, achieving nothing and taking some of the well-earned shine off the famous Galbally name.

They say in philosophical circles that 'the world is round' or 'vengeance is mine sayest the Lord', and while I felt somewhat redeemed, I also learnt that 'you can't get blood out of a stone'. I was never able to progress my legal case for wrongful dismissal as the company ceased to exist.

I started to plan and think positively again each day, there in the family home with my mother's loving support, and eventually started to see some blue sky.

Then one day, out of the blue, I received a phone call from a colleague and friend, Dick Wicks. He had once worked for Adidas in a senior promotional role, and I had got to know him through my role as captain and coach of the Kew Harriers Athletic Club. He was very generous when he was at Adidas, and each year provided us with Adidas athletic products to use as prizes for our annual fundraising BBQ. He explained that he had put together a large group of influential business people to create a major event for Australia's Bicentenary on 26 January 1988 and asked me if I would consider being chairman of the steering committee.

I never found out if he had become aware of my situation, but I have since reflected that he must have known, and to his credit was trying to help me 'get back on the horse'!

We met initially in the boardroom at Olympic Park and when I arrived the room was set up in a U shape with places for about 40 people. While somewhat apprehensive, I was impressed and a little overawed with my important Chairman's leadership role.

Well, like the Bali Bound DC-10 leadership test, I found that we all have 'latent talent' waiting to be tapped, if given the opportunity.

Everyone arrived on time and the meeting got underway with Dick taking the minutes. Dick introduced me to the other participants who represented hotels, airlines, coach companies, media, government, banks, FCL transport and Father Joe Giacobbe, the founder and Chairman of DOXA Youth Foundation Charity.

The concept for the event was to celebrate Australia's Bicentenary in January 1988 with a 200 km team's race around Port Phillip Bay to raise funds for the DOXA charity. Our first meeting was around August 1987, and it was an interesting and very stimulating project to be a part of, and act as Steering Committee Chairman.

A number of meetings followed, and found I could chair them with confidence. It was agreed that the event would consist of 100 teams of 10 runners which would set off from Wellington Parade outside the MCG. The teams would run for 200 kilometres around Port Phillip Bay and then return to finish at Olympic Park on the adjoining oval.

It was a mammoth logistical exercise which took an enormous effort from a great team of passionate business people to co-ordinate to make it successful.

After about three months it was suggested that we should try and have someone with a high media profile join the committee and I asked the members to present some names for consideration at the next meeting.

Dick Wicks suggested that John Landy MBE was returning from Vancouver after completing his role as head of Australia's pavilion at the World Expo in Canada and would make an excellent Chairman of the event. His high profile would add prestige and attract media attention. We all agreed, and Dick who knew John well through his Adidas role, agreed to approach him.

John quickly agreed and we were all introduced to him at our next meeting. I asked if he would like to take over that meeting as Chairman but he graciously replied, "I hear you're doing a great job so why don't I sit in today and assume the role from the next meeting." That leadership style, as I was to learn as time went by, was the hallmark of why he was not only a champion athlete but a champion person as well.

He was famous the world over for being the second athlete in history to break the four-minute mile, and for his extraordinary act of sportsmanship in the 1956 Olympic trial mile race at Olympic Park, when he stopped to help a fallen, fellow Victorian, Ron Clarke, before going on to catch the field and win.

I was present at this amazing event at the age of 16 and never in my wildest dreams thought that one day I would be sitting in his company as the Steering Committee Chairman of an Australian Bicentennial event!

Not long after he assumed the role of Chairman, John felt comfortable enough to invite me to dinner at his home in Camberwell where I met his lovely wife, Lynne. She had been an editor for Vogue magazine before they met and was a charming host. We therefore struck up a special friendship for several years which transcended the Bicentennial and even discussed setting up a Management Consultancy together.

We would meet secretly many times over lunch for confidential discussions about the venture while he was the Operations Director for the 1996 Melbourne Olympic Games Bid. It was at one of our lunch meetings that I learnt more about his insights, humbleness and courageous mind.

After we agreed it would be a good idea to start up our business, he made an insightful observation. "George, the only problem I can think of is that there will only be two of us and two people can become deadlocked in a decision. I think it would be better if we had a third person. A two-legged stool can fall over, but a three legged one stands up in times of a decision-making crisis."

Soon after, John was appointed Governor of Victoria, and our plans for a consultancy were unfortunately never able to be realised.

The bicentennial event was a huge success and attracted much interest in Victoria. Judy Patching AO OBE, who had been the chief starter at the 1956 Olympics, became Vice Chairman and the well-known marathon gold medalist, Robert De Castella MBE, became the Patron in Chief.

I knew the late Tony Charlton quite well from my time at the Melbourne Tourism Authority and I asked him to co-ordinate and act as Master of Ceremonies of the finish of the event at Olympic Park. He together with Su Pollard, who I also asked to assist, and who I had known for some years in event organising, enabled the coordination of the finish to go without a hitch and the event to be an amazing success.

This successful bicentennial event was commemorated the following year on 22 January 1989 with the Prime Minister, the Honourable RJ Hawke AC MP unveiling a plaque at the starting point of the bicentennial charity event near the MCG. It was a significant occasion that celebrated the bicentennial and raised over $650,000 for the DOXA Youth Welfare Foundation and a number of other deserving charities in Victoria.

Leadership Lessons:

1. In times of crisis only worry about what you can control.
2. When dealing with emotional shock just rest a while.
3. Betrayal is tough because you doubt your future judgement.
4. Remember, the world is round. Be patient and it will turn.
5. Believe in your skills, your talents and above all yourself.

CASE HISTORY 14

In Touch and In Line

Chapter 1

Foundations for a Future

The years 1987 and 1988 proved beyond doubt that the saying 'out of adversity comes advantage' is true. I was still going through the grief cycle, but I didn't realise this at the time.

Then one day out of the blue, I received a call from the President of The Melbourne Chamber of Commerce who I had come to know after joining to network for new opportunities. We had developed an excellent relationship and he had been saddened by my experience with Toyota. He said he had just returned from Sydney and overheard the guys next to him on the plane discussing an executive that had recently been terminated by Toyota.

It turned out to be the manager who wouldn't pay my company two years ago.

I was told he was eventually caught playing the same game. I didn't know he was playing with me by not paying accounts from suppliers and wanting kick backs so they got paid, and he had been sacked on the spot.

I was impressed with Toyota's honourable decision, but unfortunately, he had already brought me and my company down in the process!

In 1987, I had the opportunity to join a marketing and promotion firm, In Touch Marketing after an introduction by my old friend from Colac Caltex days, Ted Clayton. He had since left Colac and shifted to Melbourne to go into business with his long-time friend, David Roach, marketing instant Tattslotto games to companies. He had called me saying that a colleague of his, Michael Dolan, was looking for someone with experience to handle some special projects and he had suggested me.

I met Michael and we hit it off well. He was a New Zealander, who had previously worked as a magician on cruise ships before settling in Australia and had opened his own marketing consultancy business. He, like me, was also a golfing tragic and a member at Woodlands and this seemed to add some glue.

I worked with him for about nine months as Special Projects Manager to promote two Chinese Pandas visiting the Zoos in Melbourne and Sydney, planned for June 1988, and to gain sponsorship to cover the events.

Brochure describing the opportunities to sponsor the Pandas from China.

In Touch Marketing was then bought by Mojo, In-Line Marketing was then established by Mattingly Advertising, and I was appointed as General Manager.

Mattingly had many blue-chip accounts including the prestigious Myer account and were looking to increase their strategic resources to increase their perceived value to their clients. Some of their other accounts included Dunlop Olympic, Adidas, V-line, TAC and Tattersall's.

We were invited to attend a meeting one day with the Myer senior management and given a brief to help save their 'Myer in the City' flagship store as its market share was being seriously undermined by their next-door neighbour, David Jones.

I set about doing research with a colleague, Su Pollard, who I had employed to assist me as Marketing Manager, comparing Myer's standard of excellence with David Jones and we found that 'Myer in the City' was really quite mediocre, and not in any way 'excellent' in all aspects of their store's image, layout or service.

We presented our strategic report to the Myer Management who immediately went into denial and the report seemed to go down a black hole. However, I seemed to have made an impression on David Mattingly, the Chairman and Ian Herdman, the CEO. Then without warning I was advised about six months later that In Touch Marketing was to be brought into their operational set up and that I wouldn't be needed anymore as In Line Marketing would no longer exist.

Just as I was finding my feet, the merry-go-round had started up, and again it seemed I was destined to be spun off into space!

Mattingly, to their credit however, understood the humane side of their decision and gave me an empty office in MDA's building back in St Kilda Road where I could sit, think, plan my future and lick my wounds but not receive a salary.

About this time, while practising golf at the Sandringham driving range, a lady golfer I had often played with in mixed events at Yarra Yarra Golf Club, joined me, and afterwards we had a coffee and a chat. She told me she was worried about her husband, Eddie, who was becoming depressed and worried, and she felt it was impacting their family.

She was aware of some aspects of what I'd been through over recent years and asked if I would have a coffee with him. I agreed and suggested she have him call me to arrange a time to suit, but I couldn't promise I could help. I eventually received a call from him the following week and we made a time to meet in my St Kilda Road office.

Little did I know that this meeting was to become part of the foundation for my future business life some years later!

Eddie arrived and we got a coffee each and sat down. I asked him to give me his story and started to download how unhappy he was and how stressed he had become. After he had finished, I said, "Eddie, can I ask you a few questions?" He replied, "Yes, of course."

I started by asking how his health was generally. "Good", he said. How his wife's health was, "Good", he said. "Are your children all okay and in good health?" "Yes", he said. "Is your business going well?" "Yes", he said, "but can always be better." "Do you still own your house, your car and your wife's car?" "Yes", he said. "Well", I said, "You seem to be in a good position, and I don't know what you're worried about."

Then for some reason, and don't know to this day why, I said, "Let me tell you about a guy I know. This guy lost his business of 12 years, his building, his house, his wife, his staff, his superannuation, his car and couldn't see his children for six months. He lost all this in just one month!" "Wow, is he dead?" "No, you are looking at him right now."

He was taken aback and looked at me in shock and became emotional. When he recovered, I said, "So how do you feel now and how do you rate your position?" "I haven't got a worry in the world."

He got up, shook my hand, and said, "Thanks George for giving me a kick up the backside" and walked out.

This felt very satisfying, and I was proud of being able to help someone psychologically for a change. On reflection, I now realise I was drawing on the information I had learnt at Caltex, in the DC-10 disaster, in coaching at two athletic clubs and especially from the eminent speakers at the two seminars I conducted to celebrate John Bertrand's Australia II win in the America's Cup.

I didn't know it at the time, but that meeting was to become very important for me in 10 years' time.

Jan thanked me sincerely at our next golf practice session, and said Eddie came home a changed man with a spring in his step. Later I tracked his progress and found that they shifted to the Gold Coast where he became one of the top Financial Advisers in Queensland.

Leadership Lessons:

1. Your network of friends can be priceless.
2. Always give every project your best effort.
3. Learn coping skills from your experiences.
4. Be a good listener and show patience.
5. A courageous story has its own reward.

CASE HISTORY 15

Calder Park Thunderdome

Chapter 1

Learning from a Legend

The next few weeks went slowly. I sat, thought and tried to work out a plan for my future. Then one afternoon I received a call from Ian Herdman, the CEO of Mattingly, who said, "Bob Jane has called David Mattingly and was looking for a Sales and Marketing Director to work with him at Thunderdome, and David has recommended you for the position." I asked, "What do you think I should do Ian?" "Well, we both know your current situation, so if it was me, I would call him and see what happens."

I thought for a moment and replied, "Okay Ian, I'll give him a call as you suggest and please thank David for recommending me for the position." Ian gave me Bob's direct line, thought I had nothing to lose, and called him. The call was answered by a direct, gruff voice, "Bob Jane!"

I introduced myself, and we agreed to meet to explore the options and I was about to acquire a massive input of knowledge. The first interview at his new $50 million race complex at Calder Park was long and intense, yet stimulating and interesting.

Bob Jane left school at just 14 years of age, been a street kid in Brunswick, become one of Australia's champion motor racing drivers and created a racetrack called Calder Park. He helped establish drag racing meetings to get kids off the streets and onto a track. After visiting the Charlotte Motor Speedway Nascar events in America he invested over $50 million, funded in part from the Bob Jane T Mart

Tyre Centres he had set up around Australia, to build a similar type of track, called Thunderdome as part of his racing complex.

The name had been inspired by the 1985 movie 'Mad Max Beyond Thunderdome' starring Mel Gibson, Tina Turner, Frank Thring and among others, Angry Anderson.

It was daunting meeting Bob for the first time, being interviewed in his massive office with his Thunderdome oval shaped desk, lavish lounge chairs and gold fittings on the doors and in the bathrooms.

However, after our first meeting he seemed interested in what I had done in my life and invited me back for a second interview and chat in a week's time so we could both reflect on our discussion.

I arrived at the security gates about 15 minutes early for our second meeting, so I sat in my car in the car park and went over my notes from the first meeting. It was just as well I did, as the first question he asked me was what I had thought was important from the first interview. I gave him my thoughts, the interview proceeded, and this time he walked me around the office complex.

Before the tour, while I was in his office, a hidden telephone in the top drawer of his desk rang and he excused himself saying, "I need to take this call, it's very important." I later discovered that the call was from John Cain, the Premier of Victoria, who had a direct line and special phone in Bob's desk.

I met with Bob another five times and at each meeting he asked me what points from the previous interview had I found important and critical for the role.

At each of these subsequent meetings he would show me more and more of the Calder Park Race Complex including Thunderdome and would eventually introduce me to his other key executives including Grant Tillet, the Operations Director.

Finally, I was appointed as Sales and Marketing Director and arrived on the first Monday to start work at this $50 million complex only to be told I didn't have an office, but it would be okay for me to use the boardroom until Bob found one for me. The office I was supposed to use near his was being used by Bob's driver and personal assistant and he was reluctant to give it up.

It took me about four weeks of living out of a box in the boardroom before I could finally convince Bob that his Sales and Marketing Director, who he had interviewed seven times to be sure he was making the right decision, was worth the investment of having an office to do his job properly.

On the day prior to moving into my office I received an unusual phone call. I had been a member of The 500 Club for some years and on the Event Committee which created and organised the Annual Fundraising Ball. The 500 Club was created by the infamous John Elliott who acted as Chairman and the club promoted private enterprise for future prosperity.

During the previous meeting three weeks ago, we had discussed the coming 1988 Annual Ball which was to have the theme 'Monte Carlo or Bust'. The invitations were to be old style, using Hollywood art deco lettering. The meeting had discussed the possibility of displaying cars of that bygone era, in the foyer to set the scene, such as a vintage style British racing car in traditional British racing green, with a leather bonnet strap, wire spoke wheels and wooden steering wheel.

In the week after joining Bob Jane, and leaving my car for a service close by, I was walking down a street at the rear of Melbourne Grammar School on my way to a friend's office to do some work. Lo and behold, I spied sitting in the sunshine on the back of a trailer was an old vintage, wire wheeled, British racing green tourer. It was a Brooklands Riley and had a leather bonnet strap, wooden steering wheel and red wire spoke wheels. I couldn't believe my luck and wondered if my eyes were playing tricks on me.

I looked around and couldn't see anyone I could ask about the car, so I wrote a note on the back of my business card saying I was interested to talk to the owner as there was an opportunity to display the car at an upcoming function and left it under the windscreen wiper.

It was weeks before I heard anything and then this day Bob's secretary buzzed me to say she had a Janet Hider-Smith on the phone wanting to talk to me. I said I didn't know anyone by that name, and she went on to say, she has your business card which was left under the windscreen wiper of her car. I immediately asked her to put her through.

Janet owned the 1930 Brooklands Riley and she was preparing to move it back down to her father's property in Parkdale where it was usually garaged, when she noticed my business card. I broadly outlined The 500 Club Annual Ball event and said I was happy to meet with her and run through all the details and she agreed to meet, so we met at the Parkdale property at 7pm that night.

On arrival I was surprised to find this young blonde in overalls covered in grease and oil, lying under her old car. She extricated herself and I explained the details of The 500 Club event. She said that she would consider letting us display the car as long as I promised to supervise the car being delivered in and out of the Grand Hyatt. There was just one problem. She was scheduled to be in Brisbane the day after the Ball for the Australian Gliding Championships and she and her partner had intended to drive up with her 'Discus' glider on the trailer.

In view of the opportunity, I took the initiative and said we would not only invite her and her partner to the event but that we would pay the airfares for her and her partner if she could get a friend to drive her glider to Brisbane for her. A few days later Janet called to say she would let us display her car and that she and her partner would be delighted to attend the Ball.

I had pulled another rabbit out of the hat!

I attended the next 500 Club Events meeting feeling very pleased with myself and the Executive Director was delighted we could display such an iconic veteran British car. However, this was not the end of it. We immediately ran into a significant logistical obstacle. There was no access for vehicles into the Grand Hyatt and the only way to get it in the hotel, so we could display it outside the entrance to the ballroom was to remove part of the roof of the hotel and lower it slowly down with a 100-foot crane.

It was amazing that such a great and leading hotel that specialises in product launches of all kinds, including the car industry, was designed and built with no access for the products of the companies which had the biggest budgets and could generate the most income.

I explained the issue to Janet who fortunately agreed that provided I personally supervised the car's entry and exit through the roof, she would allow it. We agreed and I made sure everything was in order, especially how and where the car should be handled by the workmen and the crane.

It all worked out brilliantly. The night was a success. Janet enjoyed herself with her partner and was given loud applause when thanked by the MC. She was able to fly to Brisbane in time for the Australian Gliding Championships and went on to win her division with her Discus glider.

So began a friendship that would last 15 years, until her untimely passing on 24 June 2005, all from a chance walk down a street I had never walked down before or since.

Leadership Lessons:

1. Remember people in high places have high contacts.
2. Interviews are an investment in your 'culture fit'.
3. Appointments are investments in people power.
4. Never cease to be surprised and inspired by others.
5. Trust is a priceless personal attribute to preserve.

Chapter 2

Skating on Thin Ice

Life at Thunderdome settled down and every day brought new challenges and experiences that I had never thought possible previously.

After joining Bob Jane's business at the beginning of November 1988, I received an urgent call on 10 November from Steve Jonas, the Sales Manager. He said, "George, I will pick you up in the morning at 10am to fly to Adelaide for the Grand Prix." Bob hadn't mentioned anything to me about going, and this proved to be an insight into his unusual and disconcerting management style of keeping his people guessing when working at his various businesses.

I quickly packed a bag and we both flew to Adelaide. Then that afternoon we were transported from our hotel at Glenelg to the inside of the Grand Prix track by Bob's private Bell Ranger helicopter. I had never flown in a helicopter, let alone landed inside a Formula 1 circuit before, so I had a feeling of trepidation.

Adelaide turned out to be a great international experience, and an initial insight into the amazing world of one of Australia's most powerful and wealthiest people.

After returning to the humdrum of Melbourne, we put our energy into planning the 1989 year and especially the Moomba 200 Auscar Race Meeting.

Since joining the company in the November of the previous year, Bob had shown interest in my development and would walk around the Calder Park complex often with a guiding arm around my shoulder, as if he had plans for me to step up in some form or another. This, while appearing as a sign of confidence in me and my talents, was also a bit disconcerting as I wasn't sure what he was thinking and where it was leading in a business sense.

Bob had met his new young wife Laree at Bathurst in 1986 and married her a year later when he was 55 and she was 19 and this seemed to give him a new lease on life. More and more he brought me into his confidence and included me in his corporate meetings with his trusted T Mart and Holding company executives, Alan Coleman and Maurice Ryding.

Bob had created very close relationships with the captains of industry, and the captains of government and some government entities, so I wasn't surprised when in January 1989 he asked me to attend a meeting with him and, the then Moomba Chief Executive, Christine Whorlow.

Bob had been a sponsor of the Moomba Waterskiing event, and wanted to hold a Moomba Auscar 200 km race on Saturday 11 March 1989 as the third major Moomba event. In return, Bob could gain sponsorship monies from the Road Traffic Authority to promote the 'say no to drink driving .05' campaign as the sponsor of the Thunderdome Moomba meeting.

I was starting to see and learn how the wheels in his mind worked and realised that I was on a steep learning curve from a cunning entrepreneur. When we returned from the meeting, he said to me, "Okay, what can we do to make this Moomba Meeting special and a roaring success?" I replied, "Bob let me think on it for a couple of days and I'll come back to you."

That night I heard on the news that the 1984 Winter Olympic gold medallist ice- skaters Torvill & Dean were coming to Australia in March for some shows with the Allstar Champion Russians, and they were to appear at the National Tennis Centre. I knew from my previous dealings with Michael Edgley and his Manager, Andrew Guild, that Christopher Dean held an international Formula Ford car racing licence, so the next morning I got out my black book of telephone numbers and called Andrew.

He was pleased to hear from me again after the Toyota launch, and we explored the idea of having Christopher drive an Auscar at the Moomba race. In view of his skating commitments and the risk of injury, Andrew thought if he suggested to Christopher that he could drive say a 10 lap 'Celebrity Challenge' race, which would be more of a demonstration race, he might be interested.

He called me back later that day to say he had put the idea to Christopher, and he would be delighted and excited to take part. I asked him to confirm this in writing and finished the call feeling excited. The next day after receiving the confirmation I knocked on Bob's office door with a smile on my face. "What are you looking so happy about", he said. "Well Bob, Torvill & Dean, the world champion ice-skaters from the 1984 Winter Olympics will be in Melbourne during the Moomba period.

Christopher has a Formula Ford international driving licence and the Australian Manager of Michael Edgley, Andrew Guild, who I have dealt with before with Toyota, has just confirmed that he will drive an Auscar in a celebrity race, if that works for you Bob?" He was speechless, then in true Bob Jane style he exclaimed loudly, 'How the fuck did you pull that off George?"

I told him the story of my involvement with the Toyota launch in 1985 and about negotiating with Andrew Guild from Michael Edgley

International for Torvill & Dean to star in the launch. I explained that I still had contact with Andrew and was able to arrange the deal. I went on to explain that to confirm the arrangement it would have to be a 'celebrity race'. Bob, still in amazement, picked up his phone and called Christine Whorlow to tell her the news. She was amazed, ecstatic, and thanked Bob for his efforts.

We had all new-found energy and a spring in our step as this was much needed and welcome good news. Since returning from the Adelaide Grand Prix just prior to Christmas, Bob's Bell Ranger helicopter had crashed while on loan to Honda Australia for a sunrise advertising shoot near Thunderdome. Unfortunately, the pilot had become blinded by the rising sun, had flown too low catching high voltage power lines in the helicopter's landing skids, not realising this until the lines catapulted the helicopter into the ground.

It was only exceptional skill by the pilot that had saved those on board from death. The seats were the only things left intact on the ground. The pilot and the freelance photographer both had many broken bones, but the Honda Sales Director, who I had met at the Adelaide Grand Prix, had an amazing escape, and had managed to play nine holes of golf that afternoon after the accident.

However, we all felt a sense of loss, yet good fortune, as we had been passengers in that same helicopter just weeks before and believed that but for the grace of God, it could have been us.

The mood in the business eventually lifted and we enthusiastically started making plans for the Moomba meeting.

On the Friday of the Moomba weekend, Christopher arrived at Thunderdome for some practice laps and quickly adapted to the Auscar Holden he was to drive as well as John Sheppard's beautiful

600hp Nascar Pontiac which he took for a spin. It was obvious to us all that he was a natural racing car driver.

Later that day, Andrew Guild phoned me to ask how the practice went and I said, "Fine, thanks." He then said in a serious voice, "George, we need to make sure Christopher isn't pushed too hard by the other drivers because he is a passionate, naturally driven champion and won't want to lose his position in the field." "Okay', we'll brief the other drivers to not push him, as we don't want him crashing into a wall and hurting himself, especially with his skating commitments with the Russians."

That afternoon, after telling Bob of my phone call and concern, he arranged a formal briefing to be held on the Friday night with all the drivers after the afternoon's first Nascar and Auscar Moomba races.

Saturday afternoon I arrived at Thunderdome in anticipation of an historic day of racing and Celebrity Challenge. It was a lovely sunny autumn twilight evening when the Celebrity Challenge started at 6.15pm. I had positioned myself on the infield close to the south medical building with race executives and Christopher Dean's ice-skating partner, Jayne Torvill.

The 10-lap race, or Celebrity Challenge, commenced and was going well when on the fifth lap Christopher was pushed a bit by Kim Jane, found himself up too high on the bank and lost the rear of his Auscar at 200 kmh. He braked quickly but still went into the inside wall at 100 kmh after sliding along the grass verge.

The race was stopped, and ambulance staff raced to attend to him. Everything appeared to be moving in slow motion. I was standing next to Jayne Torvill who was in shock and began to shake. Obviously, her thoughts were for her world-famous skating partner who was possibly badly injured. I instinctively put my arm around her and said, "Don't worry Jayne, he'll be okay", without really knowing his condition. It was a weird but wonderful experience to be able to put an assuring arm around the 1984 gold medallist, something I never imagined would ever happen in my lifetime!

English World and Olympic ice-skating champion Christopher Dean survives after hitting the Thunderdome wall at 100 km/h.

Christopher was put in a precautionary neck brace and flown to St Vincent's Hospital by helicopter with Jayne by his side. He was very lucky and had no broken bones, just bruising on his shoulder and left ankle, and a dent to his pride.

The next day Christopher's crash was the lead story in all the Australian Sunday papers and even made headlines around the world. I checked on Christopher throughout Sunday and spoke with Andrew Guild who as they would say in a James Bond movie 'was shaken but not stirred'!

It had been a coup to get Christopher to drive, to have Jayne Torvill as a spectator and to have Thunderdome promoted around the world increasing the impact of Moomba in Melbourne. Yet we also were very fortunate that Christopher Dean wasn't seriously injured.

On Monday I arrived at my office at Calder Park and as usual checked my mail and messages. I had no sooner sat down at my desk when I received a call from Bob asking me to go into his office straight away.

He had a serious look on his face and asked me to take a seat. I immediately thought the worst. He looked up from his desk and said very quietly, "How is he?" "Fine, but lucky Bob." Bob replied, "Yes, Kim couldn't help himself, and pushed him too hard coming into the corner. We told them not to push him but racing drivers can't help themselves and are very competitive.

However, we were lucky too in many other ways. I've been told that we made headlines in every newspaper around the world. Thanks George, great job!"

Chapter 2   Skating on Thin Ice

Leadership Lessons:

1. Always be prepared for the unexpected.
2. Keep your key executives in the loop always.
3. Pulling rabbits out of a hat impresses people.
4. Maintain your little black book of contacts.
5. Sometimes impossible dreams do happen.

Chapter 3

Realising Reality

Over the following weeks we reviewed the Moomba weekend and in particular the Moomba race and Bob asked me to complete a total appraisal of the facilities, sales and marketing strategies. He didn't know it, but I had been doing just that since I had arrived in November 1988, so I completed my report that week and added issues I had observed over the Moomba weekend.

The following week Bob called a meeting of all directors and managers including his senior T Mart retail tyre management. I presented my report and appraisal to them and watched in stunned silence as they tried to comprehend the extent of issues that needed to be addressed, improved, researched, initiated, and implemented.

It was my opinion, that to make the $100 million Calder Park Thunderdome Racing complex become a world class entertainment venue, there needed many issues addressed and initiatives implemented. For example, patrons watching the races had no way of knowing the progressive results of any race, like a spectator could at the football, tennis, golf or any other sport, and the standards needed to be brought up from mediocre to excellent. Bob appreciated the appraisal, but others went into denial as I observed they realised that the Bob Jane T Mart tyre centres would again need to provide more of the money needed.

I had made my mark with Bob, and he kindly invited me and my three children to join him and Laree for a couple of days at his Yarrawonga holiday home over Easter. We accepted his invitation and had a wonderful and interesting time.

On my return to work after our Easter break, I learnt more and more about Bob Jane and what a clever businessman he was, but I also started to realise that working at a windy, desolate and lonely Calder Park every day in this culture of car and drag racing was not a long-term career for me. As the winter approached, it became more and more difficult to be motivated, with no changes being agreed to from my report, no racing or activities at Thunderdome and only drag racing on a Saturday night. While I hung on and tried to keep focused and motivated, I realised I was not cut out long-term for the role.

Then, as it seems to happen to me in my career, I received a phone call out of the blue from an old competitor. This former competitor asked me to meet him for a coffee as he had a proposition to put to me.

This seemed like *deja vu* as I had similarly been called by someone 25 years earlier when I was unhappy at Caltex. I had never said I was unhappy, but they had a sixth sense or ESP, call it what you will, and approached me unexpectedly with a business proposition. My competitor was the Forum Organisation who not only replaced us as the supplier to Toyota, but had pirated my Business Development Manager, Peter Dunn, away from me as well.

This was an 'off the record' meeting held at his offices and resulted in him offering me the position of Victorian General Manager with a similar salary package to that which I was receiving from Bob Jane.

In view of what I was experiencing at Calder Park Raceway I decided my career path was best suited back in the industry which I knew and had made a name for myself and my company. So, after several meetings I agreed to accept the offer at Forum and leave the Calder Park Raceway. The biggest problem I had was that I felt guilty deserting Bob after starting off in such a successful manner, and after we had developed such a warm personal relationship.

After receiving a letter of appointment, I determined an appropriate time to let Bob know of my decision to leave. I thought I should do this sooner rather than later so I asked Bob if I could have a coffee with him and sat down and got straight to the point. I told him I had learnt a lot from him and had enjoyed the role and the challenge. However, didn't believe the role was for me, or that I fitted his long-term expectations for Calder Park. I also told him I didn't want to let him down in view of the massive investment he had made in the Thunderdome venture.

I explained I had a chance to go back into the industry I had been in, and hoped that while he might be disappointed, he would give me his blessing. He looked at me and said, "I can't believe you are making this decision, but I respect you for your honesty. Okay George, I accept your resignation, but I think you must be bloody unstable to do something like this after what you've achieved here!"

We agreed I would leave in two weeks in line with my pay period, left and returned to my office at Thunderdome, looked at my oval desk and released a big sigh of relief.

Over the following days many people called me to wish me well, and then the Operations Director, Grant Tillet, told me that a farewell lunch was being arranged for me on my final Friday.

There were many issues to cover and I was pleasantly surprised by all the good wishes I was receiving.

On the final Friday, all who had been invited to the lunch arrived at the Calder Park canteen and after I thought all had arrived, in walked Bob. He took his place, and we enjoyed a lovely 'canteen style' lunch. After finishing his lunch, he stood up and made a short speech. He thanked me for my efforts in the short time I had been there and wished me well for the future. I thanked him for his generosity and everyone for their kindness.

After Bob left, Grant turned and said to me, "You know Bob never comes to a farewell lunch for an employee as he usually fires them. They don't resign and leave him!"

It was so much less stressful not having to drive half-way to Bendigo each day, and instead only travel to Albert Park.

This time I ensured my office was set up before I started, and was introduced to all the Victorian staff. They included an interesting cross section of talent ranging from a USA basketball import, to one of Edward de Bono's previous colleagues, Dr Michael Hewitt Gleeson.

However, it wasn't long before I began to realise the reason why the Managing Director had asked me to join him. He had started negotiations to try and entice Australian Airlines to buy him out, and when they weren't interested, he approached Ansett Airlines. He was aware of my previous strong relationship with Ansett and before long he included me in many of the meetings.

I was starting to see the bigger picture more and more each day and realising that I was perhaps being used as a pawn in a game of takeover chess.

I had been quietly having discussions with close friends who could see, hear and feel I was becoming disenchanted, and several had suggested I leave and start up again by myself because, as they said, I had been very successful until Toyota pulled the rug out from under me.

So, after a few months I gave him back my keys to the office and I walked out a free man again and realised I didn't really want to work for anyone else in the future but myself.

Leadership Lessons:

1. Give feedback honestly without fear or favour.
2. When you see the writing on the wall take action.
3. Listen to your heart as well as your head.
4. Always act with respect and dignity.
5. Always work at and in what you love.

CASE HISTORY 16

Norris Management Pty Ltd

Chapter 1

The Phoenix Rises

At the time I was leasing a lovely two-bedroom apartment at Hobson's Bay overlooking Port Phillip Bay, and my three children came to stay with me every second weekend and for part of school holidays. They were the source of my motivation and inspiration and gave me the strength to fight on. The only problem was how I was going to conduct this fight. I had just experienced the summit of my business career, I thought, and unsure what to do next to restart my career at the ripe age of nearly 50.

Then, as often happens to me, opportunity came knocking in the form of an unexpected visitor to my apartment one Saturday morning. I opened the door and came face to face with an Elizabeth Taylor look-a-like. She was very beautiful, was looking to lease an apartment in my building and had, it turned out, knocked on the door of the wrong apartment. She was interested to find out about the features of the building at Hobson's Bay and I invited her in for a coffee and chat.

Some weeks later she leased a sub-penthouse on one of the top floors and became a good friend. She was in a relationship with a guy from Sydney who she later married. I have to admit that not only was she beautiful, she was extremely intelligent and insightful. Also, she gave me a wonderful piece of advice, which I have since passed on to many people experiencing a personal midlife crisis, and which also enabled me to chart a new course and rise again from the ashes.

One night, while having a coffee, we got onto the topic of me and my future and tossed around a few ideas for possible ventures, such as opening a steak and fish restaurant and calling it 'Beef and Reef'. I gave her a snapshot of my career to date, and she said, "Well how do you top all that?" She sat there quietly listening and then said, "I think the worst thing you could do would be to do something very different, where you don't use your knowledge, skills and experience."

She then said, "Why don't you veer right instead of turning right?" This advice flicked a switch in my mind, and I asked her to elaborate. "Well," she said, "If you turn right you potentially could throw away all that you have learnt. Why don't you return to your core business, but focus on using the knowledge and experience you have gained to help others?" After our chat I left feeling energised, but still unsure what direction my business should take.

Some weeks passed, and as my daughters were growing up, we all needed more space, so I decided to leave Hobson's Bay and lease a three-bedroom townhouse in Elwood. It was in a court, had its own backyard and was next to a small private park and perfect for the next stage of my rehabilitation, career re- invention and safe for my children's welfare and our Corgi dog, Cindy.

The townhouse and park were an important stepping-stone in rebuilding my future and gave my three children and me room to grow together. The two girls, Nicole and Melinda were in their teens and needed their own rooms as did my young son, Campbell. Not long after I celebrated my 50th birthday and the small park next door was the perfect venue for the event.

I had invited 50 friends including my new girlfriend, Kellie, who I had met at Vic Roads whilst working at Thunderdome. I hadn't forgotten Janet Hider-Smith, the owner of the green British Brookland Riley vintage car and invited her also, but she had married a champion glider and Austrian airline pilot and had gone to live in Vienna.

On the morning of my 50th party I received an unexpected call from Ted, Janet's father. "Hi George", he said, "will you be home tonight about 9pm?" "Yes", I replied, "I am having a party tonight in the park next door so I will be definitely home." "That's good', he said, "there's a present on its way, and it should arrive about 9pm." I thanked him and said good-bye.

The party was in full swing, the BBQ was working well, the drinks were flowing, the guests were loving Bryan Ferry, and we were playing the one side over and over again of Avalon, when suddenly a taxi pulled up and out stepped Janet Hider-Smith.

It was an unexpected, pleasant surprise and present. I was astonished to see her and rushed over, gave her a big welcome hug, and introduced her to all the guests. My girlfriend Kellie, however, was not so impressed by this 'present' and so I learnt another interesting lesson in life!

It was around this time that I also decided to lease a serviced office at 580 St Kilda Road overlooking Albert Park Lake and Port Phillip Bay, and which coincidentally is next door to where I live today at 576 St Kilda Road.

Now that I had an office, I had to decide on what to call my business so I could 'veer right'. Something that had riled me over 12 years in my own business, which was now called George Norris Marketing, was the fact that business people at that time in Australia were adversely inclined to pay for creativity, ideas and strategies and would say, "Thanks, but I could have thought of that." This unfortunate attitude in Australia had meant that I had files full of ideas, suggestions, and strategies that I had never been able to charge for.

It came to me as I sat looking out the window and contemplating, that management consultants always charged for ideas, suggestions, plans and strategies because they had branded themselves to be perceived that they were providing strategic advice. Whereas, using the word marketing implied intangible 'tinsel town', unsubstantiated ideas or concepts. Marketing firms really only received payment for tangible promotional items, merchandise or in my own business case, air travel, accommodation, brochures and the like.

I wanted to be paid for 'my brain not my brawn', so I decided to start up my business again using the brand, Norris Management Pty Ltd and charge clients for my brain, advice, and knowledge. This was to be my greatest 'light bulb' moment. It had only taken me 16 years to work it out, but 'Elizabeth Taylor' had helped me to think outside the square, veer right and re-invent myself.

I had also learnt the value of completing a SWOT and had completed three on myself since leaving Thunderdome. These convinced me that my consistent strengths and attributes were strategy, communication, networking, teaching, creativity, time management, empathy, leadership, public speaking, and business presentation. My weaknesses at the time were impatience, self-esteem, taxation and accounting, computer technology, investment in stocks and shares and trusting others when I shouldn't.

So, I set about using my strengths and working on my weaknesses so that I could influence change and improvement in myself and my business.

It wasn't long before I started getting calls from friends asking if they could help me again. George Haddon's daughter Kate, who I had employed during my time with In Touch, had taken on a role with Tontine who manufactured pillows and bedding and they wanted someone to design and facilitate a series of product knowledge training seminars and award nights around Australia. Kate knew me well, knew my skill set, could trust me to deliver, so I was appointed.

During the series of seminars, I learnt another valuable lesson. In my research I found retail staff did not have the confidence to question customers about their needs to enable them to match the products they sell. They also needed to research customers' needs by using Rudyard Kipling's six words (what, why, when, where, how, who) from his well-known poem, to start open ended questions. These cannot be answered with a yes or no, only with information. The series of seminars conducted all around Australia was highly successful and gave me the confidence to kick off and rise again.

Then a friend introduced me to the Ballarat Village Conference Centre which wanted to re-invent itself and create a new vibrant image and strategic marketing program.

In the process I had also met and become associated with Bob Gorry, a director of a building firm carrying out some renovations for the conference centre and Derek Jones, a public relations expert from Currie Communication, who I still keep in touch with to this day. Bob then recommended me to the HIA and I started presenting monthly education sessions on a variety of subjects, to their members. At the same time, a squash friend, John Day, and a former colleague and management cadet I met in 1958 at Caltex Oil, Wayne Tyler, who I hadn't seen for many years, contacted me to ask if I could carry out research on their HBA retail outlets, write a report on what I observed and make a series of recommendations to enhance their presentation to the public.

These recommendations were not only implemented, but John Day in his senior role, invited me to present my report and give a presentation at their corporate conference in Echuca. As an independent advisor I could provide an unbiased, in depth review and progressive assessment of the new strategies.

Norris Management was beginning to extend its new-found wings, was gaining altitude, and I was now being paid for my brain!

A previous competitor, Ray Ellis, who was the Managing Director of 'The Event Centre', was introduced to me by a colleague who had joined me on the Melbourne Convention Bureau Committee. Ray knew of my background in the car industry and wanted me to work on a project for one of his clients, Nissan. This started a business and golfing friendship that has lasted over 30 years.

I designed a Performance Management program based on 'the Golden Arrows of Excellence Strategy' and he loved it and presented it to Nissan. However, unfortunately they thought it was too close to the Mercedes Benz Silver Arrows concept, and it wasn't accepted, but I got paid for my brain again!

Leadership Lessons:

1. When considering your future direction sometimes veer right!
2. Cocooning uses silence, stillness and solitude for Eureka ideas.
3. Value your special intellectual property because it's priceless.
4. Provide clients with high perceived value as an investment.
5. Position your business so you get paid for using your brain. . .

CASE HISTORY 17

Jetset Travel

Chapter 1

One Night in Bangkok

Norris Management was taking baby steps enabling me to re-invent myself. Then one day while presenting a 'The Psychology of Selling' session at HIA, 'it' happened again. I turned around from the group of around 20, to write some notes on the whiteboard when unexpectedly a voice from behind startled me, "Excuse me George, do you always present with so much energy?" I turned around and said, "Yes, usually. Who are you and why are you here?"

"I'm Tom Richardson, and I'm the Sales Manager of AV Jennings. I have four staff enrolled in the course, so I thought I'd come along and sit in." I asked, "How are you enjoying the session so far?" He replied, "It's just great, and I wanted to ask if you would be prepared to present a similar session to the total sales force at AV Jennings." I replied, "I'd be delighted depending on my availability." He asked me to contact him in the next few days to set up a time to discuss the topic, and some dates and times.

I called him a couple of days later and we sorted out all the details including my fee. The session went well, and I received good feedback from Tom saying it was very favourably received.

I remained focused on the new business I had gained, especially the Ballarat Village Conference Centre which was growing into a significant client.

The year 1991 was tumultuous, and as our Federal Treasurer at the time, Paul Keating, said, "It was the recession we had to have." So, it wasn't a surprise when later that year I received another call from Tom to say he had been retrenched. AV Jennings had suffered a serious downturn, mainly caused by a wrong move from their core business of building houses to trying to move into buildings for commercial use.

I tried to help Tom with a couple of suggestions for a new job including AMP who had become a good client and some other clients, but nothing seemed to work for him.

Tom was also an elite golfer, and I had helped him become a member of Yarra Yarra Golf Club, where I was also a member, so we caught up occasionally for a game and a chat.

My business had grown, I was busy, but for quite a while I didn't see or hear anything of Tom. Then, one night when driving home early in March 1993, my mobile car phone rang and surprisingly it was Tom. I was pleased to hear from him, and we exchanged the usual pleasantries. He then asked if I had time to meet up. I agreed and naturally asked why, to which he replied, "Well, I've been appointed as the National Retail Franchise Manager for Jetset Travel and have suggested you be the keynote speaker in the first week of August at our national conference in Bangkok!"

I pulled my car over on to the shoulder of the road, turned on the inside car light, as it was now dark, opened my attaché case and got out my diary. I checked the date and said, "I'm clear then" He said, "Well block the week off, and I will come back to you with the time for a meeting to discuss the details."

About a week later Tom called to set up the meeting with me. He explained that he had gained approval for me to be the keynote speaker on the opening day. I was to follow the Managing Director, David Clarke, and he wanted me to give a presentation on changes that were happening in retail in Australia.

Tom then went on to say that Jetset Travel also wanted me to present five retailer breakout sessions on the 'Psychology of Selling' using similar concepts to that which I had used at HIA. previously.

The Natcom Conference, as it was called, was a great success and as a result I was called again when we returned home. Jetset had agreed to use Hamilton Island as their retail staff training base from October 1993 onwards and I was asked if I could regularly present an opening three-hour session on 'Change in Retail' on the Friday and a further half-day session on the Saturday morning on 'The Psychology of Selling'.

These training sessions were held approximately on a monthly basis, and were well accepted. The managers and staff of their 250 retail travel shops throughout Australia reported they found them to be highly valuable as they were all very concerned about losing business to the internet.

Jetset Travel also negotiated a deal with Ansett Airlines which included free of charge return travel for all Jetset participants from around Australia. It was an innovative strategy with Jetset promoting Hamilton Island and Ansett Airlines and, at the same time, Jetset was able to train their retail people at an idyllic location.

Then 'it' happened again. I was driving alone in my car about noon one day when the car mobile phone rang. It was Andrew Richards, the National Retail Manager for Jetset Travel. "Hi George, are you free to talk?" I said, "Sure, how can I help you?"

"Well George, I don't know what you are doing up at Hamilton Island, but it's revolutionised our retail outlets and their people. However, we in Head Office are not in step with what is happening, and we need to be." "That's great feedback", I replied. "Well, we want to know if you could implement the same or similar training content for our head office staff in Melbourne."

"That shouldn't be a problem. When do you need to know and I will send a proposal to you?" "I need it by next Thursday, that gives you five days. Is that okay? I need to know when you could start, what the content will be, how many people should be in each group, how long the sessions should be, and I guess you had better include your fee for the total program!"

Leadership Lessons:

1. It's important to always be your authentic self.
2. It's satisfying to help people in life to grow.
3. Don't expect a return, but it usually happens.
4. Remember to always perform at your best.
5. The best form of marketing is 'the referral'.

Chapter 2

Success Through Service

I took a gulp, and concentrated on my drive home to Brighton where I had recently moved along with my office to larger premises as my three children were in their late teens, about to start university, and would now be living with me full time.

"Okay Andrew," I said, "To help me complete the proposal, how many people are going to be involved in the training program in total?" "Hmm, all senior management, all middle management, well, all staff really and that totals around 400 people. Also, we want you to be the only presenter, so everyone receives the same message, knowledge and style of presentation." I took another gulp and tried to concentrate harder on my driving!

On arriving home, I called Tom Richardson to tell him what had happened. He didn't seem that surprised and said, "George, you're breathing new life into Jetset at the moment. Thanks for supporting me in my role." He went on to say he thought it would be best, knowing what the culture was like inside Jetset, to present the program first to senior management, then to middle management and then to the rest of the staff. That way the change in culture would flow down from the top and senior and middle management would act as a support for staff to embrace any change.

Over the next three days I put in a lot of time and hard work, prepared a proposal as requested, and a fee which reflected the fact that they were a major client of Norris Management.

The proposal was hand delivered to Andrew and I waited and wondered what the answer would be. Then on Thursday, whilst at golf with Tom at Yarra Yarra, my mobile phone buzzed in my buggy seat and it was Andrew. I moved away to answer the call in an area where I could use my phone. He told me the proposal had been approved without any changes, he was about to go into a meeting and to call him again the next day to set up a time to meet with the Managing Director.

When I returned, Tom said, "How did you go and I just smiled and said, "It was all approved and it was unchanged." "Great work George, now let's play golf!"

The program was given the title 'Success Through Service' and commenced the following month with each group of about 25 people attending an initial half-day which was divided into two sessions. The first session was called The Challenge of Change, which set the scene for a necessary change in the culture. The second session was called The Psychology of Customer Centered Service which covered aspects of world research on why people 'love to buy but hate to be sold' and how customers can be helped to remain loyal.

In 1994, I presented some 42 half-day sessions to all 400 staff at the Jetset Head Office in Melbourne, as well as flying to Hamilton Island regularly to train and coach the retail staff from their outlets around Australia.

So, in December 1994, I celebrated an amazing year and welcomed my second daughter, Melinda to live with me full time. Like her older sister, Nicole, she was going to Melbourne University to study psychology, where her sister was already studying a double law/economics degree.

It was long awaited, and very satisfying, to have my two girls living with me again as a family. Since their mother and her new husband had taken the children away from me 12 years previously, I had badly missed them and a consistent family environment.

My partnership with Jetset grew, and in the following three years I continued to fly to Hamilton Island for the retail training sessions, flying up on Friday morning and back on Sunday, some 35 times in all. I was also retained as a keynote speaker at their next four national conferences in Darwin, Bali, Melbourne, and Hamilton Island.

In addition to this, I was asked to act as executive coach to several senior head office managers and asked to assist in writing The Jetset Way, a corporate culture program and launch it around Australia.

Meanwhile I still had other clients to assist, and during this manic period I was approached by John de Stieger, the Sales Director of Australian Pacific Tours, who had been in one of the groups I had presented to in Bangkok. He wanted me to train his management and staff throughout Australia.

The Club Med Manager for Australia, who was also in Bangkok, was fascinated by the FAB (features, advantages and benefits) product analysis technique I introduced and explained. He commissioned me to analyse the Club Med properties world-wide so they could better present them and generate increased sales more consistently.

It had been a whirlwind couple of years which confirmed to me that if you believe in yourself and commit yourself to your clients, and ensure that you provide them with value for money, they will support you, recommend you and beat a path to your door. Just make sure all your eggs aren't in one basket!

Understandably, one of my favourite songs is from the stage show Chess, "One night in Bangkok and the world's your oyster......... "

Leadership Lessons:

1. Once you have a reputation, you're on show.
2. To change culture successfully, start at the top.
3. Everything in life comes to those who are patient.
4. People don't ever buy price, they buy perceived value.
5. Always make sure all your eggs aren't in one basket.

CASE HISTORY 18

Anthony Tesselaar Plants

Chapter 1

Smelling the Roses

Sometime after returning from the Jetset Conference in Bangkok, and being involved in the training at Hamilton Island, I received an invitation to be the Guest Speaker at a Travel Agents Conference in Bendigo, Victoria.

My brief was to be provocative and challenge the agents to open their mind to change in their retail sector. They had a good attendance and my presentation seemed to be very well received, judging by the number and type of questions asked.

Then just as I was about to depart an influential agent came up to me and said, "That was very interesting George. I have a client in the horticulture business who I think could benefit from your knowledge and advice."

He asked me for a business card, and as it often happens after presentations, nothing eventuates. I said I was in his hands and interested to meet his client if interested.

The first accountant I appointed to my business, Bob Brown, who had been the Chief Accountant at Ford Motor Company, gave me a comment I have since found to be really true, "Yes's come quickly, but No's take a long time."

Well, the next week I received a call from the travel agent, who handled all the client's Australian and International travel which was considerable. He said that they would be happy to meet me and suggested I call the Managing Director to set up an appointment.

The client was one of the Tesselaar brothers, well known for the Annual Tulip Festival at Silvan. Anthony and his wife Sheryl ran a business called Anthony Tesselaar Plants.

Anthony had Dutch parents, possessed a significant knowledge of horticulture, and had acquired the rights in Australia and overseas for the unique ground covering, Flower Carpet Rose.

They had appointed breeders, growers, agents and distributors in the USA, South Africa, Japan and throughout Australia. It was a flourishing business which had grown very rapidly.

We hit it off at our first meeting, and it was agreed that I be appointed to assist them primarily for their strategic advice and planning, people management, leadership development and corporate coaching of the key executives.

Anthony, as Managing Director, was the driver and face of the business in the market place. His wife Sheryl was his Personal Assistant and accompanied him on nearly all his travels.

Rod Thorpe was the Financial Controller and Commercial Director, and Ian Smith was the Technical Director, responsible for research, development, testing and trialling of their range of plants.

The Flower Carpet Rose was the 'jewel in the crown' of their plants, generated most of their income, and had enormous potential to be marketed worldwide if their contract allowed.

Growing about one metre in height and width, it is extremely pretty, hardy and is virtually drought proof, needing only small quantities of water to survive.

It is ideal for gardens, industrial estates, and medium strips on main roads.

The business kept growing and we could see that the management structure was too thin to enable sustainable growth. I was asked to find an additional senior manager and advise on reshaping the management structure.

The business was highly successful in the USA and had significant agreements with Home Depot and Lowe's Home Improvements Stores. They also were powerful in Japan and South Africa but needed to consolidate their business in their home country of Australia. The new senior manager was given this critical responsibility.

Our relationship 'blossomed'. I was more and more trusted with the critical aspects and strategic advice and facilitated many strategic planning meetings.

At one meeting I arranged for a friend and colleague of mine, Max Grundmann, the Founder and Managing Director of the homewares company brand Maxwell & Williams. He gave an address as to why his brand was so successful worldwide and the keys for that success.

Anthony arranged several Grower Conferences in Australia, and I was privileged to be asked to present sessions on subjects including Leadership, Marketing, Communication and Lateral Thinking at many of them.

Succession planning then became an issue for Anthony and Sheryl and it was decided to bring Phillip Townsend, their nephew into the business in a senior capacity for his development in the business for the future.

Phillip was at first sight an extremely bright executive who had been educated in the Royal Australian Navy and had been a senior officer on submarine duty.

He had the right skillset which, when coupled with the knowledge of the horticulture business, would give Anthony a trusted family member in the business.

I was honoured to work with Phillip, to help him settle in and adjust his management style to fit the smaller and different business model from that of the RAN. I was most impressed with his skills in communication, people management, strategic decision making and planning. Anthony had made a wise decision, and Phillip increasingly handled areas where I had been assisting the business while it was growing.

I then introduced Anthony to one of my trusted accounting and advisory clients, Kelvin Boyd and his son Rohan who would personally handle their business. I was happy I had left them in good hands for the future.

Leadership Lessons:

1. You never know who is in your audience.
2. To help others grow, think from their position.
3. Have your client's interests at heart when making decisions.
4. Build sustainable relationships and leverage advice.
5. Have a succession plan and implement it wisely with care.

CASE HISTORY 19

Herb Herbert Pty Ltd

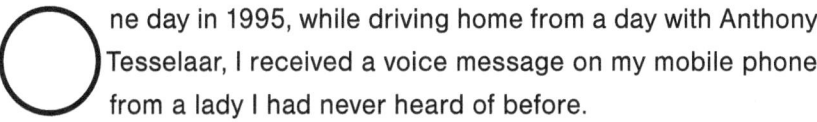

Chapter 1

The Growing of Herbie

One day in 1995, while driving home from a day with Anthony Tesselaar, I received a voice message on my mobile phone from a lady I had never heard of before.

Her name was very difficult to decipher, but the message asked me to call her, so I did. She answered and I meekly asked her to slowly say her name as when she said it quickly, I couldn't understand her. We both laughed which broke the ice of an awkward moment for us both!

Her name was Zelma Wyatt, and she was the Managing Director of a business quaintly called, Herb Herbert. It was run from their offices at Monbulk in the Melbourne Dandenong Ranges, not far from Tesselaar's. I apologised for not being able to understand her phone message.

Zelma mentioned that she was in a plane returning from an appointment in Perth, and Sheryl Tesselaar was sitting next to her. She also mentioned to Sheryl that they had been using a business consultant in Perth but had been thinking of changing. Sheryl very kindly mentioned my name, and that I had commenced working with them. She gave Zelma my contact details.

We set up a meeting and met in their quaint log cabin in Monbulk, which had once been their home. In the meeting we were joined by her avant-garde husband, Neil, who was the Creative and Marketing Director.

They explained their business which was a clever concept. Like Anthony Tesselaar Plants, they had a network of growers in Australia and around the globe, but instead of growing flower plants, they grew herb plants.

These were marketed under a licence agreement and packaged as Herb Herbert Herbs. Neil had created a cartoon character of a little old white-haired gardener called 'Herbie' who had become the Disneyland 'Mickey Mouse' of the Herb Herbert brand.

He was available for retail and nursery promotion days in the form of a life size dress up suit. Neil would often wear this, and his image was used in point-of-sale material, the website, other communication vehicles like cookbooks, children's colouring books, on the pots housing the herb plant and especially on the identification tag standing in the pot describing the type of herb and it's best use.

They had cleverly captured a market segment with a brand they had created and were on their way to owning that market segment on a global scale.

They appointed me as their Corporate Strategic Advisor, and we met on a regular basis when possible as they were often away around Australia and overseas. They too had arrangements with Home Depot and Lowes Stores in the USA and Bunnings in Australia. They had grown their brand by maintaining a strategy of staying close to their retailers.

I was then often asked to present business education sessions at their various Grower and Retailer Conferences in Australia and our relationship grew and grew just like their herbs!

In fact, our relationship grew to such an extent that we became close friends and in 2000 they bought a rundown farmhouse in the seaside town of Biarritz in France with a view to renovating it and holidaying there to relax.

As time went by, and my business morphed into Corporate Coaching and Management Mentoring, they asked me to give some advice on those areas as well as corporate strategic advice.

So, in 2001, at one of our meetings, I asked Neil how he felt about what he was doing, and was he achieving his full potential and doing something that he really loved. He stood bolt upright and said, "Follow me George. I'll drive you up to our house and show you my answer!"

I sat in his car, and he drove up the hill to the amazing home they had built, that I'd never seen before. It was on a grand scale, had a somewhat medieval appearance inside with a very tall knight called David in a full suit of armour, and a grand staircase like in the film, 'Gone with the Wind'.

Neil showed me around, then we climbed the staircase and entered an impressive library/office where Zelma worked on their private matters.
He then went over to a button and in true James Bond style the bookcase spun around to reveal another room which was his painting studio.

It was a special moment in time for us both. He just looked me square in the eyes and said, "George this is what I'd love to do virtually full time, paint as an artist!" There were several large paintings, some completed, some just started and one of his wife Zelma nearly completed.

It was a breathtaking revelation, I was enthralled and in return looked him straight in the eyes and said, "Well Neil what's stopping you, just do it!" He did, and his career as an artist flourished and grew.

Then one day early in 2005, after having lunch with me at my town house in Brighton, he asked a strange question. Would I give him a few golf lessons to start him off in the game so he could go to a golf professional with some confidence after learning the basics.

I agreed, then he went on to say, "If you're prepared to do that for me, I'd like to paint your portrait in return." I was flattered and agreed to be his subject. He quickly took some digital photos with the camera I hadn't known he'd brought with him, and then left.

Over the next six months we got together for his basic golf lessons. I can't remember ever asking how my portrait was coming along, probably because I didn't think I should be so forward and ask an artist to push his project along.

Then in September 2005, Neil called me and asked if I was available one Saturday morning to give him another golf lesson. He then said that he would present me with his portrait of me afterwards.

When we returned to my place, he asked me to go to another room while he set up the painting. I duly obeyed and then, after a few long minutes, he asked me to come back as he was ready.

When I entered the room there was this massive lifelike full colour portrait of me propped up on a chair with a spotlight shining it. I was flabbergasted by its size, detail, and the unusual treatment to cast shadows across my head, face, and jacket.

It was an immensely powerful painting, and I was somewhat taken aback.

In some sort of shock, I asked why it was so large and powerful. Zelma, who really was now Neil's manager, explained that Neil was going to enter the portrait in the 2006 Archibald Prize in Sydney. They had thought I was a good subject to paint, but deep down I also felt that Neil wanted to say thanks for helping him embark on a career that he loved.

The painting was duly framed and entered but unfortunately did not win. It now hangs proudly in the foyer of my Melbourne apartment, so I see myself every day and remember Neil's very kind and meaningful gift. In fact, the portrait is the background for the cover of my business autobiography book you are now reading.

Neil and Zelma have since sold their amazing house in the Dandenong Ranges and have settled in France where they live in their renovated farmhouse in Biarritz. They have recently opened Neil's own Art Galarie in Salies-de-Bearn, a commune village in the Pyrenees only one and a half hours away from their home.

Neil's painting business is growing in leaps and bounds just like Herb Herbert herbs and 'Herbie' grew once upon a time.

Leadership Lessons:

1. Leadership is weighing up options and making courageous decisions
2. Humour can save face in moments of potential emotional conflict.
3. Give your business a personality for a point of difference and power.
4. Try to ensure you do what you love in life not only what you like.
5. Live your dreams, think high and you can rise to exciting heights.

CASE HISTORY 20

General Motors Holden

Chapter 1

Renewing Relationships

After such a great three years and living in six different houses, apartments, and town houses, I was able to buy a house again. That was interesting as I was still busy flying around Australia for Jetset and other clients and I really didn't have time to dedicate to the task. Today, I guess you would employ a buyer's advocate.

Instead, I decided to take a calculated risk and delegate the task to my daughter, Nicole. It was an opportunity for her to use her new found legal skills and knowledge to help us as a family and she revelled in the challenge.

During the following weeks, I was completing a series of business programs for General Motors titled Marketing to Women which I had been working on at the same time as Jetset's program.

They say the world is round, and one night in late 1993 I again received a phone call out of the blue.

My original contact at Toyota had seen the light and had been poached by 'The General' to help achieve for Holden what he had achieved for Toyota. I had always got on well with Jeff Martin and I knew he had felt badly about how the new Manager at Toyota had treated me after the Corolla car launch. Jeff invited me to his Holden office and set out his plans and how I might help. It appeared from research that females to the car market in Australia were worth an enormous $1.6 billion in retail sales, but the male culture of dealerships, their management and staff was such that this was largely untapped.

He wanted me to create, design, develop and present a series of training seminars around Australia to set the scene for the project, educate the management and sales staff of the dealerships in the current situation, and give them the knowledge and skills to feel comfortable and confident to tap this lucrative market.

It was a huge market, a huge problem, and a huge opportunity for the first manufacturer to take this initiative and 'own' the female market.

I was naturally keen to be involved as the key presenter. Jeff also engaged a behavioural psychologist, a lady from Tasmania who had recently moved to Victoria. It was planned for us to conduct a series of seminars in each state's capital city and at my suggestion, based on my Jetset experience, we would present to the dealer principals and sales managers on the first day, and sales staff on the second and third day if required.

The research we carried out was invaluable and I was privileged to take part in this study as the knowledge I gained was not readily known at the time, and highlighted the differences in 'wiring in the brain' between males and females. For instance, females have a double conduit between the left and right parts of the brain, and they can think 'logically AND emotionally' at the same time. Males on the other hand have a single conduit between the left and right parts of the brain and can only think 'logically OR emotionally' at the same time.

This biological difference enables females to multi-task easier than males and probably why females often get more emotional when discussing issues whereas males seem to remain in a more logical mode. I also found from research that when a female says to a male, "You're not listening to me", what she really means is 'you don't understand how I feel', which is her emotional feeling together with the logic of the issue. The male doesn't usually understand this statement of emotion and logic and usually replies, "But I am listening", because he is not letting her know that he knows how she is feeling. It's complex, but critical in communication between a male and a female.

So, what we learnt is males should try harder to understand how a female 'feels' as well and not just listen to the 'logic' of her words.

I also learnt that the female eye can see a wider range of field of approximately 180° whereas the male eye can only focus straight ahead on a narrow range of approximately 90°. This eye performance has apparently evolved from the early cave dwellers, where the male required a sharp focus to hunt for food while the female would stay with the children and watch out for animals and predators to protect themselves and keep safe.

This seems to be the main reason why waiters, flight attendants and other customer service roles are often better performed better by females who have a broader peripheral vision and can see customers waiting for attention, more easily.

We also discovered that in the male dominated retail car sales industry, females can easily see a male looking at them in an inappropriate manner or unprofessional way and this immediately puts a barrier up between the female customer and the male salesperson.

The research we undertook for this program was interesting and enlightening and proved that Australian car retailers at the time didn't understand how to tap the female market and, in my opinion, still really don't today.

To qualify the findings of the research, GMH gave a female researcher $20,000 and asked her to purchase a car on a Saturday at one of the Sydney dealerships along Parramatta Road. On the following Monday she returned with the same $20,000 and said no salesman had wanted to sell her a car! We also interviewed many female drivers and prospective purchasers. They provided overwhelming evidence that the male dominated sales force in the retail car industry lacked the social skills, empathy, communication skills and manners to make female buyers feel comfortable and confident they could make a wise decision to trust these male salespeople.

GMH made a video with us as presenters explaining the research, and the interviews promoting the program. We showed it to dealerships around Australia, and sent it to the GMH head office in Detroit, USA. I compiled a series of photographs of typical Holden dealerships for my presentation which included their retail floor display and sales office layouts so the sales managers and sales people could see at a glance that the internal environment was also not conducive to marketing to women.

As could be expected, some dealer principals didn't like seeing the truth of the raw evidence of the facilities even though no names were mentioned. Also in Melbourne, during the lunch break on the first day of the program, a dealer principal left in a huff saying he didn't believe the research, and the problem, even though his own sales consultant was featured in the video.

However, just to prove that the evidence is in the eye of the beholder, when I presented the same first day program in Sydney to the dealer principals and sales managers, one of them approached me at the lunch break. He said, "This presentation is brilliant George, do you have space for an extra three of my sales team to attend tomorrow's presentation?"

Two very different reactions from two very different dealer principals!

The program resulted in GMH, stealing a march on their competitors at the time and my relationship with Jeff Martin again was forged at GMH like it was in the early days at Toyota.

At the conclusion of the program, Jeff asked me to present some sessions at the GMH annual conference in Canberra and if I would approach John Bertrand to be the keynote speaker and present 'The Importance of Focus'.
I was able to confirm John, and his presentation proved to be most significant. He was the final speaker at the Canberra conference, spoke for nearly an hour, and had the audience in the palm of his hand.

At the end, he stunned everyone, except me, by forcefully making the provocative point that, "I thought I never really won the America's Cup, Dennis Conner lost it!" You could have heard a pin drop in the auditorium. He had never made these comments to the wider Australian audience, except in his self-deprecating presentation at the two conferences that I had organised in October 1983, some 12 years previously.

As 'focus' was the theme, he explained in great detail how, when a yacht is in the lead and going up the final leg of a triangle course with the wind coming from behind, that all that yacht must do is cover every move the second placed yacht makes, and in normal circumstances it simply can't be beaten.

However, with Australia II tacking every 30 seconds or so, the Americans became lax and actually became somewhat arrogant and ignorant, and lost their 'focus'. They also didn't realise that John, like his late grandfather, had the gift to 'see wind on the water' when others couldn't and when Australia II went out wide, Dennis Conner thought they were mad and didn't focus on covering Australia II.

The result was that Dennis Conner lost the 'unloseable' America's Cup and became the first American Skipper to do so in 132 years, but if he had stayed 'focused' he would have won!

Leadership Lessons:

1. If you have a successful business, people follow you.
2. You can make people famous because of your skills.
3. Female eyes see wider and differently from males.
4. Females think emotionally and logically simultaneously.
5. Staying focused on the task at hand enables success.

Chapter 1   Renewing Relationships

CASE HISTORY 21

Telecom Mobilenet

Chapter 1

Searching for Excellence

Also, during 1993, Telecom Mobilenet which had been a sponsor for the Australian Marketing Institute, invited me to a meeting at their offices in Collingwood. I had become close to them in my role as an AMI board member and had developed a good business relationship with their senior management.

When I arrived, I was surprised to find Bob Ansett in attendance. I had only met him fleetingly before on a couple of occasions, once with John Day when my friend worked at Budget as a State Manager and secondly at an Australian Customer Service Association conference after Bob had become President following the demise of Budget Rent A Car.

The meeting started and I had no idea what it was going to be about until the Senior Telecom Mobilenet Manager said, "Bob why don't you give us the background to the meeting?"

Bob, in his normal eloquent manner, set the scene as ACSA president and mentioned that the Association was bringing out to Australia one of the icons of the world supermarket industry from the USA, Stew Leonard Jnr, the son of the founder of Stew Leonard's Dairy. This was the second case history in the documentary film 'In Search of Excellence' which was based on the book of the same name that I had introduced nine years earlier to Toyota in Tahiti.

I knew about him, and his dad. The business was in the Guinness

Book of Records for having the highest sales per square foot of any dairy/supermarket in America. In fact, I had used the film for numerous presentations since showing it to the Toyota dealers, and had also recommended several their strategic marketing initiatives to clients.

The meeting continued, and I still wasn't aware of why I had been invited. Then it was announced that Stew Leonard Jnr, was going on an Australian tour and that Telecom Mobilenet was going to also sponsor the tour and erect mini 'Expo' exhibitions at each venue. Tim from Telecom Mobilenet then looked at me and said, "George, we would like you to act as MC for each event and act as supervising coordinator with Telecom Mobilenet, to ensure that each venue was presented as planned."

I was surprised and flattered, yet at the same time elated that I would have the opportunity to meet and work with one of the supermarket icons of the world.

Stew Leonard's Dairy, as it is known, started out as just that, a dairy, and because of their unique customer service initiatives they were forced to build 27 extensions to cater for their customers' needs.

In many ways it is based on the Disneyland philosophy that people want to have fun and an adventure when they shop as most people feel supermarket shopping is pure 'drudgery'. They entertain the customers from the time they enter the dairy/supermarket until the time they leave.

Stew Leonard Snr initially acted as a maitre d' in welcoming customers to the store, mixing with them while they shopped inside and saying good-bye to them when they left. They also have 'Wow the Cow' interacting with the children who shop with their parents. It is a family affair with Stew's son, Stew Jnr as President and CEO, his brother Tom as CEO of their second store in Danbury, Stew

Snr's daughter Beth as the founder of Beth's Bakery in the centre of the store, and her daughter Jill as Vice President of Culture and Communication.

The business was started by Stew Snr's dad, Charles, as a milk dairy and the cow became a symbol of freshness as one was positioned on the front of his milk trucks above the front window and would make a mooing sound when delivering milk in the neighbourhoods.

Some of their unique initiatives are, wider than normal aisles, larger than normal trolleys, a wall displaying photos of customers on holidays around the world holding Stew Leonard shopping bags, a suggestion box that is emptied each day and by 10am all the suggestions and feedback are typed up, highlighted and distributed to the managers of each respective department.

Each customer is immediately sent a reply to their suggestion to let them know their point is valued. Every week they hold a customer focus group of about 10 customers selected at random. They sit at a round table, so no-one has a power position, and Stew Jnr asks the customers to say what they like and don't like about the store.

A famous story he told many times during his Australian tour is of the shy lady customer who didn't say anything for over an hour. When finally asked what she didn't like about the store, she took a big breath and blurted out that she didn't like their fish! When asked why, she went on to say that she didn't think it was fresh because it was cut up and supermarket packaged. Stew explained that it was actually freshly caught and asked how she bought her fish. She replied that she only bought her fish fresh off the ice.

So, in true Stew Leonard fashion they built a new counter near the packaged fish with whole fish displayed on ice and as a result they more than doubled their fish sales.

Stew explained to the audience in each capital city in Australia that this 'Focus Group' strategy taught them many lessons:

1. That perception is reality – packaged fish was not perceived to be fresh.
2. That the lady had to shop at another supermarket, therefore putting her loyalty and their income at risk.
3. That customers have ideas and can give you valuable feedback provided you make them feel comfortable and confident.

Another amazing piece of information is that the typical supermarket stocks an average 30,000 items, whereas Stew Leonard's stocks only 2,200 items. The reason he gave in answer to the many questions from each event's audience was amazing yet so simple, that they know these are the items the customers want to buy!

The family-owned business has a special and passionate approach to customer service and at the front entrance to the store is a large rock on which is carved 'Rule 1: The Customer is Always Right! Rule 2: If the customer is ever wrong reread Rule 1'.

We all left the meeting that day feeling very privileged to be part of such a unique event.

I especially felt at this difficult time in my life that it was a vote of confidence by the business world in my ability, and I set about building a close working relationship with Telecom Mobilenet and Bob Ansett.

The venues were spectacular, and every event was a sellout. The Telecom Mobilenet Expo looked and worked very well and I was given very generous feedback that my MC role, facilitation of questions and coordination of the events was done well.

The final presentation by Stew Leonard Jnr was at the Melbourne Concert Hall at the Arts Centre and some 2,500 people attended. I never thought I would be standing in front of so many people, and especially introducing such a world-famous guest.

It all went well however, even though in the hustle and bustle of parking, negotiating the traffic and the 'rabbit warren' backstage complex, I inadvertently forgot to pull up the zipper on the fly of my suit pants.

After introducing Stew to make his presentation I went backstage and thank goodness on checking my suit I noticed the unfortunate dressing malfunction. Without a word to anyone I fixed the problem with a deft touch, and the night went off without another 'hitch'.

Leadership Lessons:

1. Being on boards lets others see your talents in action.
2. Others often see your depth of talent better than yourself.
3. Always aspire to perform consistently with excellence.
4. Remember you can always acquire new knowledge.
5. As a carpenter once said, "Measure twice, cut once."

CASE HISTORY 20

The PGA of Australia

Chapter 1

The Business of Golf

Golf has been a passion of mine since my father George William Norris, took me to watch him play at the Yarra Bend Public Golf Course. I was hooked, and at about 12 years of age would often go with him and putt on the practice green while he played the first nine holes then I would walk the second nine holes with him.

I eventually found an ancient set of my grandfather's clubs hidden away in the loft of our garage that included niblicks, mashies, an old putter and a wood. They were so ancient they had hickory shafts. I had them restored and still have them with the 150-year-old bag they were in. So, I have been playing golf since I was about 13 years old, and practised by clipping the daisy heads off their stems when they shot up in our back and front lawns, much to my mother's concern for the lawn.

With that passionate background I often played at Yarra Bend, Ivanhoe and Albert Park public courses until I moved to Colac and joined my first private club. I then joined Warrnambool when Caltex relocated me, then Croydon after I was married and had moved back to Melbourne and started my own business consultancy.

I then became Golf Captain of The City and Overseas Club in Windsor, and although the club had no course, each month we were able to play one of the famous Sandbelt courses. This allowed me to meet some of the members, and in 1977, two Yarra Yarra Golf Club identities, Keith Walker and Harold Little, invited me to join their club. Since then, Yarra Yarra has been a second home for me. In 2000, I joined The National Golf Club on the Mornington Peninsula as well since I had bought a holiday condominium at Cape Schanck and for 10 years, I enjoyed spending weekends playing there.

However, this love of golf led me in 1997 to call the Executive Director of the Victorian branch of the PGA, an astute man called David Healy. He was planning a series of business workshops for the resident PGA professionals of Victorian golf clubs. I was appointed, and in my element conducting these workshops which ran for nearly seven years, and successfully lifted their business standards.

David was an enthusiastic executive and asked me to be a judge for the Victorian PGA Golf Shop of the Year awards. This was an interesting position which afforded me more research opportunities and an insight into where the PGA members needed assistance, especially in knowledge and skills. David then introduced me to the NSW and Queensland PGA executive directors, and I conducted business workshops for their members. This evolved further as I became known among the P.G.A. members and culminated in being asked over three consecutive years to be a keynote speaker at the PGA Education Expos held at Sanctuary Pines on the Gold Coast.

On the third occasion, I was asked to give a presentation on 'Leadership in Business'. While researching and preparing my presentation, I read a fascinating article about how Jack Nicklaus used to practise and play golf. Jack, when interviewed, stated that on 'every' shot, whether practising or playing, he would visualise in colour, first where his ball should finish, second how it would travel there, and third, the shot or action he needed to achieve the first two goals. Just like a business sets its targets, then its strategies and then its action plan.

In other words, I found out what most golfers didn't know, that Jack Nicklaus 'played golf backwards' or just like a successful business operates. First, set the target, second, decide the strategy and tactics and third, make an Action Plan to execute it!

So, after the first session and before morning tea, I set out the foundations for the presentation with a session on 'The Challenge of Change' and the importance of overcoming the RCF or the resistance to change factor in order to grow.

Invitation to The 500 Club 1998 Presidents Cup Dinner which was compered by Tony Charlton after a car crash on the way!

Research shows that the older we get the more we resist change, yet to remain relevant we must change or be left behind. A key to being open to change is to be able to think outside the square. It comes from an exercise in 'psycho cybernetics' a 1960s book by Maxwell Maltz in which he states that 'low self-esteem is like driving through life with your hand-brake on'.

His exercise comprises nine dots and illustrates how to solve a problem by 'thinking outside the square' which is what most people draw in their first attempt to solve the problem.

After morning tea, I introduced the professional golfers to the various aspects of leadership of which there are 12 major ingredients: clarity, commitment, courage, confidence, character, communication, active listening, self-esteem, empathy, consistency, trust, and respect. I then outlined Dr Stephen Covey's 'Seven Habits of Highly Successful People' and explained the first habit of proactivity and using your initiative to start change. However, when I outlined the second habit, 'Begin with the end in mind', I explained how the world's most successful golfer, Jack Nicklaus, played golf and illustrated his process on the whiteboard. I thought most of the professional golfers present would have known this, but instead they went very quiet and listened intently.

When this session concluded and I thanked the 30 odd participants for their effort and attention, three of the international professionals from Asia came up to me and asked what I was going to be doing in the afternoon. I replied I was going to walk around The Expo and just have a rest. "Why do you ask?" They said, "Well we wondered if after lunch you'd like to play nine holes with us."

"I'm a 14 handicapper and you are all at least scratch golfers, why would you want to play with me?" They replied, "We found the session enlightening as we hadn't heard anything like that before, especially how Jack Nicklaus played golf and we'd like to pick your brains!"

I agreed, we had an enjoyable nine holes and a good chat. I answered a lot of questions which I was surprised they needed to ask. They explained that the tuition they were receiving to play and work in the golf industry mainly focused on how to play golf technically and physically, not as a mind strategy.

This observation was borne out when I was acting as a judge for the Victorian PGA Professional Golf Shop Awards. To qualify for the Best Pro Shop of the Year Award, golf shop professionals had to submit their own entries. The criteria required included name tags for all staff, golf shop shirts in the same colour for all staff, changing room facilities for females with a full-length mirror, clear pricing on all merchandise, staff product knowledge, cleanliness, lighting, etc.

One year, the finalists were visited by the judges, the Executive Director of the PGA, another board member, Trevor McDonald, and myself. We travelled together in my car and started with the professional at Portsea Golf Club. All the staff were wearing matching polo shirts with name tags, but we couldn't find the female change room, let alone a mirror because that didn't exist. On our way back into the pro shop a couple of members entered and exclaimed, "Why are you guys all dressed up today in matching shirts with name tags?" The professional was duly embarrassed as one would expect. The next visit was to the professional at The National Golf Club at Cape Schanck. We proceeded to look around, as he would have expected to check his entry. We found the ladies change room with a full-length mirror, but also stacked to the ceiling with crates of full soft drink bottles and not one piece of displayed merchandise was priced. We were all shocked as this pro shop had previously won the annual award on two occasions before I became a judge.

Dumbfounded, I asked him if he could explain why there were no prices on any merchandise in his whole pro shop. He replied, "George, we don't believe in putting prices on anything so we can negotiate with the member!" I said tongue in cheek, "Well I had better tell David Jones, Myer and Target as they don't seem to be aware of this new trend." He had obviously been caught out and looked very sheepish about wasting the time of the judges.

This research proved significant and instructive in the way I designed my future business management courses and enabled me to better understand the style, character, leadership, and business acumen of the PGA professionals. It also resulted in being retained by the PGA in Queensland, NSW, and Victoria.

Also, several individual golf clubs appointed me to implement specific training for their golf shop PGA professionals and their staff. These included The National Golf Club, Peninsula Golf and Country Club, Yarra Yarra Golf Club, Portsea Golf Club, Barwon Heads Golf Club, Tallwoods Golf Club and The Royal Sydney Golf Club.

Invitation to my 25 years business anniversary. Caricature by four times Walkley Award artist, George Haddon.

Leadership Lessons:

1. Think in business like Jack Nicklaus played golf.
2. It's good for your mental health to have a hobby.
3. We all can easily become creatures of habit.
4. As Englishman, Francis Bacon said, "Knowledge is Power."
5. Never try to cheat in business awards, as you'll never win

PART 3

THE CORPORATE COACH

CASE HISTORY 1

Grey Advertising Pty Ltd

Chapter 1

Insights in a Bubble

In 1997 I received a surprise call from Ian Herdman, a long-time colleague and advocate. In the years since I had left Bob Jane's Calder Park/Thunderdome, Ian had left Mattingly Advertising and had been appointed as the CEO of the New York based Grey Advertising. I had met Ian back in 1980 when he was Marketing Director for Dunlop Olympic Tyres and became a client for a short time. He then left them after the difficult and unusual merger between Dunlop and Olympic Tyres, and as CEO helped David Mattingly form Mattingly Advertising.

After 11 years at Mattingly, he was disenchanted with the firm's senior leadership and joined the New York based advertising firm Grey as their Australia/Pacific CEO. We hadn't caught up for quite a while and he simply called and said, "Mate, can we catch up for a coffee?" I agreed, but little did I know that day would change my business life forever.

In his new role as CEO, Ian wanted to weld the team in Australia and New Zealand together and had decided to hold a joint company conference at the Rocks in Sydney to create a new corporate culture.

The brilliant documentary 'When we were Kings', had just been released and Ian wanted to use the final two words Muhammad Ali says in the film when he is addressing a university. 'Me/We', was the theme of the conference, meaning the person is inseparable from the team.

The film was about the famous 'Rumble in the Jungle' world heavyweight title fight between Muhammad Ali and George Foreman. It was an epic match in 1974, fought in Zaire, now the Democratic Republic of the Congo.

It was the world title fight where Ali introduced the now famous strategy of 'Rope a Dope', where he lay against the ropes allowing Foreman to waste his energy by continually punching him the stomach while Ali protected his head. Foreman didn't know that in Ali's training his trainers had been dropping heavy medicine balls onto his stomach to build-up his muscles, and after Foreman had gone into muscle 'oxygen debt' and had no strength left, Ali took him apart with punches Foreman couldn't counter.

It was, and still is, a brilliant strategy which is used in sport, and in business to achieve a position of 'stealth power'. We decided to show the film to the conference participants the night before the conference commenced and use the lessons about Me/We the next day in the conference sessions.

At the conclusion of the conference, Ian took me aside and said, "George, you've changed and learnt a lot of high performance leadership stuff. Thanks, that went really well, and we achieved our goal. Look we've got a leadership problem in our New Zealand office in Auckland, and I was wondering if you would be prepared to try and fix it." I said I was prepared to go over and give it a shot provided the Managing Director, who was present at the conference, was happy to approve the program. 'Well, Marco will be in our Sydney office next week so why don't you fly up and discuss the idea with him."

The next week I flew to Sydney, only to find that Marco was just about to leave their Sydney office for the airport that I had just flown into from Melbourne. We met as I checked into the foyer of the office, exchanged pleasantries and he apologised for having to leave, but circumstances back in Auckland demanded he take an earlier flight to New Zealand.

I had learnt something already about him, and his style of leadership, as he hadn't even thought to contact me to let me know his predicament even though he knew he was leaving early and that I was especially flying up to Sydney to meet with him! So, we shared a taxi back to the airport and discussed the situation. He agreed that I could accompany Ian Herdman on a visit to his Auckland office in a couple of weeks, and we departed on the understanding that I would confirm the details.

The trip was illuminating, and I realised after meeting with all the partners, and reflecting on my Sydney meeting experience, that Marco was the primary cause of the leadership problem. In his former role he had been the Creative Director and now needed to act as the Managing Director, resist from micro-managing the team, and be the leader of the firm with more focus on his broader responsibilities.

I had allowed four and a half days to meet all concerned, but it turned out that I really needed two days alone with Marco to help him understand that he needed to change his management style, show more leadership and trust, and delegate more to his other directors and managers.

However, the other directors and managers also had to realise they had to 'catch the ball' and become more accountable and responsible and support the firm in their performance. Everyone I spoke and met with agreed, and Ian and I left Auckland in the weeks prior to Christmas feeling that a lot had been accomplished to solve the problem.

Flying back in a Boeing 747 and sitting in the quiet of the upstairs 'bubble', I was reading, and Ian was dozing. Suddenly Ian opened one eye and said, "George, how could you do in three days what we at Grey couldn't do in three years? You should do this type of work more often as you have a gift!" I thanked him for the compliment and his observation and went back to my book, but his comments stayed with me in my sub-conscious over the Christmas holidays.

We touched down in Melbourne, and before departing agreed that I would return to Auckland at the beginning of February after the Christmas holidays to track the progress of the New Zealand office.

I spent the Christmas break with my children, mowing the lawns, doing some gardening, playing a few games of golf, and generally re-charging my batteries. As February approached, I prepared to fly back to Auckland as planned.

Checking into the Qantas lounge on that Monday morning, I found it was very busy, there was only one seat available to use, and I had a 40-minute wait before my flight was called. The seat was located between a group of 6 guys sitting together and I decided not to take it as one of them may have temporarily vacated it. However, seeing my plight and as the seat was not being used, they beckoned me over to sit down with them, which I did and thanked them.

Being convivial I asked them where they were going, and they replied, Wellington, New Zealand. I flippantly retorted windy Wellington and then possibly too rudely asked, "Are you going for a conference?" "No, we are going to take over a company." "Oh, and who do you work with?' "GE", they responded. I smiled and replied, "Well GE seems to be taking over everything lately." We all laughed, thankfully. Then the leader of the group turned to me and said, "And what do you do?"

I have no idea where my reply came from, other than my sub-conscious, and I quickly replied, "I'm a corporate coach." The group went quiet then he leant forward and replied, "That must be so interesting and satisfying. I'd love to be a corporate coach one day!"

I was stunned by their reaction to my 'off the cuff' answer and hoped they didn't ask me for a business card as mine said 'Management Consultant'. I was saved by Qantas calling my flight to board early and so I breathed a sigh, said goodbye and thanked them for the seat.

I boarded the plane, took my seat, and made a note to call my personal assistant when I arrived, and to change all our corporate stationery and digital communication to read George D Norris, Corporate Coach.

The strategies we had put in place in Auckland were starting to work well and the senior management team was showing more cohesion and teamwork. The whole firm was starting to calm down and the productivity and morale was on the rise.

I spent some more time with Marco who was still finding it difficult to 'let go creatively' and 'throw to grow' or delegate, and this 'All Black' style metaphor seemed to hit home and he 'caught it'.

I returned home to Melbourne satisfied that I had made a difference to a lot of people at Grey, New Zealand, and was very satisfied that I had also embarked on a new career and potentially exciting business future.

Leadership Lessons:

1. If your brand is authentic people remember you.
2. When asked to take on a new project, stretch yourself.
3. Some executives when promoted find it hard to let go.
4. Remember to delegate and 'throw to grow' your people.
5. Love what you do, not like what you do, then 'just do it'!

Chapter 2

Many Shades of Grey

It seemed that New Zealand was progressing well. Ian then asked me to coach and mentor him as well as Paul Gardiner, his General Manager and their CFO, Raja Kanniappan, and manager of their in-house digital creative department, David Crothers.

A few months later, Ian suggested that I might be of help to one of their clients, Colliers Jardine, now Colliers International, a large international commercial real estate firm with offices in all Australian capital cities. He introduced me to Bill McHarg, the Managing Director and his Sales Director, John Morasco. They were interested in me coaching their key sales consultants in the art of sales psychology, creative thinking, time management and leadership.

I researched, created, and developed a program for them and progressively implemented it over a number of months. It was working well and then I was asked to present a morning session to all their sales people at their Glen Waverley office.

It was during this session, while I was explaining the benefits of 'cocooning' and using the three S's of Silence, Stillness and Solitude, which creates an environment of peace and tranquility to open the right brain to enable 'Eureka' or 'Light Bulb' moments, that Bill McHarg asked if he could interrupt and tell a story.

Naturally, I agreed, although it was an unusual request from a client to want to interrupt a presentation, to tell a story, yet in this case it was extremely useful. I had just made a provocative point, that if anyone had an office it was okay to shut the door to create your own cocoon and the three S's. However, it seemed in Australia the culture was that you weren't working, were on the phone to the TAB or having an extra marital affair.

Bill came up to the front and said, "I know you are all finding what George is saying hard to believe, so let me tell you a story because I once did too!"

He began, "A few years ago, I mustered up courage and had lunch in my office with the door closed. I asked my PA to hold all calls and I turned around and looked out the window, while eating my lunch in total quiet. Suddenly I noticed the building opposite our office on the corner which I had walked past often and thought, what a great opportunity. If it was refurbished, that building would be great. It was obvious that the exterior could be enhanced with a better finish and it was set back from the building line with space for this to happen. It could also have an atrium created inside to give it presence. The windows could be modernised, and there could be a turret erected on the roof.

I buzzed my PA and asked her to call the managing director of Capital Finance, who owned the building. She did and put me through to David Greatorex. I explained that I had just been looking at his building and wondered if he had time for a coffee to explain my ideas and thoughts. He suggested I come over when I had finished my lunch.

I explained my vision of enhancement for their building and the rest is history!
The enhancements were made, and Colliers Jardine was given the opportunity to lease space in the newly revamped building on the south west corner of Collins and William Streets, Melbourne where our city office is located today. Thanks George, I couldn't let the opportunity pass without letting you all know that having the courage

to cocoon can enable you to come up with new ideas, suggestions, strategies and plans for the future to enable Colliers Jardine to achieve our vision."

He was given a resounding round of applause, and I couldn't have asked for a more authentic example of how cocooning works to set the climate for creativity and thinking outside the square.

Grey Advertising became an integral part of my new found direction and role as a Corporate Coach. Ian then introduced me to Dr Martin Vogle, a Corporate Mentor, who had been counselling Ian from time to time. Martin and I became good friends and colleagues and I even helped him with advice to grow his business until his untimely death in 2018.

My relationship with Grey continued to flourish for the next 18 months until one day I arrived to meet Ian for a coaching/mentoring session only to find him in the lift foyer with his bags packed, waiting for me to arrive. It was to be his last day as CEO and I later learnt that the chairman in New York felt Ian was gaining too much influence and power. I offered to drive him to his solicitors, and we chatted along the way. He didn't see his demise coming, and was in shock, but then I had been through a similar experience so was able to give him my best advice. Be calm, don't answer calls straight away, use the 24 hour rule, take time to think of the future and work on your golf swing!

Ian found it difficult to handle being a CEO one minute and unemployed the next, as had many other senior executives in the business world. He was and is what I call a business architect. He is a visionary that with the right opportunity can see far into the future and is prone to often get ahead of himself.

My friendship with Ian now covers 42 years and I will never forget his thoughtfulness in giving me the opportunity to become the Corporate Coach and Management Mentor I am today.

I continued to work with some of the remaining executives at Grey and helped the CFO, Raja Kanniappan, and the Digital Manager, David Crothers, to keep focused in the aftermath that followed Ian's departure.

Paul Gardiner then became CEO of Grey Worldwide, as it was eventually rebranded, and the powerful President of the AFL club, Melbourne, the oldest football club in the world. It's ironic that Ian was his original mentor at Mattingly and then asked him to come and work with him at Grey, but as they say, 'that's life in the fast lane'.

Leadership Lessons:

1. Remember when you're referred 'you've already got the job'.
2. Cocooning is very powerful, but you need to know how to do it.
3. It's critical to create an environment 'to think outside the square'.
4. Stories help to accelerate and confirm understanding and change.
5. We can all be a rooster one minute and a feather duster the next.

CASE HISTORY 2

BMW Australia Ltd

Chapter 1

The Beauty in the Beast

During this time, I was asked to become a board member of the Australian Marketing Institute. I had been a member for several years and this gave me the opportunity to enhance the institute, and work closely with the Executive Director, Keith Richardson.

When at an AMI member function, I received a call from Ray Ellis, the Managing Director of The Event Centre. Ray wanted to know if I was interested and available to present an Australia wide series of business breakfast seminars for one of his clients and to follow each seminar with nine holes of golf with each group of four participants.

Apparently, he had approached a number of PGA golfers who were interested to play the nine holes, but none were able to present the breakfast business briefings. I didn't have to think twice, and agreed.

The client was Colonial First State, one of Australia's leading wealth management groups.

The series started in Perth at Joondalup Golf Resort, then travelled to Adelaide, then to Cairns in Far North Queensland, followed by Brisbane and concluded in Melbourne.

The former, well known 3AW Breakfast host, John Blackman was the MC chosen to deliver some humour and I was the serious corporate coach/speaker and 'golf coach'. The concept worked really well, and the Colonial First State agents learnt valuable business information, some new golf tips I had researched, and enjoyed their golf on the course.

When we arrived in Brisbane to play at the Indooroopilly Golf Club, I met Lori Vanston, the Training Manager for Colonial in one of the groups playing golf. She mentioned that she had received excellent feedback on my Breakfast Business presentations and suggested we catch up when we were back in Melbourne.

After the final presentation in Melbourne, I called her, and we agreed to meet at her office in the city. However, on the morning of our scheduled meeting I received a distressed call from her telling me to cancel our meeting as she had that morning been retrenched along with a number of other managers and staff. It appeared that Colonial First State had merged with the State Bank of New South Wales and the new Managing Director, Peter Smedley, had made the decision to cut the total Training Department and utilise the State Bank's Training Department.

A few days later, when the dust had settled, I met Lori for a coffee, offered my support and a 'shoulder to cry on' or 'someone to watch over her' if it was needed.

Lori was a very professional and intense lady. She was married with a couple of children, and revelled in the stimulation of her business role. Prior to working with Colonial First State, she had a been appointed in a senior training role with General Motors Holden.

We kept in touch over the next 18 months, met for the odd coffee and Christmas drink, and then in July 1998, she called and asked me to join her for lunch. I agreed and she asked me to join her at the bistro at BMW Head Office. "Why the bistro at BMW?" She happily replied that she had just been appointed National Professional Development Manager for BMW Australia Ltd.

We arranged a date and time and I drove out to their Head Office in Springvale Road, Mulgrave. Back in the 1980s, Ron Meacham had built this office after he arrived from South Africa.

On arrival Lori met me after I had cleared security and we went to the bistro, selected our lunch, then settled down at a corner table. During lunch she mentioned that BMW was embarking on a World Best Practice Quality Management Business Program and wondered if I knew of a corporate coach that would be interested in being appointed to implement the program in Australia.

It took a few seconds for it to sink in that she was asking me if I was interested in applying and to present my case to the selection panel. I quickly said, "Yes!"

After lunch she invited me to meet the National Leader of the Program, David Williams. The name sounded familiar, and as soon as we met we both realised that we had previously met when David was employed by Renault Australia when Renault was a client of mine for five years in the late 1970s. It's a small world!

David explained that the program was called QMA, short for Quality Management for Autohaus or Assurance as I called it, and it was designed to be implemented by BMW worldwide. He had been appointed to lead the program and asked me a few questions regarding my experience in working with business performance diagnostic tools.

I replied that when employed by Caltex Oil (Australia), and for some years later, I had extensive experience in training and coaching up to 30 businesses using similar diagnostic tools and providing retail improvement recommendations. I couldn't believe my luck, as I never thought all the training experience and knowledge I had gained at Caltex Oil would again be of use in my career in a similar way.

We concluded our informal chat and I left BMW with the knowledge that Lori would contact me shortly to arrange the next step. This she did and she informed me that I was one of several people who would be invited to present to the selection panel. Apparently, I would have a 30-minute window where I could make a presentation and then answer questions. The panel would consist of Derek Hale, the HR Director, David Williams and the Financial Director, Jeff Yapp.

I set about researching BMW's position in the world and found that in the USA they had slipped down to position 100 in the Fortune 500 list of companies based on their customer satisfaction ratings, with Mercedes Benz at No. 1. In addition, I had not been favourably impressed with the service of my BMW some years ago, when I had paid for the air conditioner to be serviced only to have it break down a few weeks later, and then discover it had not been serviced at all.

So, I prepared my evidence and an appropriate presentation and gave it my best effort, making sure that I spoke softly and slowly, wore a dark suit, white shirt, and conservative tie, just as Lori had suggested.

I was successful and appointed the first QMA coach in Australia. The second coach was a former New Zealander, Brian Clark, who specialised in organising and leading business tours to companies of excellence around the world.

I received the news in July 1998 while at home and excitedly told my son, Campbell, who at the time was living with me while he was studying for his degree in Mechanical Engineering at Melbourne University. He congratulated me and said, "Dad, what happens now?" I replied that I would be travelling to Germany to BMW in Munich for an intensive three-week World QMA coaching course. He then asked, "How will they advise you?" Having some fun with him I replied, "They will probably send a letter saying you will attend this course in Munich!" He laughed, not believing my suggestion. Well about two weeks later I received a letter in the post from Karl-Heinz Ebeling, the World QMA Coach saying simply, "You will attend the QMA Course in Munich on Monday 7 September 1998."

I laughed to myself, amazed that my light-hearted, off-hand comment on the wording and letter had come true and raced up the stairs to show Campbell that what I had predicted had come true. We both had a laugh as he thought I was joking, and I had to admit I had been.

So, the wheels were set in motion for three weeks of intensive study in Munich with 25 other QMA Coaches from around the world.

My two daughters had both studied German at school and gave me a crash course in the language to help me survive the experience. In addition, my youngest daughter, Melinda, contacted the Kühn family who lived in Trostberg, and told them I would be visiting. They then invited me to stay with them for the second weekend which we would have at leisure.

The Kuhn family had hosted Melinda for a three-month student exchange with their daughter Babette Kühn, so I looked forward to meeting and staying with the family who had played 'pseudo parents' to her.

It was a long, tiring but comfortable business class flight with Qantas to Singapore then Lufthansa to Munich and by the time I arrived at the Radisson University Hotel in Munich I was quite exhausted. However, my adrenalin was high, and after checking in I decided to go for a long walk to see my surroundings and get some exercise. I walked for about 90 minutes before deciding to return to my hotel. The only problem was I had lost my bearings and had no idea where I was or where my hotel was located. An interesting experience in a new city on the other side of the world!

I asked a few people as I walked, but most spoke only German and the crash course in German my daughters had given me did not prove to be much help. I finally had the good fortune to ask a guy whose English was good, but he was also a visitor and had no idea where the hotel was either. However, he suggested I ask one of the young attendants at the next service station as he knew that young German university students worked weekends at the petrol stations.

I found one a few blocks further on, and sheepishly asked the attendant if he could help me and give me directions back to my hotel. To my utter embarrassment he smiled and said, "Oh, you're right behind it. Just go up to that road and turn left and it's about 200 metres from the next intersection." I thanked him and smiled to myself feeling guilty for walking so far, a bit dumb for getting lost, but impressed that I had actually started walking back to the hotel without knowing it. It was a good, self-deprecating story to tell a few of the BMW/QMA participants when we met for the first time the next day.

The course started with an insightful introduction by the BMW World QMA Leader, Martin Gerecke, who then introduced the BMW/QMA World Coach, Karl-Heinz Ebeling, who was even more insightful.

There was an international cross section of participants from Italy, France, Germany, Holland, England, Brazil and of course the two of us from Australia making a total of 25.

Leadership Lessons:

1. Fate can be an amazing phenomenon sometimes.
2. Helping people can be a cathartic, rewarding experience.
3. Remember the past because the future has opportunities.
4. Mirror your dress style as well as your voice style with clients.
5. When you're lost, be courageous and think creatively.

Chapter 2

Breathless in Bavaria

Martin had made some interesting comments in his introduction, advocating that if BMW didn't change the way their retailers were doing business they would be bought out by another powerful company. It appeared that while BMW was No.1 in the world for research and development, they were well down in the lower ranks for providing consistent customer service, and this was eroding their position in world markets.

The course opened with each of the participants giving a brief background profile and this set the foundation for an interesting, insightful, and inspiring three weeks.

The topics, or more aptly described, subjects ranged from Group Dynamics, High Performance Psychology, Change Management and Effective Communication. We role played potential real-life situations with dealer principals introducing the QMA program process and focused on overcoming resistance to change with management styles.

Karl-Heinz made an interesting comment in his opening session which he repeated throughout the intense three-week Harvard style course, when in answer to a participant's question he forcefully said, "In my experience the dealer principals try to get the QMA coach to do a lot of the QMA work to lessen their involvement. However, you must resist this pressure and let them know I will not work for you!"

It was an interesting 'German Way'. I believe in saying in our

'Australian Way' I will work with you but not for you, as you and your people need to own the policies, processes, and procedures, not me!

The group got on well, and we enjoyed meeting at nights for group meals when we had time between completing projects and studying. The French and Italian participants seemed to especially enjoy interaction with Team Australia with our quaint accent and weird sense of humour.

On the first weekend I was met at the hotel by Mr and Mrs Kühn who showed me around Munich and gave me an insight into its history. They also showed me many of the places my daughter had visited with their daughter, Babette and even took me to a lake where the girls had skated when it had been frozen. We dined together on that Saturday evening before spending the night at their place and meeting Babette's grandmother who they called Oma in German.

The next day we visited Salzburg and they showed me many beautiful sights including Mozart's residence in the market square. It was then time to catch the train back to Munich in the afternoon and prepare myself for another five days of BMW/QMA education. Unexpectedly, when saying goodbye to Gesa and Eberhard Kuhn, I felt particularly emotional. It was difficult to explain, other than to think my past had come to seize me, in that I was saying goodbye to the pseudo parents of my daughter for three months and that I had experienced a special relationship and moving experience I had not expected to feel.

The train trip back to Munich was very cathartic, and a beautiful one, as the scenery with the mountains and snow took my breath away.

The second week of the course was more intensive than the first, and it was interesting to witness the way the various personalities were starting to be exposed.

Karl-Heinz kept up his focus and feelings, which were quite assertive at times, and could often see that some of the participants were even offended or threatened. Two additional lecturers arrived from Italy, and they focused on the psychology of communication and I learnt for the first time that 93% of all communication is unspoken verbally and only 7% is the actual words.

The exercises we participated in proved this conclusively, as did the additional knowledge of VAK or visual, auditory, and kinetic language. In other words, see, hear, and touch (or feel).

I was receiving and absorbing some great knowledge and was unaware at the time would be referring to, and using for many years to come as a corporate coach and management mentor.

The next weekend I had planned to travel by train to Vienna, meet Janet Hider-Smith, the glider pilot friend who had settled in Vienna with her husband Wolfgang, and stay the night with them.

Brian Clark, the other Australian QMA coach, asked if he could join me on the train trip as he would be by himself.

We booked a first-class cabin and took in the magnificent mountain vistas and stunning landscapes along the way to Vienna. I had a surprise for Brian when we arrived, because there waiting beside her British racing green BMW Z3 sports car was none other than the diminutive blonde, Janet Hider-Smith, beaming away and seeing me for the first time in about five years. Being her welcoming and hospitable self, she made room for Brian in the small back seat, and we spent the night with her and her husband at a winery overlooking Vienna.

We all met up the next morning and had a traditional Viennese morning tea before catching the afternoon train back to Munich. It was a great mental break from two weeks of nearly non-stop studying, and we both welcomed the much needed, rest and recreation.

The final week was even more intensive, if that was possible and we were all becoming mentally tired and irritable, and possibly becoming somewhat homesick. On the Wednesday night my mobile rang at about 2am and woke me with a start. I immediately thought the worst, yet it happened to be Ian Mannix, the ABC Radio Program Director in Melbourne wanting to talk to me about a potential part in the John Faine morning show. He had been listening to me on 3MP with my 'Shots of Inspiration' vignettes and thought I might be able to give the program a business feel. We agreed to meet when I returned, and he apologised profusely when he realised I was answering my mobile in Munich.

On the second last day, Martin Gerecke asked each one of the QMA coaches to give feedback on the course and take the opportunity to ask a question. When it was my turn, I commented on the valuable knowledge we had been provided, then asked my question.

I explained that I had been appointed to implement a similar, yet different program for Jetset's retail network throughout Australia. They had been placed in an embarrassing position as their own head office staff of over 400 people had been out of step with their retail network and forced to implement the same program of consistent customer service themselves. So, I asked Martin the important and fundamental question, "When did BMW Head Office plan to implement the QMA program so they were leading the retail network worldwide by example?"

He was very interested in the point, and as the Friday morning was at leisure, arranged for me to meet the World Divisional Zone Manager for QMA for Australia so I could explain my strategy for BMW to benefit from the Jetset Travel model and experience. Later that afternoon I received a message asking me to meet with the BMW executive and suggested a time, but Brian wanted to tag along again and join me, and it was awkward for me again in the circumstances to say, "No!"

The meeting started well, then Brian took over the meeting and it became mostly about the business he was conducting. I was disappointed, but as time went by, found out that he would often let his passion take over at BMW meetings.

Leadership Lessons:

1. Leaders and coaches must resist 'doing it' for others.
2. When you are giving advice make sure to use empathy.
3. Communication is 93% unspoken with only 7% being the words.
4. If you can, mirror your audience using VAK communication skills.
5. Humility and self-awareness are critical attributes for relationships.

Chapter 3

The Benefits from the Brand

The Munich BMW Four Cylinder building was an interesting construction in that it had been built from the top down and jacked up as it was built. It was a very revolutionary technique at the time, and I daresay for the future.

On my return the next day, Martin asked me how the meeting went, so I replied with 'sensitive diplomacy' which was difficult for me to do.

The three weeks enabled me to learn from a number of significant, awkward and distressing behavioural science events that taught me valuable lessons in leadership.

The first happened on our trip to Dusseldorf to visit one of the newer and larger BMW/QMA Dealerships. I noticed that each salesperson worked in tandem with a sales secretary. The salesperson sold the car, and the sales secretary completed all the accounting and accessory details. I asked our German host why this happened, and he told me that in Germany they had researched that salespeople are 'right brained people oriented' and their weakness is they often don't record the accounting, accessory details and prices correctly as this is a 'left brain task oriented' skill. Wow! I just learnt something that I could initiate and use in Australia in the future.

The second happened when we were on our way to Regensburg, some 125 kilometres from Munich, to visit another smaller German BMW/QMA dealership. Early that morning, Karl-Heinz, the QMA

Head Coach drove Brian and me in his BMW 325i station wagon to visit this BMW dealership. We started out at a sedate pace till he reached the Autobahn then he quickly accelerated up to 200 kph. I had never been in a car going this fast for so long and I was somewhat tense. This was not helped when he kept turning around to talk to us in the back seat!

To relieve my stress, I decided to call my office in Melbourne as the time difference worked out well and in answer to my PA's question of, "Where are you at the moment?" I answered in an anxious voice, "In Karl-Heinz's BMW travelling at 200 kph, and he is looking at me on the phone talking to you!" He got the subtle message.

The third was the heritage for the BMW logo and what it represented. It was revealed that BMW, which stands for Bavarian Motor Works, was originally created to build aeroplane engines in 1922. The logo roundel is in fact two propeller blades against the blue sky. Not a riveting idea, but what has turned out to be a lasting logo for a car manufacturer that challenged Mercedes-Benz when they were losing their way in the 1960s and 1970s and so gained a foothold in the prestige car market with a destiny to be a market leader forever.

The final session in the QMA three-week course was very interesting as each one of the participants was asked to give a summary of the three weeks they had experienced.

A point of contention had kept entering my mind. When we, as BMW/QMA coaches had implemented the program in a retail business, over say a two year period, who was going to have the role of maintaining the Quality Management Assurance program after that time? So, when it came to my turn to give my summary, I gave what I thought was a good overview of the course and said, "I have a question that is bothering me. Once a dealership is accredited in BMW/QMA, who will help them to carry on the program once the QMA coach departs?"

It was at this time, that as a finishing touch to my son's question many months prior, Karl-Heinz Ebeling looked at me and said, "The BMW Area Manager." I replied, "Well for them to maintain the QMA program, it assumes that they will be as qualified as we are, for them to maintain its focus on excellence."

The real German personality in Karl-Heinz then was on show for all to see and hear when he loudly and bluntly exclaimed, "What do you want George, BMW to provide you with an old age pension!" I chose to not play a backhand to that powerful serve and let the ball pass for an uncontested German winner!

The fact of the matter was, that BMW had not realised that unless their Area Manager had the time, the inclination and the knowledge to ensure its on-going implementation, the QMA program, as brilliant as it was, would eventually die and fall away. Hence, it would become redundant instead of remaining viable and vibrant as a positive strategic business initiative.

BMW/QMA Diploma of Quality Management from Munich

Nevertheless, we returned home to Australia much the wiser for the knowledge, experience, skills, and friends we had met and made during the three weeks in Munich. As Ian Herdman, the CEO of Grey Advertising at the time said after I was appointed as BMW's first QMA Coach in Australia, "George this will be the most significant appointment of your business career." It was.

After debriefing with David Williams, I was asked to sell my beautiful Honda Legend Coupe as BMW wanted the coaches to drive BMWs. After some serious negotiations they agreed to put the QMA coaches on the BMW Management Car Plan, where we would be able to virtually drive the car of our choice, changing them over every six months. BMW would totally own the cars, service, repair, register and insure them and we, as coaches would only put in the fuel. I was proud of my negotiating skills after securing that wonderful arrangement.

The next critical exercise was for BMW to match up BMW dealer principals with coaches. My first dealership was Bruce Lynton BMW in Southport, Queensland. Bruce was the first exclusive BMW dealership appointed in Australia. He had left Sydney as a car racing driver and had married the star of the water ski review at Surfers Paradise, the lovely Margaret. They had two children who both worked in the business, Beric, as General Manager, and Chelsea who worked in an administration and development role.

I met Bruce in November 1998, and two and a half years later they became the first accredited QMA dealers in Australia.

It was a good match. Coincidentally Bruce and I were around the same age, height, hair style, golf handicap, had children of similar age and our businesses had been operating about the same length of time. We soon became good friends and still are. He eventually asked me to mentor his son, Beric so he could take over the business to allow him to retire. I worked for the Lyntons for 18 years, and they became the longest established client of my new business.

BMW/QMA Dealership Accreditation Trophy replica presented to QMA Coaches

I was allocated another six dealerships and in order they were Robert and Dean Kurz at BMW Caloundra, Nat Zanardo at BMW Canterbury, Phil Rodriguez at BMW Silvania, Chris Stillwell at BMW Brighton, Brian Joseph at Rolfe Classic BMW in Canberra and Greg Duncan at Autohaus Classic BMW. All became accredited after much effort, energy, patience and resilience with the exception of BMW Canberra whose QMA leader departed unexpectedly and the Dealer Principal, Brian Joseph, decided not to continue in the program as I believe he was paranoid BMW, and I would catch him out in some strange way. His attitude reminded me of my Caltex mentor's great saying, "You can always tell a paranoid except you can't tell them much!"

I was also allocated BMW Sydney at Rushcutters Bay. This was BMW's largest dealership in the southern hemisphere and was housed in the converted Australia Post Handling Exchange. The Dealer Principal was also paranoid that the QMA program was out to get him, so he kept BMW at arm's length by turning over three QMA coaches so they wouldn't make him transparent and vulnerable. He unfortunately had what I would call 'small man syndrome' and was a bully to all his managers as well as me and the next two QMA coaches appointed to this dealership.

We all tried hard to implement the QMA program with him, but after his Parts Manager took me to lunch and asked for my help, he asked BMW for another coach as he thought that I had taken the Parts Manager to lunch to spy on him. However, the experience taught me another powerful coaching tool to help other clients, and especially myself. Coaching makes the person being coached 'transparent and vulnerable' and some people can't cope.

Originally my agreement with BMW, which I thought might last three years, eventually lasted 12 years and in that time I had the good fortune to drive 28 new BMW cars of all models. I worked with many colleagues, made many friends, and learnt many valuable lessons along with new skills and knowledge. David Williams kindly wrote an emotional testimonial in my first book 'Winning with Wisdom' and we have kept in touch all these years.

Glass Apple presented to the Author in New York

Chapter 3 The Benefits from the Brand

I continued working as Beric Lynton's management mentor in Southport, and as corporate coach to all his department managers at BMW and Land Rover until they sold the business in 2018.

Of course, I kept playing golf with his father, Bruce, as often as possible together with his many golfing friends he had introduced me to over the years. These included a charming Scottish gentleman, Stephen Fenton, with a golfing pedigree from Carnoustie and a professional's swing to match.

It was on one of my early trips to visit him that another amazing coincidence happened. After I had boarded my Ansett plane for the Gold Coast the well known, back to back premiership Adelaide Crows AFL Coach, Malcolm Blight, boarded last and sat opposite me.

He disembarked first and I never saw him again at the airport. I was picked up by my hire car driver and dropped off at my hotel at Broad Beach. After checking in and unpacking, Bruce called to say he was downstairs waiting to collect me and my golf clubs for a game at Southport Golf Club, as my business at his dealership started the next day.

I changed, went down to meet him, and found sitting beside him none other than Malcolm Blight. I was again speechless, as I had been so often in my life, and mentioned I had sat opposite him on the flight. It turned out that he was a neighbour of Bruce, and they often played golf together. We had a great day, a very interesting discussion, and became friends playing often together.

Then Malcolm was unexpectedly appointed Senior Coach of the Melbourne AFL club, St Kilda. That came as a shock as he had confided in us he wouldn't because of their off field culture. We would play golf each Thursday on his one day off, at my club Yarra Yarra, where Malcolm was a reciprocal member from The Grange in Adelaide.

He was then shocked when, after being appointed, gained seven top players because of his coaching talents, a $1 million sponsorship from Pura Milk and an increase of the membership by 23% because of his appointment, he was terminated without notice because he supposedly didn't have a 'business plan'. Not the way to treat an AFL legend!

We have kept in touch all these years and have a game now and again when we can fit one in. Life certainly has 6 degrees of separation!

Leadership Lessons:

1. Right brain salespeople need left brain detail assistance.
2. We are all a bi-product of our environment at 200 kph.
3. It's important to know the heritage and culture of a brand.
4. Building lasting relationships is an investment not a cost.
5. Be resilient, focused, and with respect for other people's opinions.

CASE HISTORY 3

Radio 3MP 1377

Chapter 1

A Shot of Inspiration

In 1998, I achieved another lifelong ambition.

Ever since I watched Michael Parkinson in his interview series, I had a desire to be involved in the media. I had done my radio apprenticeship, so to speak, many years before with my weekly chats on 3CS Colac with Doug Jennings and had often thought I would like to be on radio again.

Then 'it' happened. One morning while walking our corgi, Cindy, I started to think about what I could do to promote my business, and at the same time achieve my goal. An idea popped into my head. Perhaps I could present a thought for the day on radio to inspire people to achieve their goals or their ambitions. The problem was I didn't know anyone in radio, so I parked the idea and finished the walk.

That afternoon I played golf in the twilight 'nine and dine' competition at Yarra Yarra, and later saw my colleague and close friend, Dick Wicks, 'The Magnetic Man', and went over to say hello. He was sitting at a table with a large group, and in his usual social way, took the trouble to introduce me to his guests. One of his guests was Dean Matters, the breakfast announcer on Radio 1377 3MP, who I incidentally listened to each morning. When Dick introduced me to Dean I simply remarked, "Hi Dean, it's lovely to meet the man I listen to each morning. You've got a great voice!" He was gracious and flattered and I left the group to enjoy the evening. I really meant what I had said because he did have a superb voice rich in timbre for radio.

The next day I cheekily thought why not ask Dick if he could set up a meeting with Dean to discuss my idea of a radio spot. Dick thought the idea had merit and offered to call Dean to float the idea. Dick called me back within minutes to say that Dean was keen to meet me and would call me after finishing his broadcasting commitments that morning. He duly called as promised and we arranged to meet that afternoon.

We met at my house, and I outlined my concept to which he immediately replied, "George, we have many listeners who often call in for some inspiration, and the segment you're suggesting could be just what we need. I have an idea, why don't you write three demonstration one-minute segments which we in the industry call vignettes. Then you can come down to the station and record them. I will set up a time in one of the recording studios with Peter O'Callaghan, the Production Manager, and we'll see how they sound." He then went on to say, "We could call them say, 'A Shot of Inspiration.'"

I wrote three pilot segments, we recorded them, the station loved them, and so started a two-year relationship. The interesting thing was they thought they could be positioned at 8.45am daily to hopefully stop listeners from switching over to the news on 774 ABC radio.

They also taught me the power of 'white space' in a one-minute segment. If I filled up the one minute with copy, the listeners wouldn't 'get the meaning of the message', so I had to learn the lesson that 'less is more' when it comes to radio communication. It seems that not many advertisers understand, that if they 'fill their spot' with talk and noise, the listener feels bombarded and the message loses meaning.

I learnt the lesson and went on to record a weekly 'Shot of Inspiration' for two years until the radio station was bought by new owners.

After taking over, the new owner asked me to change the format so I suggested a short version of the successful Michael Parkinson format where I could interview successful 'captains of industry' for a three-minute segment. This was agreed and was to become the new format for the year 2000. I set about interviewing some interesting leaders, only to be told some months later that the radio station was going to change its format again to only music, and 'Moments in Management' would finish.

These two years were very rewarding, and over 250 companies contacted me after hearing my vignettes or 'Shots of Inspiration' and those calls resulted in a number of new clients and corporate presentations. It was a win/win for me and for the station.

In addition, I was often asked if I had thought of writing a book so after finishing my time at 3MP 1377 I re-wrote the 200 radio scripts and published my first book in 2004 titled 'Winning with Wisdom' which contained all the scripts. The first edition hardback format sold out and was reprinted in a soft cover format which is still available today. Little did I realise that my career in radio was just beginning.

Leadership Lessons:

1. Walking in solitude can generate great ideas.
2. It never hurts to flatter people if it's true.
3. Your contacts will always help you if you ask.
4. It's courageous to chase down your dreams.
5. We don't realise how many people need inspiration.

CASE HISTORY 4

Melbourne and Hawthorn AFL clubs

Chapter 1

Coaching the Coaches

In 2002 I re-married after being single for 16 years, so I guess it can't be said that I rushed into marriage again. We combined a honeymoon with a conference in New York where I represented the Australian BMW/QMA coaches. We then flew to Paris, Edinburgh and London before sailing on the QEII from Southampton to New York, courtesy of my ex-manager's wife who was the Australian Manager for Cunard, and then on to Hawaii before returning to Australia. It was the trip of a lifetime.

After being married for 15 months, I needed a heart bypass. The surgery was a success and I called my wife after seven days in hospital and excitedly told her that I was allowed to go home.

In 2003, some exciting business opportunities also came my way. Firstly, Neale Daniher, the recently appointed Senior Coach of Melbourne Football Club, had relocated from Fremantle where he had been mentored by Ric Charlesworth, the well-known Olympic Ladies hockey coach. After moving to Melbourne, he found it too difficult to catch up with Ric in Perth and asked the CEO of Melbourne FC, Ray Ellis, if he could recommend a mentor in Melbourne. Ray kindly recommended me, as I had been mentoring him for some years.

Ray gave Neale my mobile number and we decided to meet at a restaurant in Fitzroy Street, St Kilda, not far from the Junction Oval where Melbourne FC trained at that time. We had coffee and a general background chat, and he said he would consider me for the role.

He then surprised me by saying, "Look George, I've got to go back now to what will be an aggressive media conference. Do you have any thoughts on how I should handle it?" Melbourne was going through a torrid period with some poor performances, and this was a good test case for me.

I replied, "Neale, there are three things I would advise you to do. Smile all the while, keep your chin up and look directly at the camera, and only give the media good news." He replied, "Why, what will happen?" "Well, they only want bad news, they really want you to be distressed and they want to be in control of you. If you do as I suggest they will stop hounding you and pack up and leave."

We both left and went our ways with Neale saying he would get back to me. Later that afternoon, around 4pm, he called me. I asked, "How did you go?" "Well, I did what you suggested and you were right, they stopped, packed up and left. You're hired. When can we meet to start our mentoring sessions?"

So began a close business relationship that has lasted until 2018 when Neale was sadly diagnosed with Motor Neurone Disease.

While Assistant Coach at Fremantle, Neale had instituted a new way of recording AFL game statistics and was a very clever IT specialist. He was also a 'stress carrier', as I was informed by Chris Fagan, the Melbourne FC Manager, as he took every loss personally, and found it difficult to let go and divorce himself from the loss.

Then at one session, Neale asked me to observe his performance on match day in the rooms prior, in the coach's box, in the rooms at half time and after the match. I was happy to oblige and the next week went to the MCG for their match against St Kilda.

I observed Neale's performance in the rooms before the game where he had given a stirring address. Then, as the players were running down the race onto the ground, he came up to me in his laconic way and asked, "Ok George, what did you think?"

He had made mention of a lot of things in his address, so I replied, "Let me ask you Neale, what do you think the players are focusing on as they run onto the ground?" "Mate, I've got no idea." I said, "Well, you could be in a lot of trouble." He then asked, "Why do you say that?"

I replied, "Young footballers like them can probably only remember at most three things of importance, so I suggest you'd be better to focus on less volume of strategic information on match day to get a better performance and result."

I then mentioned the lesson I'd learnt on radio at 3MP that 'less is more'!

Later I observed a further surprising communication experience in the coach's box. The situation became very stressful during the first half and I noticed that four times Neale, in the heat of battle, spoke to the 'runners' by phone to give instructions to players. The runners would leave the phone and take off, however Neale continued to give them further critical instructions, but in fact he was talking to no-one, as they had gone onto the ground.

This situation happened four more times in the second half and when I pointed it out to the General Manager Football, Danny Corcoran, he mentioned it happened often in stressful situations.

Melbourne won by 1 point, but I thought it could have been more with faster moves and all of them actioned!

On the Monday, I debriefed Neale as requested. He was naturally in disbelief that this had happened and asked me what I thought would be the best solution, because in the heat of battle, it's easy to lose your poise and your self-awareness.

I had already given it some serious thought and cheekily replied, "Neale you need a simple process that the runners must implement in the heat of battle. I suggest that you tell them not to leave the phone until you say GO! He laughed and said, "George what a great idea!"

He was, we both worked out, mainly a left-brain task oriented person and not a right brain people oriented person. On a scale of 0 to 100 he thought he was about 25% along the scale, midway through the task oriented left brain skill section, when he thought he needed to be about 75% along the scale with more right brain people skills.

We set about working on these right brained people skills over that year and the next, so much so he was given a new nickname by the media, 'The Reverend', due to his new found confidence and people communication skills.

During my early time with Neale in 2003, I received a phone call from Ian Dicker, the President of the Hawthorn AFL Club. I had written to him prior to being asked to mentor Neale, and he was interested in me mentoring their Senior Coach, Peter Schwab, mainly in communication and presentation skills.

I mentioned that I had just started mentoring Neale Daniher, but I would ask his thoughts on me mentoring the senior coach of another AFL club at the same time. I indicated that it would be acceptable since I conducted all my coaching sessions on a strictly 'doctor/patient' confidential basis.

I met Neale the following week and mentioned that I been asked to also work with Peter yet reassured him that all our meetings and discussions would be strictly confidential. He thought for no more than 30 seconds, then to his credit said, "George, that's fine."

I called Ian Dicker the next day, told him of Neale's answer, and he agreed to set up a meeting between Peter and myself for a chat.

We met at Georgio's restaurant in Malvern, chatted for an hour or so, and after a couple of more meetings, Peter agreed to appoint me as his mentor.

Peter was happy to work with me as he felt I had some sensible things to suggest, and he warmed to my help as the first few meetings progressed. Hawthorn was going through a tough time that season, and by meeting at Peter's home I was able to 'unlock some doors in his mind' to assist him.

When I arrived for the first of my fortnightly sessions, I met his lovely wife Jenny and their two boys, William and Michael. I also observed the many photos of their daughter, Emily.

The following sessions were important in our relationship and I was able to challenge Peter about where he could change. He adjusted his communication style and focus, and Hawthorn won the next 10 games!

Peter gave me feedback that he valued someone unbiased listening to him. He could download his thoughts, ideas and frustrations and receive advice on matters related to how he was performing in his role as a coach, and in his relationships with the players, staff and administration.

He was also interested in feedback on what he was doing well, what initiatives he could consider implementing, and how he communicated with all these people, especially the media.

Later in the season he invited me to hear his address on match day and appreciated the suggestions I gave him to better connect with and influence the players' actions and performance. He found that he also received benefit from being helped to see himself, and his abilities, in a more positive light.

Mid-way through the 2004 season, Peter was concerned with the communication and reaction time of his instructions regarding player moves during games. He then asked me to join him in the coach's box to observe proceedings and to go down to the players' area on the boundary line and observe proceedings as well.

I observed in the box that not only were player moves being considered in an urgent, stressful state, also I thought that the assistant coaches were trying to be noticed and impress Peter as Senior Coach.

Later I told him it resembled how I thought an airport control tower would be at the busiest times of landings and take offs, but with no process in place to prioritise the importance of decision making.

After half time, at Peter's request, I positioned myself at the end of the boundary line players' box to see what was happening. I observed some amazing and unprofessional processes for an AFL club. Peter would send moves to the main person with the earphones, and he would write them on yellow Post-It notes and stick them on his bare leg!

Then suddenly, a strong wind blew them off his leg and over the ground and under the seats, and he and the runners started desperately looking for them. After what seemed like an eternity, they thought they had recovered them all and started trying to work out what to do!

I was shocked that this was the process which a leading AFL club would use to make strategic moves to try and win games. This was especially so, given the serious financial consequences associated with running a significant AFL business, turning over many millions of dollars, let alone putting the coach's position in jeopardy.

When I debriefed Peter, he too was shocked as he had not previously 'audited' this area of the coach's communication methods, trusting those in charge to act responsibly, professionally and with accountability.

As a result, he implemented a new process in the coach's box to highlight the importance and priority of player moves, and a new professional process to record player moves and quicker action from the players' box.

Near the end of 2004, Peter told me he had selected seven 'Young Hawks' to become the next leadership group and asked me to implement a leadership program with them. They were Sam Mitchell, Luke Hodge, Michael Osborne, Chance Bateman, Campbell Brown, Nathan Lonie and Nick Rees.

I set about conducting group sessions and showing leadership videos by David Parkin and a couple of other eminent coaches of Australian teams, Joyce Brown, and Tim Sheens. Each player would then meet me every two weeks for a session of about 30 to 45 minutes and we would work on his strengths, weakness, opportunities, and threats, and set some goals to achieve.

It was a stimulating leadership program and I received good feedback from all players on how it had developed them as leaders. In fact, Ian Dicker said to me a year or so after Peter had departed, that he thought 'The Young Hawks' Leadership Program was the most significant initiative that Peter had implemented in his tenure as Senior Coach of Hawthorn.

Premiership winning evidence has since proven that was true!

Leadership Lessons:

1. Adversity can give you strength to draw on lessons learnt.
2. In the heat of battle, processes protect your performance.
3. To be effective, left brain Leaders need right brain soft skills.
4. Corporate coaches must work as in a doctor/patient relationship.
5. Stories can help quick understanding, acceptance, and change.

CASE HISTORY 5

Radio Magic 1278

Chapter 1

The Life Coach

As my first book 'Winning with Wisdom' had just come off the press in September 2005, we decided to take the opportunity at the book launch to also unveil the portrait of me painted by Neil Wyatt.

A client, the flamboyant Tony Rabah was a part owner of the new restaurant, 'Feddish' in Melbourne's Federation Square. To promote his new restaurant, he offered to host the book launch and unveiling of the painting.

I asked Peter O'Callahan, the previous Production Manager at 3MP, who was now Production Manager at Magic 1278, 3AW's sister station, and who was also hosting their morning show, to act as MC. I also asked Neale Daniher if he would be the guest of honour and guest speaker to launch the book and unveil the portrait.

It was a successful evening with some 150 people attending. Before launching the book, Peter introduced myself and Neale. In his introduction Peter spoke about how he had met me at 3MP through Dean Matters, how my segment had been positioned to stop listeners switching stations to listen to the ABC news on 774, how this had been very successful, and lastly how the advertisers had flocked to the station either side of my daily segment.

3MP didn't pay me directly for the segments, but had given me credits at the 'top and tail' which had brought enquiries, new clients and increased income.

Neale in his laconic way spoke like 'The Reverend' he had become and kept his comments to a light banter with the final sign-off, "You should buy his book, because his fees are so high, you'll win!" The painting was then unveiled to the surprise of all.

After the launch Peter came up to me to say goodbye. I thanked him sincerely for his kind words and role as MC. He asked why I was not still on radio. I replied that after 3MP changed hands I was quite busy, and didn't know anyone in radio I could ask. "Well, you know me. Tomorrow I'll mention you to our General Manager, Gary Hoffman at Magic 1278, and ask him to call you."

He left, and true to his word, the next morning at 10am I received a call from Gary Hoffman. We agreed to meet later that week and I looked forward to seeing what opportunities might be in store. Initially I suggested a weekly segment similar to what I had recorded for 3MP 1377, but Gary told me that to keep it fresh and vibrant he would prefer a daily segment. After much discussion we agreed on a daily segment or a one-minute vignette introducing a different topic each day.

Even though he knew my clientele and business expertise extended way beyond that of the average life coach, he wanted a short, snappy and easily identifiable name and so my segment 'The Life Coach' was born.

The segment was broadcast continuously for over 8 years and in the course of the program I wrote over 1500 different radio scripts or vignettes. These have since been published in three more books which have been sold out and reprinted twice.

The format for Magic 1278, which proved to be a winning concept, was to take a quote from a famous person and then for me, as 'The Life Coach', to explain how the meaning of the quote related today to people in everyday life, business, and sport.

Again, destiny I find seems to reside in the hands, minds and actions of others who see someone's courage, consistency, commitment, conviction, creativity, caring and communication skills and want to support them to achieve their goals so they can be the best they can be.

Leadership Lessons:

1. Confidence + Comfort + Trust = A wise decision to agree.
2. Always expect the unexpected in life, business, and sport.
3. People love to be loved and given credit for their talent.
4. If you want to be on radio, or write a book, you must be disciplined.
5. Time management is the key discipline that enables all others.

CASE HISTORY 6

National Foods Ltd

Chapter 1

Food for Thought

In 2003, several interesting new business opportunities opened up. Some I initiated, and others on recommendations.

One initiative I took was to contact Max Ould, the Managing Director of National Foods to see if there were any opportunities to coach and mentor his executives.

He had been mentioned in some magazine articles and I had worked with Max when he was previously a client working at Bowater-Scott and then at Gillette. I noticed he was making his mark at National Foods and gaining attention for its growth in the business world.

I wrote a letter to Max and true to form he called me and suggested we meet for a chat. We met in his executive suite at National Foods, and we caught up with the latest on both our careers. He then surprised me by saying he was due to retire in about 18 months and thought it would be a good idea for me to spend some time coaching and mentoring his CFO, and second in charge, Peter Margin, who was earmarked to be his successor, and Max thought needed to fine tune his people skills.

We worked out a strategy so that Peter could meet and chat with me first so that he didn't feel as though he was being pushed into a situation where he was forced to appoint me. Max would invite me to the next board meeting and allocate me time to present my credentials and answer questions. I attended the meeting, my presentation was well received, and I answered several questions, but none from Peter Margin.

However, a week or so later David Clark, the HR Director, contacted me to ask me to meet with the Sales Director, Geoff Byrne who was interested in participating in an executive coaching program with me.

We met, there was a good fit between us, and so started a business relationship that has lasted over 17 years.

Geoff retired from National Foods after successfully integrating Berri Fruit Juice into the company. He then decided to become an executive coach himself and sought the advice of Peter Margin who had by then left National Foods and become Managing Director of Goodman Fielder.

In 2010 Geoff called me and asked if I would train him to become an executive coach and mentioned that he had discussed this with Peter Margin who, even though he had never personally worked with me, had kindly given me a glowing recommendation.

I designed a comprehensive 40-hour intensive course, based on my 40 years of experience, and worked closely with Geoff to ensure he understood the psychology involved and was able to successfully start his own consultancy. Geoff finished the course and became the first fully accredited Norris Management Executive Coach.

Around the time Geoff was departing National Foods, another executive who had been in the board room meeting that day, Keith Mentiplay, the National Foods Operations Director, also contacted me and asked me to include six of his key high potential managers in his team in an executive coaching program.

These executives worked with me for the next seven years and I am proud to say all went on to take very senior executive roles at National Foods, Murray Goulburn, Simplot, Bega Cheese, Kraft Foods, and Foster's Brewing. In addition, Keith invited me to be a guest presenter at several conferences to educate his team on emotional intelligence and soft skills.

During my time with National Foods, I observed another corporate culture phenomenon. There were successive takeovers, firstly by San Miguel, then Kirin and finally Lion Nathan. What I noticed, as with a previous takeover between Dunlop and Olympic Tyres, is that it can result in a 'clash of cultures'. Also, the 'acquiring company' is suspicious of the 'acquired company' and immediately puts in place a 'spy' to report back on contentious issues.

This then breeds distrust in the new owners, and the culture of the existing business becomes toxic, people become unhappy, productivity drops, the new senior executives are not respected, and the more established and previously loyal senior executives start to leave. The result is that the human intellectual property (IP) asset, that the new owners bought, is diluted and the outcome is a lose/lose for all concerned.

To enable successful takeovers to prosper, companies who do more due diligence on the human asset base, show more trust and recognise the IP knowledge of the employees they have acquired, create a more sustainable corporate culture. Hence, the people respect their ability more, and generate more consistent results.

Leadership Lessons:

1. Take a risk and contact past good clients.
2. Be careful because people are watching from afar.
3. The 'fit factor' is critical in coaching and mentoring.
4. There is a delay factor in coaching and seeing results.
5. A clash of cultures creates a toxic environment.

CASE HISTORY 7

Royal Sydney Golf Club

Chapter 1

The Cellar Dweller

I received a call in late 2004 from a long-standing golf friend, Keith Russell, who had moved back to his home in Sydney.

He mentioned that the General Manager of the Royal Sydney Golf Club, Bill Francis, who he knew well, had asked him for a recommendation for a coach and trainer to help implement a corporate culture program for the management and staff to support the $27 million refurbishment of the clubhouse and changes to the course.

Keith had recommended me as we had worked together previously when he had appointed me to coach and train the management and staff of the Australian Club in Melbourne, and the University and Schools Club in Sydney, while he was General Manager of the clubs.

I called Bill Francis and we made a time to meet at Royal Sydney GC to discuss the project. The meeting went well, and we decided to start the program in August. In the meantime, I would design the program and we would meet again in a month's time.

The main objective of the program was to give the management and staff of the various profit/member centres, the knowledge, and skills to complement the newly refurbished clubhouse and course. I was to especially help the long-time head professional and his staff to feel comfortable and confident to work for the first time as part of the club, and not as an independent contractor running their pro shop. This was a big goal of the club, because not having a professional shop as a club integrated profit centre was weakening the total consistent brand, corporate image, and culture of the club.

I returned to my office in Melbourne feeling very stimulated and proud that I had been selected to reinvent and retrain the employees at one of Australia's most prestigious golf clubs.

To put Royal Sydney GC into context, the club is situated in Rose Bay and was founded in 1893. It is one of Australia's premier sporting and social clubs featuring a championship golf course, championship lawn tennis courts that have hosted the Davis Cup, squash centre, lawn bowls, croquet, swimming pool and an extensive golf club museum. It also has private suite accommodation, three restaurants, several function rooms, golf academy and an enormous and well stocked golf professional's shop.

We agreed the program would be called 'Achieving Your Future Vision' and after completing the contents and format, I arranged to meet Bill and present the outline of the program to him at his office.

However, on arrival I noticed a few police cars arriving at the entrance and police incident tape being put up. I entered Bill's office, and as we sat down his very efficient PA came in and said, "Mr Francis, I need to see you." "Not now", said Bill, "George has just arrived from Melbourne and we are about to start a meeting to discuss the program he has been working on."

She persisted, "I am sorry Mr Francis, it's extremely urgent, the police are here and they need to see you now!" Bill looked at me, and I said, "Go Bill, don't worry about me, I've got time, I'll wait." He apologised and quickly left his office.

I sat there going through my presentation of the program and drinking the coffee his PA had given me. After about 30 minutes a stressed looking Bill returned, his face as white as a ghost. "What's the problem", I asked, "You look like you have seen a ghost!"

He looked at me with a shocked and ashen face and said quietly, "They've found the body of an indigenous person in the cellar. I urgently need to make some calls and arrangements with a number of people."

I looked at him and simply said, "Bill, I totally understand. I'll get a cab back to the airport and fly back to Melbourne. Give me a call after the dust has settled and we can discuss the program on the phone. I will leave you a copy of what I have prepared for you to digest." The incident could have had serious ramifications, and this was heightened by events at the time and discussions in the media regarding native land title. I left Bill's office saying, "Good luck Bill."

The program was eventually approved and implemented. The senior golf professional and his staff agreed to stay and become a new profit centre of the restructured RSGC. The other managers and staff of the various other sporting precincts all enthusiastically joined in the spirit of the new 'one team' culture, the new restaurant overlooking the first fairway, which is floodlit at night, became very popular.

Surprisingly, so much so, that after the initial training program was concluded, Bill called me back as more training was needed so the management and staff could 'handle' the members who in the past had never needed to book, but who now needed to book for dinner. Due to its new popularity, they could no longer walk in for a meal at their leisure, as they had done in the past.

The additional training concluded in July 2005 and Bill invited me to have breakfast with him on the final morning. We met at 8am, had a lovely breakfast and convivial chat. During coffee he mentioned that on 14 November, the Golf Course Managers Association of Australia and New Zealand would be holding their annual conference at the Sydney Wentworth Hotel. He went on to say that in view of my program's success at Royal Sydney, he had recommended me to the steering committee as a keynote speaker and asked if I would be interested and available.

The theme of the conference was 'Leadership–Embrace the Challenge' and the topic they wanted me to speak on was 'The Rights of Business Success'. The golf club industry I had noticed was changing, becoming more business based, and more professional in its leadership and management. My presentation was to follow the opening address by Rod McKeogh, the main keynote speaker and who had been instrumental in successfully negotiating with the IOC to have Sydney appointed as the preferred city for the summer Olympics in 2000.

I was honoured to be asked, and set about preparing my presentation which was to cover about an hour then followed by questions.

Unfortunately, life never runs smoothly. On the Friday prior to the Monday conference in Sydney, I came home to find an empty house. My wife had decided my heart by-pass and stroke was too much to cope with, and had packed up and left!

My Sydney presentation went on as planned and was well received, even though I was in numb shock and can't remember much of the weekend, let alone what I said in my presentation.

Leadership Lessons:

1. As an Australian Prime Minister once said, "Shit happens."
2. Never give up and people will admire your strength.
3. Know when to leave. Read the situation and act.
4. Betrayal is the cruellest form of deception.
5. The show must always go on with pride in yourself.

CASE HISTORY 8

Kelvin Boyd Advisory Pty Ltd

Chapter 1

A Watching Brief

In 2000, I joined The National Golf Club with the idea of one day retiring to Cape Schanck. I found a condominium overlooking the course with views over Gunnamatta Beach, Sorrento, across Bass Strait, and to Lorne and Anglesea.

In 2004, my first book 'Winning with Wisdom' had been published and launched and The National Golf Club Head Golf Professional, Henry Cussell, who I had known for many years, suggested I display the book and sell it to members, many of whom had listened to me on 3MP 1377.

One Sunday, my wife and I played a four-ball game of golf with another couple, Kelvin and Jan Boyd who we didn't know. Around the 15th hole it dawned on Kelvin that I was the author of the book he had just purchased from the professional's shop before our game. After the game we shared a bottle of red and a coffee, I signed his copy of the book, and we all parted.

I did not see or meet Kelvin again for some three years and then 'it' happened again. In October 2007, I attended the Annual General Meeting of the Yarra Yarra Golf Club. At the conclusion, I went to the bar to order a drink and Kelvin came and stood beside me. He looked over and said quietly, "Hello George, do you have a business card?" As it is not protocol at the club to tout openly for business, I said I would come past his table later and discreetly give one to him. I asked him why he wanted it and he thought I could help him personally and in his business. He said he would call me the following week and arrange lunch. He called and we arranged to meet at The Stoke House overlooking St Kilda beach.

Kelvin had booked a table in a relatively private nook overlooking Port Phillip Bay. After catch-up conversation, he began by saying he needed help with some business issues in a dairy business which were greatly distressing him. He was also interested in gaining some advice for his accounting practice. I asked him why he thought I could be of assistance, and he mentioned that he had enjoyed my company at golf, enjoyed my book, and had watched my performance at AGMs at Yarra Yarra and The National over the past two years and thought I acted well and consistently.

I explained how I thought we could work together in a corporate coaching and mentoring program, and he agreed we should start working together after he returned from Christmas holidays.

Kelvin, I discovered, had an interesting background. As a young ambitious 20-year-old boy with a Maori heritage, he had left his father's sheep station north of Auckland and made his way to the vast land of opportunity, Australia. Once here he studied accountancy and tax law and with dogged determination, had made his mark as one of the most respected taxation advisers in Australia.

Our sessions were held every month for one and a half hours, and I was able to help him with a number of critical areas, especially in removing himself from his distressful involvement in the dairy partnership. I was also able to help him with some sensitive personal issues.

We kept working together, and then he announced that he was going to move offices from St Kilda Road to the IBM building at Southbank. This move was to simplify his business and focus on three core components, his accounting practice, his advice to high net worth individuals in off-shore taxation matters, and in global pension advice matters.

The last one had 'popped out' of a session with me. His young son, Nick, was working in the business and had started managing this area, marketing its image, and growing this specialised business to capitalise on his father's unique knowledge, experience, and advice.

It has now become the 'head of the arrow' for Kelvin's business future.

Leadership Lessons:

1. Beware, your profile and performance are being watched.
2. Due diligence is a discipline much over-rated at your peril.
3. Writing and publishing a book lifts you out of the pack.
4. Polishing the gem in your business can provide a new focus
5. Invest in 'outside the forest' thinking and knowledge.

CASE HISTORY 9

Greystone Wines

Chapter 1

A Strategic Solution

Then 'it' happened again. I was nearing completion of some programs, and had some availability coming up when I was asked by a client if I would meet the CEO of a New Zealand wine brand the next week when he was in Melbourne.

It was to be an interesting meeting. The winery business was about an hour's drive from Christchurch in the South Island of New Zealand.

At our meeting he painted a colourful picture of a winery that needed more focus and sales. He also mentioned in his presentation that there was a large storage of bottled wine undelivered in their warehouse.

I then gave a brief background of myself, and after doing so, was asked the big question. "So George, what observations have you made after hearing the background brief?" I said, "Well, it would appear that the business is not controlling its own sales destiny as currently all sales are being made by agents who no doubt represent many brands, and unfortunately yours may be way down their lists.

It would appear you need to appoint a Sales and Marketing Director in Australia who can help you control your own sales destiny in Australia, New Zealand, and Asia, where the market really is.

Also, in view of the amount of product in storage, I think you're acting more like a bank than a winery as you have locked up what I would call 'lazy money' or a large amount of valuable working capital."

We then had a light lunch in the boardroom and a general discussion during which the CEO suddenly mentioned he needed to leave for the airport to catch his flight back to Christchurch. I offered to drive him so we could have a chat along the way, and he could ask any more questions, so we set off.

I could see he was thinking as we drove along and when we were nearly at the airport, he looked over to me and said, "George, I like your analysis and your candid comments and would like to appoint you to help make the business more successful." I duly received his appointment letter, and I started to plan the strategy that would enable the initial and gradual rise of the brand.

The first thing was to appoint a Sales and Marketing Director and after much due diligence, Ed Davis was appointed. He was an astute, wily, well connected, and understated person, perfect for the role. I had known Ed since he was General Manager of Marketing at the Melbourne Tourism Authority. He then went on to become the Sales and Marketing Director of the Radisson Hotel in Melbourne near Albert Park Lake and then the General Manager of the Radisson Hotel opposite the Flagstaff Gardens. He had recently had a change of career direction and oversaw the finishing of the building and launching of the RACV Resort at Inverloch after opening a Ramada Hotel in Korea.

His background had been on the 'purchasing side' of wines for hotels and it was considered his experience, contacts and knowledge in Australia, New Zealand and Asia were perfect, so he was appointed as Sales and Marketing Director.

It was then considered critical to conduct a strategic workshop near the winery in Christchurch. I was asked to facilitate the workshop and it was agreed I would use a strategic formula I used with BMW to cover five steps for the future success of the business.

Step 1. Decide and discuss the current situation.
Step 2. Discuss the desired sales outcome and goals.
Step 3. Analyse the current situation.
Step 4. Brainstorm ideas and strategies to achieve the desired goals.
Step 5. Agree on an action plan to execute the ideas and strategies.

The workshop was duly planned. I then located an Australian winery expert to assist us with unbiased, specific knowledge which was considered critical in enabling the team to understand a bigger picture and put a plan in place for future success.

It was an interesting workshop and I learnt that the owner had the inspiring goal of growing 'Great Pinot Noir', had developed a 'Rolls Royce' vineyard, but as yet, they didn't own a winery and simply leased one when required.

It was agreed the best strategy was to move the current stock as fast as possible into the right market niche and at the same time promote the brand.

On returning to Melbourne, I found an opportunity for Greystone to sponsor the Australian Institute of Company Directors' conference in Christchurch later that year, 2010. Members of the AICD were considered in the right market segment to promote the brand. The sponsorship package would include naming rights for the breakout sessions, a display, and a tasting stand at the conference. It also came with a guest speaking and MC role at a session in the Gondola Restaurant on the mountain top overlooking Lyttelton Harbour, and the opportunity to display the brand's logo on all conference printed material as well as sample bottles of wine as room gifts.

It was agreed that this was a strategically sound sales target market opportunity to launch the brand and it was planned with great precision.

The MC, John Mangos or 'Two Dogs' of Graham Kennedy television fame, and more recently as a Channel 10 newsreader, promoted the wine with daily lucky number giveaways. The Prime Minister of New Zealand, the elegant and astute John Key attended the conference, visited the stand, and tasted the wines with the CEO, whom he had attended University with some years previously.

When the Conference concluded, the opportunity was analysed and found that the AICD strategy had been a resounding success.

Sadly, on 22 February the following year, 2011, Christchurch suffered a 6.3 magnitude earthquake which killed 185 people, injured several thousand and caused immense structural damage to buildings including the Gondola Restaurant which was obliterated and vanished.

Ed Davis had started to make great sales strides in Australia and Asia, so it was agreed to again sponsor the AICD conference the following year in Beijing. It was suggested we produce a 'Corporate Wardrobe' that the key people would wear at all times during the conference and that we give away Australian slouch hats with the logo on the front, as it would not be possible or practical to bring bottles of wine into China with any certainty.

The conference went even better than in Christchurch. At the final dinner on the closing night, directors from the RACV head office approached me and asked how we had pulled off the impressive Greystone Wines sponsorship coup. They, as a team were very impressed.

The Beijing experience was a lesson in creative teamwork, and the

Australian slouch hats were visible everywhere around the Beijing Hotel and the airport on the final day of departure.

We were now on course with the owner's vision, the wine brand strategic structure had been set up correctly and Ed had increased sales in clubs, restaurants, and bottle shops throughout Australia. He had even created a sponsored Golf Classic Corporate Tournament at Yarra Yarra Golf Club and this prestigious club was now stocking the brand.

It was then advised that the business owner, who had recently completed a wine course in America, was inviting the support team to a workshop to let us know what he had learnt and what he believed could be achieved for the future success of the brand.

We all flew into Christchurch, which was still recovering from the earthquake crisis, and attended the workshop. He shared his new knowledge, and what the brand could become, based on what he had learnt at the wine course. It was a very informative, and enlightening presentation.

The next annual AICD conference was to be held in Darwin and it was agreed that the brand again would be a sponsor, but only a minor sponsor compared with the concentrated critical mass achieved in the two previous years as a major sponsor.

This sustained innovation in strategic thinking, by incorporating the brand with a sponsorship opportunity of an Australian institute, whose members fitted the target market, confirmed it can be a valuable launch pad for a product's sales and marketing success. The ROI is considerable in comparison with a normal advertising campaign which can usually cost many more times the budget and still not be able to deliver the same measurable result.

The brand has now stretched its wings, is really flying, and with the owner's valuable guidance has become a wine success story in New Zealand and Australia.

Recently I celebrated a milestone birthday and took a group of 26 out for dinner to one of Melbourne's leading Italian restaurants. It was pleasant to discover that when my guests ordered wine, they were able to order Greystone and made suitable glowing comments on the brand afterwards!

Leadership Lessons:

1. Lazy money can put your business at risk and impede growth.
2. For success, a business needs a vision, mission, and values.
3. Think outside the square and leverage your business.
4. Think creatively and be market and customer focused.
5. Strategic sponsorship can be a high ROI sales solution.

CASE HISTORY 10

Cookers Bulk Oil System Pty Ltd

Chapter 1

Cooking with Canola

In May 2010 it happened again! Sitting at my desk, day-dreaming and thinking about my business strategy, the office telephone rang and I heard in the distance my Executive Assistant, Christine Griffiths having a humorous and animated conversation with someone. She then buzzed my extension and said, "There is someone on the phone you have known since he was a young boy and would like to speak with you."

Not knowing who it was, I took the call only to find out it was Peter Carter, the eldest son of my former Caltex Sales Manager and mentor, the affable Eric Carter, who had worked with me in 1978 in the role of General Manager.

"Hello young Peter", I said, "How are you, and to what do I owe the pleasure of this call?" Peter Carter went on to explain that he had joined a new company as the Queensland State Manager, that they were planning their first national conference and that he had recommended me to the Managing Director to present two afternoon sessions if I was available. He went on to say, to move the business forward they needed to be challenged to change in the way they thought about the business and the way they thought and planned their sales strategy. I was available on the date and we quickly agreed on the presentation format, content, and my fee.

From an early age Peter had been an above average AFL footballer and had played for the famous South Melbourne 'Bloods' or, as they are currently known, the 'Sydney Swans'. He was a fast and creative player.

They were a challenging couple of sessions to present. The business was only about three years old and had grown quickly under the watchful eye of the Managing Director, Peter Fitzgerald. It was obvious Peter had managed the business very well, while at the same time maintaining a healthy relationship with the financial backers, a group of astute Jewish men who owned the Peerless Foods Group.

However, I could see a couple of significant issues that could provide further growth opportunities for the business. The most obvious being for the sales and marketing team to focus on achieving 'a point of difference' to Cookers competitors by emphasising that it was a total 'bulk oil system' and not just another cooking oil.

The system was enabled because Cookers set up their own bulk oil tank, delivered the oil by secure hose from a purpose-built truck/tanker, monitored its level, monitored its oil quality, picked up the waste oil after use and gave the client expert advice on the many quality aspects of their cooking oil.

The conference participants quickly picked up on this strategic opportunity and changed their focus to 'What business Cookers was really In'.

The second opportunity I saw was to include each person's title and position on their business card. I couldn't believe this had not happened before as it powerfully enables each employee, when face-to-face with buyers, customers or clients, to be quickly understood along with their expertise and influence. This enables doors to be opened more easily, as I had found out many years earlier with my own business and my Manager in NSW.

There was some resistance initially to my recommendation, yet it soon became clear and obvious that it assisted customers to ascertain the role of the Cookers representatives and increased their self-esteem and self-confidence.

It turned out I had made a significant impact on the Cookers management team and I was then asked to present various workshops around Australia for sales, operations, drivers, and state managers over the ensuing eight years.

My involvement also included mentoring several state managers to help them be better equipped with leadership, strategy and personal communication skills.

Today I am more of a confidant to the Managing Director, Peter Fitzgerald, and we often have a one-on-one strategic chat in his office over coffee or over the phone.

Cookers Bulk Oil System has become one of Australia's best entrepreneurial success stories and has grown to become the major cooking oil supplier in Australia.

Peter Carter has grown to become one of the leading state managers in the company and Peter Fitzgerald has shown his visionary, leadership, entrepreneurial and innovative skills with many 'cutting edge' strategies. One such strategy was installing Cookers own 'wind turbine' at their Melbourne operational head office to generate cheap electricity for the various operational areas.

The business has expanded across Australia and is the preferred supplier of canola cooking oil for restaurants, hotels, casinos, clubs, cafes, and bistros and many business in-house cafeterias and kitchens.

It was a privilege to be asked to assist in the fledgling early days and to remain connected to keep the culture cooking at Cookers with a unique system that gave them 'Sur/petition', or as Edward de Bono would say, a point of difference and a position of power that keeps them above their competitors.

Leadership Lessons:

1. You can only lose the business when you're referred by others.
2. To be successful, your business must have 'Sur/petition.
3. Sur/petition, as de Bono says, gives you 'a value monopoly'.
4. Brainstorm your business 'raison d'etre' to remain relevant.
5. Value the 'Circle of Influence' with your business relationships.

CASE HISTORY 11

Victoria University

Chapter 1

Worshipping Wisdom

When in Christchurch in 2010, at the AICD conference final dinner at the Air Museum, I met an interesting and delightful lady from Melbourne. Barbara McLure was a Fellow of the Australian Institute of Company Directors and happened to sit on my client, Greystone's, table. Barbara mentioned that she was on the Advisory Board of Victoria University and was able to provide the CEO of Greystone Wines with valuable insights as to what his nephew should do and who to contact regarding a sports management degree.

Barbara and then I swapped business cards, agreed to catch up for a bite of lunch when we returned and had settled back into our work routine, and debrief the conference.

She was a passionate and energetic business woman, and we agreed to meet at a trendy Yarraville restaurant. As the lunch progressed, she seemed quite interested in my role as a corporate coach and suggested that I should meet Dr Damira Lopez, the Director of Business Studies at Victoria University, as she thought she could utilise my experience and expertise. As we left the restaurant, she said she would talk to her and get back to me soon.

It didn't take long for her to call me and a meeting was arranged with Damira. She was a delightful Russian with the fine porcelain complexion of a 'china doll'. It also helped that she had been listening to my daily vignettes on Magic 1278 for many years.

At our first meeting she indicated that Victoria University had the opportunity to implement leadership training and a coaching program for the Shepparton City Council executive management team as well as their middle and junior managers.

Our meeting was timely as she was looking for a coaching group who could work with the trainers at Victoria University to continue the knowledge input to ensure the participants were able to understand the detail and implement the program within their specific roles in the Council. I had recently established a Norris Management Coaching Group, so I was able to build into our proposal that two associate coaches and I could work with the trainers at Victoria University to implement the program.

The proposal was submitted and accepted, and we were asked to join her to present the Victoria University Leadership program to the Shepparton Executive Management group with them presenting the training segment and me presenting the coaching segment.

I drove up to Shepparton with a Victoria University colleague and on the way, he gave me an interesting insight into how a University operates, and the idiosyncrasies of their people. He studiously pointed out that Universities don't focus on profits, but on how many 'papers' their people can publish to show their knowledge and that of the University. This was a very new concept for me to come to grips with, but one I would soon discover that was deeply entrenched.

Our presentation went well, and we were appointed to perform the executive coaching role. I then selected the two most suitable and experienced coaches from the Norris Management Group to support me in my role. These were Geoff Byrne who had completed the 40-hour accredited Norris Management Coaching Course with me, and Tom Richardson who had left Jetset Travel after asking me to work with them many years earlier and had embarked on his own coaching career.

Dr Damira Lopez briefed the three of us together with Gerard Glennon, the Victoria University Leadership Trainer, on the requirements of their leadership program and I further briefed Geoff and Tom on their specific coaching requirements.

It was agreed that I, as the principal coach would coach the senior members of the City Council Executive Group. Geoff would coach the next level of senior managers, and Tom would coach the middle and junior managers.

After experiencing the 190 km journey taking three hours by road for the presentation, I suggested we travel up and back by train so that we were mentally fresh when we arrived and saved expenses on petrol and car maintenance. It was agreed we would meet at my office where we would leave the cars, take a taxi to the Southern Cross Station, then travel by first class rail.

This we did monthly for the nine months of the program, staying the first and second nights at a suitable motel near the Council offices.

The program went very well, and Shepparton City Council was happy with most facets. The interesting insight gained by me and my coaches was that Victoria University, which had previously operated as a TAFE College, was still thinking, acting, and speaking like they were still a TAFE College.

The client really wanted their participants to be trained and coached in a leadership program which was presented by a University and not a TAFE College. It was with some reluctance, after sitting in on the group training, that I had to take the significant, calculated risk and remind the presenters of this fact. I also had to convey this sensitive message to Damira, to ensure the University was seen in the 'right light', and the client remained happy with the program. She appreciated the feedback, thankfully any unfortunate perceptions from the client were avoided, and the program concluded successfully.

Shortly afterwards, Damira called me to another meeting in her city office. She explained that Victoria University would soon be hosting a group of visiting university associate professors from China wishing to experience the benefits of what Victoria University could offer. She invited Geoff Byrne and me to the launch function at the Victoria University campus in Footscray and to a welcome dinner for the delegation, and for us to present a series of coaching sessions for seven of the associate professors during their visit.

It was a great honour for Norris Management to be invited to present such a critical part of the Victoria University program. It was an engaging project and one that required the assistance of Chinese interpreters to enable the sessions to be delivered successfully. The seven associate professors were all delightful, open, sincere people and the sessions were very well received.

However, it wasn't all smiles. We experienced some tears and sad moments when the program sessions were ending, and a couple of the female Chinese delegates broke down and cried. Worried in case I had offended them, I stopped and consoled them and asked what the problem was. To my surprise they said they had thoroughly enjoyed the sessions on communication strategy, but while they understood the benefits of the communication techniques, they were sad because they believed their superiors in China would not let them use the knowledge they had acquired.

It appeared, without it being said, that their superiors were totally influenced by their way of thinking and would not be open to this western style of leadership communication. I explained to them that they shouldn't let this aspect of their culture overcome their passion and that they should try, with great respect to their superiors, to influence them to change by using the 'Benefit Bridge' I had taught them.

This approach seemed to work wonders with them, and they all recovered their composure and wanted us to pose for group photos as a lasting reminder to celebrate their stay in Australia before flying home.

The following May 2011, my New Zealand wine client was again the main sponsor for the Australian Institute of Company Directors Annual conference in Beijing. So, I decided to follow up with the seven Chinese associate professors to catch up with me while I was in Beijing.

I received one reply from the associate professor who had acted as interpreter on several occasions for the Victoria University program. She was the Deputy Dean of the University of Agriculture in Beijing and asked me if I would have time to present a half day workshop for the lecturers. She was prepared to again be my interpreter, and the topic she wanted me to present was surprisingly, 'Implementing Change through Effective Communication'.

We agreed that I could present the workshop on the Sunday afternoon, prior to the AICD Conference, as we would have all our sponsorship details completed in the morning.

She arranged for me to be collected by a chauffeured limousine to take me to the university, where a tour was arranged, and I would present the four-hour workshop. It was really only three hours of content, but because of her consistent translation, it took four hours to present. The lecturers were passionate participants, and the session went very well with many interesting questions asked.

Following the workshop, I was their guest of honour at a traditional Chinese banquet before I was driven back to my hotel. The experience taught me a valuable lesson in that, 'China Worships Wisdom' whereas the 'West Wastes Wisdom'. The Chinese defer to grey hair (or none) and respect and value their elders. I thought it was a significant lesson the western world could learn, that instead of making those with wisdom feel under-valued by being banished to retirement, they should harness their wisdom and use it.

Leadership Lessons:

1. There certainly exists a six degrees of separation phenomenon.
2. Being on radio helped cement a business relationship.
3. Universities are not run like a business for profit performance.
4. When an organisation changes brands, its people must follow.
5. Asia worships wisdom, but Australia wastes wisdom. .

CASE HISTORY 12

AFL Coaches Association

Chapter 1

Meeting the Master

In October 2011, I was asked by the AFL Coaches Association to present a keynote address at their annual conference. The topic I was asked to present was, 'Getting the Best from your Players through Effective Communication'. I compared an AFL team to a commercial business, as well as using the 1960 Olympic Games victory of Herb Elliott in the 1500 metres gold medal world record race, and the comments by his coach, Percy Cerutty as supporting examples.

The presentation was to over 100 AFL coaches, mostly assistants and judging from the number of coaches who spoke with me afterwards, the address and provocative messages I delivered were well received.

About three weeks later, I arranged a debrief with the then CEO, the late Danny Frawley. He told me that the conference went well, my presentation was very appropriate, and that Neil Craig, the former Adelaide Crows Senior Coach had expressed the opinion that it was of great value. He went on to suggest that I should give Neil a call, and he gave me his mobile number.

By this stage Neil had left Adelaide to take up the position as Director of Sports Performance at the Melbourne Football Club with Mark Neeld as Senior Coach.

Neil and I agreed to meet for coffee at the clubrooms and had a good discussion. We then decided to meet confidentially a few times at the Hilton Hotel near the MCG, to continue our discussions and soon formed a trusting, healthy, and respectful relationship.

Just before the start of the 2012 AFL season he finally felt comfortable to ask me to act as his coach and mentor.

This arrangement continued during 2012 and into the 2013 season when he was asked to become the caretaker coach after Mark Neeld was sacked as Senior Coach. Then in 2013, Neil was asked to join the Essendon Football Club which was experiencing a difficult time due to the fallout from the 'Supplements Affair'. He asked for my thoughts and I simply said, "Well, Melbourne is a basket case, and if you go to Essendon, you'll learn a lot about their culture and issues. Then perhaps be able to use the experience to write a book or go on to the speaking circuit."

Neil agreed and was initially appointed as Head of Coaching, Development and Strategy and in 2014 was promoted to the position of General Manager Performance, which meant all coaches reported to him in their various roles.

Neil then tried to assist Mark 'Bomber' Thompson who had been appointed as 'Stand in Coach' when James Hird was stood down because of the scandal.

When James Hird returned for a period before he stood down, Neil could see that his role was not tenable due to a clash of personalities. Then in 2015, the CEO of Carlton Football Club, Stephen Trigg who had been the CEO of the Adelaide Crows during Neil's time as Senior Coach, asked Neil to join Carlton to support their new young Senior Coach, Brendan Bolton, as Director of Coaching, Development and Performance.

After helping Carlton in this demanding role for two years, in August

Chapter 1 Meeting the Master

2017 Neil announced he would retire from his AFL career and in October, was appointed as Director of High Performance for the 2019 England World Cup Rugby team. He was to be a 'critical friend' to Head Coach, Eddie Jones, who he had worked with previously, and his focus was to win the 2019 World Cup in Japan.

The England team performed skillfully, magnificently winning their way into the finals, but were unfortunately beaten in the final by the brilliant South African team.

After acting as his mentor for nearly seven years, I now consider him to be a good friend as well as a client and he has recently joined as a member of my golf club, Yarra Yarra. He loves his golf, is an above average golfer on a 13 handicap and enjoys trying to put his high-performance knowledge to good use in his own competitive way, on the course.

It was after he and I played at The National in 2017 that he asked for my thoughts on whether or not he should leave Carlton and join Eddie Jones as the Director of High Performance for the 2019 England World Cup Rugby team. I had bought a new Mustang GT and had driven us both to The National. Stopping outside his house on our return, Neil said, "Okay George, what do you think I should do?"

I looked him in the eye and said, "I will ask you a couple of questions and want you to listen to your answers." "Okay, shoot', he said. "What is Carlton?" He replied, "A suburb of Melbourne." "Who runs Carlton?" He replied, "A mayor or in the case of the AFL Club, a president and CEO." "What is England?" He replied, "A country in Europe." "Who runs England?" He replied with a chuckle, "The Queen." I looked at him and simply said, "Neil, it is a no brainer, but you've got to want to love to do it." He picked up his golf bag and said, "Thanks George, it's an interesting way to weigh it up and make a decision."

He called me later that week to say he had accepted the position with England subject to the right remuneration and conditions being agreed. The next Chapter in his illustrious sporting career was about to begin, but the negotiations had to also begin to enable this to happen.

We met again for an update strategy meeting when I suggested it would be advantageous to meet a colleague and client of mine, Kelvin Boyd, the global accounting, and taxation guru. I arranged a meeting at my office where they could meet and as Kelvin is a New Zealand All Black 'tragic,' the meeting went exceptionally well with good natured teasing and banter from both sides.

Kelvin agreed to negotiate Neil's contract details which he did skillfully and with much patience. Later, Neil's position as Director of High Performance for England Rugby and his remuneration package was confirmed for the World Cup.

It was an amazing ride not only for Neil but also for me as his mentor. We were in regular contact by mobile phone, text, and emails during the 24 months or so he spent immersed in the campaign.

I knew little about rugby, but became a self-educated student of the game and religiously watched and analysed each England match and offered my own 'non-expert' observations to Neil. While I am sure he was amused by some of my comments, he admitted that having someone 'outside the forest' giving insights with a sporting and high performance leadership knowledge and background was often very helpful.

He also gave me a memorable piece of wisdom that we all should use when we're getting over an injury or an operation, 'If you want to be back at your best, you've got to get lots of rest!'

Leadership Lessons:

1. Performing on stage makes you transparent and vulnerable.
2. Performing as a guest speaker puts you on notice to prepare.
3. Be patient and take time to develop a working relationship.
4. Use analogy and metaphor to help people make decisions.
5. Bring in the experts when negotiating contracts and money.

CASE HISTORY 13

Mercedes Benz Dealers

Chapter 1

The Silver Stars

In 2010, my contract with BMW Australia finished and I was free to coach and mentor dealer principals from other car manufacturers.

Then 'it' happened again!

Christine Griffiths, my Executive Assistant was talking on the phone to the tenant who had leased her mother's house. When she finished her call, she said, "Oh, Libby Miller said she knows you from the days she worked at Brighton BMW. She said to say hello and suggested you give Geoff Quirk a call as he has recently been appointed Dealer Principal at Mercedes Benz Brighton and perhaps could use your help."

It's a small world. Geoff had been the General Sales Manager at Brighton BMW when I was their QMA Coach, and we had a good working relationship.

I waited a few days then called Geoff's mobile and we arranged a time for a talk. It was perfect timing as he was 'under the pump' to perform, and he asked me to meet with their HR Manager, Matt Britten, as the business at that time was owned by the South African company, Barloworld.

Matt and I met, and he introduced me to the Barloworld CEO, Alan Carter, who was a very tough and forthright executive. He briefed me on the situation, and they agreed to appoint me as Corporate Coach to assist Geoff in his progress as the new Dealer Principal.

As time progressed, I was asked to coach and mentor all their senior department managers. Then in 2016, Geoff showed interest in a leadership program like the program I conducted for Peter Schwab when he was Senior Coach of the Hawthorn AFL Club, called 'The Young Hawks,' for his own emerging group of leaders. He asked me to create, design and implement a program to develop the younger 2ICs in each of their departments so they could step up, lead, and manage with maturity when needed. At the same time, we believed this would build their loyalty to the business.

So, in February 2016, we implemented a leadership program called 'Leaders of the Future'. The program consisted of a series of six group sessions covering the topics of change, leadership, emotional intelligence, culture, communication and relationship marketing.

After the six group workshops, each of the 10 participants met with me for one-on-one coaching sessions for six months to help reinforce the knowledge acquired and help them personally with leadership, management and even personal issues. The program was well received and provided a foundation for 'The Leaders of the Future' at Mercedes Brighton.

My executive coaching role continued with the senior managers though 2017 and 2018. Then towards the end of 2018, Geoff said he was interested in implementing a 'Corporate Culture Innovation' program, something that I had mentioned earlier in the year, and he also wanted to celebrate the 40th birthday of the business with a program I called 'Vision 2020'.

The program was designed and launched at the annual Managers Conference in January 2019 so it could be rolled out progressively during 2019.

The program was based on the successful 'Circle of Innovation' program I had implemented some years earlier for Ferntree Gully Holden, one of the group's dealerships. This program was designed to 'Tap the Talent of the Team' and harvest the staff's suggestions and ideas to improve the business. This successful program had resulted in over 200 suggestions and ideas of which many were implemented. That Holden dealership went on to win a national award for the best improving dealership in Australia.

The Brighton Mercedes Benz program was divided into nine groups, new cars, pre-owned cars, finance and insurance, service, workshop, parts, panel shop, marketing and lastly, but most importantly vision, mission and values. Each group consisted of a cross section of participants from various departments which met twice during the 12 months for a one and a half hour 'Innovation Session' with me as the facilitator.

After each session I collated all the suggestions and packaged them into a management report which was then presented to the dealer principal, the specific department manager and the internal program co-ordinator for feedback and action. Each participant received a printed copy to see that the dealership had listened to their suggestions and ideas, and valued them as an asset.

As the year progressed another group was added as it was agreed the 40th birthday milestone needed a specific taskforce and action group.

The program welded the total workforce together and resulted in a 40th birthday special logo and a birthday launch night the week before the 2020 Melbourne Grand Prix, with Mercedes Benz Australia management in attendance.

Unfortunately, immediately after the launch in March, the Coronavirus pandemic changed the lives of people throughout the world. Even though the 40th birthday celebrations were put on hold, the Vision 2020 program enabled the morale and winning culture to survive.

Shortly after I commenced working with Barloworld Brighton, now Mercedes Benz Brighton, I was asked to coach and mentor another manager, Steve Gardiner, Manager of the Pre-Owned Vehicles Department. He was recovering from a major car accident when he was hit from behind and suffered serious mental trauma and neck whiplash. This had impacted on his self-confidence and I was asked if I could help him. This started a special relationship which has now spanned 10 years.

After working with Steve for about 18 months his self-confidence soared to the point he was nominated as the best performing Pre-Owned Mercedes Benz Manager in Australia. He was then head hunted for the critical new role of BMW Dealer Principal of a brand-new purpose-built Waverley BMW retail dealership.

Not long after he 'got his feet under the desk', I received a call to ask me to coach and mentor his New Car Sales Manager, Pre-Owned Sales Manager and their After Service Manager. These assignments lasted for three years.

Steve was having some difficulties with the dealership owner and then was head hunted by the Stillwell Group. He left and accepted the role of Dealer Principal of Stillwell BMW in South Yarra. This was a plum appointment in the BMW Group as the name Stillwell was revered after the Australian champion racing driver Bib Stillwell, who was the founder of the business.

Shortly after Steve joined Stillwell, the business was sold to the Bayford Group and unfortunately the culture changed significantly. It was no longer conducive to the character and style that Steve was used to, and three years later he was again head hunted. This time he was to return to the Mercedes Benz brand as the Dealer Principal of Silver Star Mercedes Benz Doncaster, Ringwood and Burwood. It was a huge appointment for Steve, but one that set him both business and personal challenges.

Then 'it' happened again!

One day, driving to golf, my mobile rang, and it was Steve Gardiner. "George, how are you doing?" "Well thanks, how can I help you Steve?" He said, "I think I need your expertise, guidance and wisdom in this new role. It's got some big challenges, and after two years I need you to hold my hand for a bit."

So began another assignment with Steve which we both believed I could ethically handle as the Mercedes Benz Brighton and the Doncaster, Ringwood and Burwood dealerships were not geographically competitors in the marketplace. In any case, all my coaching and mentoring assignments, as all my clients know, are strictly confidential as in a doctor/patient relationship, so everyone was happy.

It was not long before Steve asked me to coach and mentor his Ringwood General Manager, New Car Sales Manager and his Doncaster New Car Sales Manager.

Both Geoff Quirk and Steve Gardiner, I am proud to say, both wrote great testimonials in my fourth book 'Moments on Management'. I'm also proud to say that have both grown as people, managers, leaders and astute businessmen and are currently steering their 'business ships' carefully through the corona virus crisis.

Leadership Lessons:

1. Your brand is priceless so guard it carefully.
2. It's critical to invest time in forward thinking.
3. Your people are carrying around 'pearls of wisdom'.
4. When people are asked for ideas, they feel their best.
5. Value your people, and value them as an asset.

CASE HISTORY 14

HLB Mann Judd Pty Ltd

Chapter 1

Taming the Tiger

In April 2012, I joined a group for a week's golf in Tasmania. I only knew the two organisers, but I decided to live on the edge and go. We were scheduled to play a few different golf courses including Launceston Golf Club, Tasmania Golf Club, Barnbougle Dunes and Lost Farm.

On the first day I played with a group which included one of the organisers, Brett Bridgeman, and his father Wayne Bridgeman, both scratch handicap golfers, and a young accountant, Aaron Murden. We each played a different course each day and on the last day played the famous Barnbougle Dunes, the best known of the courses designed by world renowned Tom Doak and Australia's Michael Clayton.

The young accountant was again in my four, and we had a great day with plenty of laughs. When we had finally hit off the 17th tee, Aaron politely said to me, "So George, what do you do with yourself back in Melbourne?" It had happened again. I offhandedly replied, "I'm a corporate coach and management mentor." "How does that work", he asked. "I work with leaders and managers in business to assist their development in leadership, strategy and communication. I have also worked with a number of AFL senior coaches."

"That sounds very interesting, do you have a business card?" I replied, "I have one in my luggage, and I'll give it to you when we finish, why do you ask?" "I work for an accounting group", he said, "and we have been considering having a coach or mentor for a while, so I'll give you a call and perhaps we could have a coffee and chat in more detail about how it works."

We finished our game, collected our luggage and I gave Aaron my card before flying back to Melbourne with some of the others from the group. Aaron, who originally had lived in Tasmania, stayed on to visit his family.

It had been a very enjoyable week of fun, sport and social interaction and I returned home to Melbourne in good spirits and with a possible new client, but as I said to him, I won't call you, you call me if that's ok.

Several weeks later I received a call from Aaron, and we arranged to meet for a coffee at the RACV Club in the city. He explained what he wanted to achieve, and I outlined how a coaching/mentoring program worked, and agreed to send him a formal proposal.

The proposal was accepted, and we started a corporate coaching relationship that is still on-going. Aaron has made the journey from Junior Accountant to Senior Accountant, to Partner, to Equity Partner and who knows, perhaps in the future, Managing Partner. It has been a rewarding trip together.

Then in April 2015 'it' happened again!

I received an email from Aaron saying that Janelle Manders, Managing Partner of HLB Mann Judd Gold Coast office, would like to meet me when I was next visiting my client, Bruce Lynton BMW the Southport dealership. I contacted her and we agreed to meet over lunch and have a sandwich.

On Tuesday 28 April I met Janelle, a bright and astute woman who explained that HLB Mann Judd had done research that showed they needed to 'future proof' their business, especially their Business

Advisory Services departments and that Aaron had recommended me to her. She was the Chair of their National BAS Group and wanted help to implement a program to achieve this goal and to influence change in the culture of the business.

I prepared and presented a submission to Janelle and she and Aaron agreed that Norris Management would be the creator, designer, presenter, producer, and implementer of the program. After conducting some research, I suggested that the corporate communication and client program should be called 'The HLB Way'.

I still had in my archives a copy of 'The Jetset Way' which I had helped produce in 1995 and its basic content, strategy and goals were still relevant and similar to the goals of HLB Mann Judd in 2015, some 20 years later.

They agreed and set about introducing me as the architect of The HLB Way starting with their Sydney conference in May 2015. While my conference presentation was short, it enabled the national BAS participants to meet me, understand the research and needs of the program, and perceive the benefits of the program. It concluded with a Q&A session so they felt involved in its direction.

With positive feedback, the program was approved to proceed to final planning, with the National Managing Partner, Tony Fittler, agreeing to fund and launch it at the next conference in Adelaide in May 2016.

For the next 12 months I was consumed by 'The HLB Way' as well as assisting my other clients. It was a very busy year!

To achieve the best long term result I decided the best strategy was to appoint and train two 'HLB Way Champions' from each office in Australia and New Zealand prior to the launch. This would enable a similar support strategy that I had seen work well in 'The Jetset Way' model.

The plan was again approved by the BAS Board Chairman, Janelle and my 'HLB Champion', Aaron, so I set about writing, researching, creating, designing, and producing the material for the champions' manuals.

Then out of the blue I received a call from Janelle. The National Board was having second thoughts about the budget and wanted to own my IP as part of the total figure.

I agreed, and allowed my previous experience to dictate my strategy, explaining that the only way the firm could own my IP in the program was to pay for it, like any other commercial contract. They agreed and we progressed profitably.

The official launch was still to be at the 2016 national conference in Adelaide. A vital component was to train the office champions prior to my keynote address which was to be the second last segment on Friday 20 May. The two day 'HLB Way Champions' course would set the foundation for a successful launch in all offices. However, I found that training 'left brain' oriented accountants to try and think like 'right brain' people oriented client advisers was more difficult and draining than I first expected. Nevertheless, we achieved our goal and I slept well.

The next day, with Aaron Murden's assistance, I presented to several breakout groups and explained the objectives, methodology and benefits of The HLB Way.

Tony Fittler, the National Partner, introduced me later that afternoon and I gave a short keynote address on the virtues of The HLB Way to the 250 people from their offices in Australia and New Zealand. Tony's address was very supportive and The HLB Way was launched.

The following 12 months were quite exhausting, yet at the same time exhilarating, exciting, educational, stimulating, and very satisfying.

The first roll out of The HLB Way was in Adelaide in October, followed by Perth in November, Brisbane in January 2017, Melbourne in February, the Gold Coast, Head Office, Sydney and Woolongong in March, and finally Auckland in April.

A year or so prior, 2014, was also the 40th anniversary of my business and to celebrate I bought the 50th anniversary model of the Ford Mustang which was released the same year. My son, Campbell, a mechanical engineer in charge of dashboard design at the Melbourne Ford Design Centre helped me buy my dream machine through their staff family buying scheme.

I decided to track its journey to Australia on my iPhone app and was thrilled to discover my beautiful 5.0 litre V8 Ruby Red Mustang was in the vehicle carrier 'Figaro' on route from Baltimore, USA, to Melbourne and moored in Auckland Harbour whilst I was presenting 'The HLB Way' to their office. I was hopelessly excited, and like a small child actually carried the colour brochure in my briefcase.

I returned from New Zealand, and in anticipation of the arrival of my dream machine and on Easter Monday morning, 17 May, opened the blinds of my St Kilda Road apartment to watch 'Figaro' arriving in Port Phillip Bay to unload my Mustang. What an unbelievable Easter egg to receive!

In May I presented a summary of the outcomes of the various presentations to the National Advisory Board and later at a special presentation at their 2017 Annual Conference in Melbourne.

What a tumultuous five years of challenge, endeavour, planning and energy. Again, it had all started with a game of golf!

The HLB Way broke new ground in the accounting sector as it was designed to provide tools for 'left brain' task orientd accountants to use to help them move more easily towards becoming 'right brained' people oriented advisers.

They would therefore become more confident and able to grow and maintain client satisfaction, and help 'future proof the business.

Leadership Lessons:

1. The game of golf shows your character, 'warts and all'.
2. Being your authentic self is your true brand on show.
3. It's very satisfying to watch the career of a client grow.
4. Value your IP and experience in negotiating it's worth.
5. It's good for your soul to celebrate like a child now and again.

CASE HISTORY 15

Renault (Australia) Pty Ltd

Chapter 1

Renewing the Connection

The world of technology moves at a frenetic rate. By 2014, I had created a profile with background on my 'Linked In' app as a new means of marketing myself as a corporate coach. Soon after I connected with the Managing Director of Renault, the French car manufacturer, I gained as my third client back in 1975, just after launching my own business.

His name was Justin Hocevar. While I had never heard or met him previously, he had heard of me when he was working previously for BMW Australia, through the QMA retail program I was implementing.

To develop a feeling of a 'fit' we met several times for coffee and chat, and then he finally asked me to send him a corporate coaching proposal which he duly accepted.

The first few sessions were very important and enabled me to gain an insight into his intricate personality. He was an introverted, guarded, and shy person who was predominantly 'left brain task oriented'. To be successful I suggested that he needed to acquire significant 'right brain soft skills' to become more people oriented and the complete MD package. As our relationship progressed the more confident and people oriented, he became.

He was able to delegate and trust his senior executives to execute their strategy for Renault Australia, and the business grew as he grew. I was privileged to be able to coach and mentor the Australian Managing

Director of one of the world's largest automobile manufacturing companies and help him to influence change. My background in oil and the motor industry once again stood me in good stead.

After about six months he asked me to also coach and mentor their Marketing Manager and later, the General Sales Manager. This meant working closely with the HR Manager who was a fountain of knowledge about the background strengths and weaknesses of all of them.

Over this period Renault grew and grew. It grew at such a rate that the business, which had been operating from leased premises in a business park, needed its own purpose designed building and Justin earmarked a suitable property nearly next door to be the new Melbourne head office for Renault. The building was the latest in design and technology to portray the degree of success achieved and laid the foundations for the brand's future success in the country.

My relationship as coach and mentor lasted five years. The business had grown to such a level that the French head office sent in their own Managing Director, as is often the case world-wide and Justin took a 'golden handshake'. Although sad, it was well earned and deserved.

Leadership Lessons:

1. Invest time and patience in first building a relationship.
2. The 'Fit Factor' is now a critical key for people success.
3. Speaking the same language in business is a powerful asset.
4. As John Paul Getty said, "The key to success is taking a risk."
5. Be careful of success unless you're the same nationality.

CASE HISTORY 16

Logic Information Systems

Chapter 1

Flying High on Golf

In October 2015 I was invited by a golf friend, Trevor Main, to join a group to fly to Bangkok for a week of golf in Hua Hin. We were booked to play the famous Black Mountain Golf Club and four other prestigious golf courses with five other golf tragics from The National Golf Club and an old school mate, John Keeble, from the Rosanna Golf Club.

We all left Melbourne in business class on the new hi-tech Boeing 787-9 Dreamliner bound for Bangkok. After take-off, the tall man sitting next to me worked for a while on his laptop, went to sleep for a few hours, then woke up as the evening meal served. Neither he nor I had spoken up until then, and he looked over and said, "Hello, are you going to Bangkok for business or pleasure?" I replied that I was going for a week's golf with five other guys on board.

I then asked him the reason for his trip, to which he replied that his firm had an office in Bangkok, and he was going to a meeting and to spend some time at the office with his new manager. We then exchanged names and he, Brad Kliegl, said, "George, are you retired or still working?" I replied, "Still working four days a week." He then asked what work I did, and told him I was a corporate coach and management mentor. He seemed interested and asked me a few more questions over dinner regarding the type of clients I worked with, and their industries.

I then asked what his business was, and what position he held, to which he replied, "I'm the Vice President of Logic Information

Systems, a retail advice specialist firm." We talked about his business, which he mentioned worked in conjunction with the large American software firm, Oracle.

During our conversation he also mentioned he enjoyed playing golf with a friend at Yarra Yarra Golf Club. I couldn't believe it, and said completely surprised, "That's where I am a member. What a small world." He then asked if I had a business card, and I promised to give him one after we landed as they were in the overhead locker in my bag.

When we landed, we exchanged business cards and we parted after travelling for nearly nine hours together with the plan that he would contact me on his return to Australia, to see if there was any opportunity to work together.

'It' had happened again, in an aeroplane at 35,000 feet.

We had a wonderful week of golf. The courses were simply stunning and the accommodation right on the beach, owned by the daughter of the King of Thailand was priceless. The scenery was breathtaking, the food was amazing, the company was great, and even the standard of my golf was above average.

We all spent the last night together in a street market where we ate at an interesting street restaurant, even selecting our own lobster! Afterwards we ventured to the feet nibbling and cleansing fish attraction to experience 'first foot' the unusual sensation. We then packed our bags ready for the return trip back to Bangkok airport.

Our Jetstar Dreamliner return flight was again pleasant, and we all agreed that calling the Jetstar 'Business Class' was a bit of a stretch because the seats were not that comfortable, wouldn't recline fully, and we were really forced to virtually sit up the entire nine hours to Melbourne.

After about two weeks, I received a welcome email from Brad Kliegl, suggesting that we meet for a coffee to continue our discussion. I was pleasantly surprised, because often people you meet on a plane, or elsewhere, may never contact you again.

We agreed to meet at a café in South Melbourne for coffee. It was good to see Brad again. He was a very impressive, athletic man of about 195 cm who had also been a successful college basketballer. He was also a quiet, unassuming man who I suspected was a deep thinker.

We met a further time in my building's boardroom to discuss the proposal I had sent him after our coffee, and he agreed to start our coaching and mentoring program.

Our sessions went well and like most 'left brain task oriented' accounting, processed, and focused people, he had an appetite for the 'right brain oriented' people soft skills. He especially found the psychology of benefit related language, Kipling's six open question words, and the aspects of emotional intelligence not only fascinating but helpful. In fact, he thought so much of these 'right brain' soft skills that he then asked me to conduct a series of communication workshops for his workforce in Australia so they could focus on delivering better client service.

As a guest speaker I invited my client Neil Craig, an AFL coach, to one of these workshops and he contributed his thoughts and experiences to give a further dimension about a learning organisation.

The workshops were very well received, and we also continued our coaching and mentoring sessions. Then Brad mentioned he had received such a positive response from the workshops in Australia, that he'd like me to present a one-day workshop for his staff in Thailand at their Bangkok office.

A date was set for April 2017 when I would present a morning session, 'Creating a Culture of Innovation' and in the afternoon session, 'The New Age of Retail Business'. These workshops were designed to be in parallel with those in Australia so all Logic people were 'singing off the same hymn sheet' for a consistent outcome.

It was to be a flying trip in many ways as I would depart Melbourne on Saturday around 3pm, arrive in Bangkok that evening, have lunch with the Bangkok Office and Area Manager on Sunday, present the workshop sessions on the Monday, then fly back to Melbourne on Monday evening, and arrive at approximately 7am on Tuesday morning. It was tiring, and I was for a week afterwards!

However, the workshops were successful for Logic Solutions, and enabled Brad to make some important strategic decisions as a result.

Logic Solutions was again another client gained from creating a relationship in flight and reinforces the point that people are always weighing up 'the risk' of working with others in a business relationship.

It also proves to me that just being yourself, and being humble in your presentation, are key ingredients for helping others make wise decisions about your value to their business, and them personally.

Leadership Lessons:

1. Airline flights are relationship building opportunities.
2. Try to be a 'counter puncher' and not the first to talk.
3. Travelling in Business Class is an investment not a cost.
4. Left brain task oriented people are globally in need of soft skills.
5. Coaching and mentoring are now perceived as critical professions.

CASE HISTORY 17

m3property

Chapter 1

The Vision Equation

One day in February 2017, I received an email out of the blue.

It was from the Secretary to the Managing Director of a firm in Melbourne I'd never heard of before, called m3property. They wanted to conduct their Victorian conference at a winery near Lancefield, past Tullamarine Airport and they needed an MC who could also present a number of specific sessions.

I was surprised to be asked, as I had never been aware of the company, so I asked how they had found me. They said they had found me through a Google search, so I got an answer.

We arranged to meet and discuss their requirements and it was agreed that they needed a session on change, a session on innovation, another on communication and a final session on leadership.

These topics were decided, and I was able to introduce some innovative individual and group syndicate exercises to encourage participation.

The conference went well, and we achieved the objectives.

Later I attended a debriefing meeting and was asked if I could also MC and facilitate the National Directors conference later in the year.

It appears that their previous conferences had been disasters and the Victorian conference had opened their eyes to new ideas, new thinking, new methodologies and had given the Managing Director, Grant Jackson, new confidence for the future.

The National Directors conference was to be conducted at the historic Werribee Mansion, and it was a great setting to bring all the Australian directors together.

However, at dinner on the night before the conference was to commence, and after the directors meeting, the director from Brisbane, stood up, said good-bye, left the group and flew back to Brisbane.

I was in shock, as he had been included in several syndicate groups as a leader, yet soon found out that this was far from the truth, and it immediately put a damper on the group's enthusiasm. When I asked the Managing Director why he had left, he embarrassingly replied, "He just said he was busy, and had to go!" I looked at him in surprise, but chose to not pursue the matter as it was really none of my business.

The next two days went well in spite of the hiccup the night before, and we introduced the need for leadership to be implemented, what this meant and why a vision, mission and values needed to be developed.

The syndicate group exercises also went well, and developed teamwork and interaction to a great degree.

However, I discovered a major weakness in the directors' abilities that had been appointed to act as syndicate facilitators. They couldn't facilitate effectively, since instead of enabling the syndicate members to contribute, they took over the groups and forced their views which stifled discussion. So, rather than encouraging the group to participate, it created a climate where the individual directors went into their shell and shut up!

The highlight of the first day was Neil Craig who was the guest speaker after dinner. Neil at the time was Director of Coaching, Development and Performance for the Carlton Football Club.

He gave an insightful presentation which focused on the benefits of a business becoming 'a learning organisation'. This term implies that 'anyone can come up with a new idea without fear or favour and not be criticised for their input'. The organisation therefore gains the insights from all employees or players and can implement new ideas 'to see if they work or not'.

The debrief of the conference with Grant Jackson, the Managing Director, was positive and gave the company a lot to ponder for the future.

They say if you perform well with a client focus, prospects will beat a path to your door.

Well, in 2018, I was contacted again by Grant to ask me to facilitate their next year's conference. He told me, the conference in Sydney two years earlier had been a disaster, and the recent conference concept, content, topics and energy, had breathed new life into the business.

They had selected the brand new RACV Resort at Cape Schanck as the venue, and wanted to unveil their new vision, mission and values which they had commissioned a South Australian firm to research and design.

Many meetings were held with his PA, and finishing touches were agreed and completed for my presentations to the participants.

However, when I arrived on the afternoon prior to the welcoming dinner, I was informed by Grant's PA that in his absence, as he was on annual leave, the South Australian firm had changed the final presentation and deleted the vision component.

I was shocked, astounded and embarrassed for Grant, who wasn't aware of this extraordinary development, and went back to my room to contemplate how I would overcome this major flaw in the presentation I had prepared covering his brief.

It just proves a saying that my dear old dad used to say to me when growing up, "A little knowledge is a dangerous thing."

Anyway, the next day went well, and I was able to gloss over the mammoth mistake the firm had made and achieve our objectives.

The evening dinner was again the highlight of the conference as the first AFL coach I ever mentored, Neale Daniher, had agreed, in spite of his debilitating motor neuron disease, to be the guest speaker.

Leadership was the topic, and the theme of the conference was 'Leadership: Your Choice', so I briefed Neale on the theme, and he gave a great presentation.

It was interesting for him to say to the director delegates that if you, as a leader, want to encourage change in your organisation, you must explain to your people 'why they should change', not just tell them to change.

It was a stunning performance by a man in great trouble, and showed the depth of courage he had to fight MND with all his might.

His presentation inspired everyone to realise it was 'their choice' and their role to implement the leadership skills needed for change.

It's your choice to have the Power as long as you realise it's Fragile!

Leadership Lessons:

1. When a client's last experience is poor the only way is up.
2. Leadership is all about decision making and managing risk.
3. Once you show a client your best effort, their risk is reduced.
4. Elite sport success has many parallels to business success.
5. Vision, mission and values are critical for sustainable success.

CASE HISTORY 18

First National Real Estate

Chapter 1

Putting Culture First

In 2008, I received a surprise call from my longtime colleague and golf friend, Ray Ellis, who had resigned as CEO of the Melbourne Football Club, and had worked for some time afterwards in America.

He had just been appointed as CEO of First National Real Estate, a national network of co-operative offices. Their profile had been languishing and Ray's brief was to lift the national profile, the number of offices, and expertise in sales, marketing, management, client service and leadership.

He wanted to discuss how I could assist him, his management team, and the national network of offices to improve their performance in those areas.

Ray had a powerful leadership background in having operated his own performance management and corporate events company for many years prior to his appointment at Melbourne FC.

We met, and he briefed me on his vision to implement a coordinated program of professional development to support the marketing and image profile initiatives he had planned.

So, in 2008 I started a business relationship which lasted until 2020, and I trust beyond. The many programs we have implemented include:

- 2006 – Sales Champions and High Achievers Seminars.
- 2006 – The Psychology of Advanced Selling Program.
- 2007 – Lateral Thinking for New Sales Opportunities.
- 2007 - Guest Speaker at the Annual Conference – Coolum.
- 2008 - Guest Speaker at The Heritage 'Growing a Business'.
- 2009 – Creating a Winning Culture Session – Richmond.
- 2010 – Guest Speaker WA Quarterly Awards – Perth.

Then in 2011 Ray thought the head office management team would benefit from a more proactive and client focused approach and asked me to implement a corporate coaching and management mentoring program.

This was to cover leadership, management, time management, effective communication, and strategic thinking. He also felt they were working too much in 'silos' and needed to be more 'one team' oriented.

In 2013, I was then asked to present a retail management course in Brisbane. This was a great success and focused on Barack Obama and his style of leadership. Approximately 40 principals attended the all-day course.

Since 2013, First National has lifted its marketing profile, business acumen, client service and especially leadership, and is now considered one of the leading real estate agent networks in Australia.

Ray is a dynamo CEO leading the charge and the change, and along with a progressive board, they are working on continual improvement for the group.

I have been honoured to have now presented leadership programs and other presentations around Australia in such places as

Kalgoorlie, Broken Hill, Perth, Adelaide, Sydney, Hunter Valley, Brisbane, Coolum and Melbourne.

In March 2019, I was asked by Ray to give the guest speaking presentation in Sydney to the esteemed 'Chairman's Circle' awards event for the top sales people, and 'Diamond GEM Award' winners which incorporated the 'First National Women of Influence' luncheon.

The presentation focused on being agile in today's market and building trust and value in the First National brand. It also introduced the importance of building self-worth within their office teams, and especially in the value of building each office's point of difference.

We also discussed the importance of mental health for all office people, not knowing at the time that we were going to experience a global pandemic in 2020.

As a result, a leading Victorian CEO and office principal, Rob Westwood, contacted me afterwards to assist him in a corporate coaching and management mentoring program to help him and his business to reach the next level.

To help people at First National 'get back on the horse' and back to work, they asked me to conduct a series of 'Coping with Post COVID' sessions in December 2020. It was interesting to hear how the lives and well-being of the various participants had been affected by the Corona virus lock down measures. Their stories brought home the reality of the effects of the first pandemic in over 100 years, and the support they needed.

In May 2021, I was invited to present three sessions at the Canberra convention to continue helping First National to keep its culture remaining first.

Leadership Lessons:

1. Leaders recognise the value of knowledge and their brand.
2. A winning corporate culture is critical for sustained success.
3. Leadership emotional intelligence is the major key attribute.
4. Self-worth and mental health is the real wealth for the future.
5. Business sales strategy today is helping people to buy value.

EPILOGUE

The People's Pandemic

Then 'it' happened again!

While trying to get back to normal after Christmas 2019, it was announced that a virus had escaped from the wet markets in Wuhan, China, and was starting to sweep the world.

The virus quickly became so overwhelming, that in March 2020 the World Health Organisation had no option but to declare it a world pandemic. Many communities were ordered into lockdown, with employees working at home if possible. Schools were closed, and students also started working at home.

Panic buying started in supermarkets, and some states in Australia locked their borders. Virtually all flights, cruise ships and trains were halted, as was playing sport.

The Coronavirus has, at the time of writing, affected over 200 countries around the world, with over 153 million Coronavirus cases resulting in over 3.2 million deaths. Thankfully, nearly 90 million people have recovered.

Since the pandemic was declared, many people have taken to meeting by 'Zoom' and other internet conferencing programs which allow individuals and groups to connect by video worldwide for meetings, coaching sessions, etc.

As stated previously, 'out of adversity comes advantage', so as I write this epilogue to my book, and the future of the world hangs in a precarious state, we can still communicate, laugh, learn, love, and play golf in the future, even if it is with 'Fragile Power'.

Leadership Lessons:

1. Life is a journey not a destination, so focus on the journey.
2. Experience is lessons learnt and retained for resilience.
3. Be your best self and learn to love yourself unconditionally.
4. When you can be kind to others you will be well rewarded.
5. To cope with adversity, focus only on what you can control.

www.ingramcontent.com/pod-product-compliance
Lightning Source LLC
Chambersburg PA
CBHW051827230426
43671CB00008B/871